Sport Mana[...] the Middle East

CW00732851

The Middle East is one of the fastest growing and significant markets in world sport, as well as a powerful source of investment in sport. Bids for the Olympics in 2020 and the soccer World Cup in 2022, as well as remarkable investments in Formula 1 motor racing, horseracing and English Premier League soccer clubs, demonstrate the strength of interest, the depth of resource and the technical expertise maintained by sport business interests in the region.

Sport Management in the Middle East is the first book to offer a serious and in-depth analysis of the business and management of sport in the region. Written by a team of world-leading researchers in Middle Eastern sport and illustrated in full colour throughout, the book examines the importance of sport in the Middle East and introduces its particular management processes, structures and cultures. As well as providing an overview of the region's sporting strategy and key stakeholders, the book offers a number of detailed case studies of sport in individual Middle Eastern countries. A unique guide to sport management in a region of fundamental importance in world sport, this book is essential reading for any serious student or scholar of sport management, sport business, Middle East studies, or sport and society.

Mohammed Ben Sulayem is one of the most famous and successful sportsmen in the Middle East. He received his Doctorate from the University of Ulster in 2012 and combines scholarly work within sport management with practical engagement in the field.

Sean O'Connor has an established research publication record in the field of sport management. He completed his PhD by publication in 2011 and has over 25 years' professional experience in the marketing and communication of sport, in particular in the Middle East region.

David Hassan is a Senior Lecturer at the University of Ulster, Northern Ireland. He has published seven academic books on sport studies, has authored over 60 scholarly articles in peer-reviewed journals/edited books and has presented at international conferences around the world.

Sport Management in the Middle East

A case study analysis

Edited by Mohammed Ben Sulayem, Sean O'Connor and David Hassan

Routledge
Taylor & Francis Group

LONDON AND NEW YORK

First published 2013
by Routledge
2 Park Square, Milton Park, Abingdon, Oxfordshire OX14 4RN

Simultaneously published in the USA and Canada
by Routledge
711 Third Avenue, New York, NY 10017

First issued in paperback in 2014

Routledge is an imprint of the Taylor & Francis Group, an informa business

British Library Cataloguing in Publication Data
A catalogue record for this book is available from the British Library

Library of Congress Cataloging in Publication Data
Sport management in the Middle East : a case study analysis / edited by
Mohammed Ben Sulayem, Sean O'Connor and David Hassan.
p. cm.
1. Sports–Middle East–Management–Case studies. 2. Sports administration–
Middle East–Case studies. I. Ben Sulayem, Mohammed. II. O'Connor, Sean. III.
Hassan, David.
GV664.S66 2013
796.06'9–dc23
2012035287

ISBN 13: 978-0-415-67730-1 (hbk)
ISBN 13: 978-1-138-83770-6 (pbk)

Typeset in Univers LT 8.5/12.5pt
by Fakenham Prepress Solutions, Fakenham, Norfolk NR21 8NN

Contents

List of figures

List of tables

List of contributors

Hisham J. Al Masari was Head of Promotion at the Arab Games 2011. A marketing communication practitioner with over 27 years of diversified professional experience, Masari has worked with established multinational and locally nurtured commercial brands in various market sectors, and across a wide geographical region, including countries in the Arabian Gulf and selected Arab countries. He holds a Bachelors degree in Microbiology from Louisiana State University and an MBA in Marketing from Benedictine University, Lisle, Illinois.

Awista Ayub, MPA, is the author of *Kabul Girls Soccer Club* and is an expert on issues related to Muslim women in sports. Previously, Awista has published articles in a range of well known publications including *Glamour Magazine*, *San Francisco Chronicle*, *Washingtonian* and *USA Today*

Mohammed Ben Sulayem (Co-editor) is President of the Automobile and Touring Club of the United Arab Emirates (ATCUAE) and Vice President of the Fédération Internationale de L'Automobile (FIA). He is one of the Arab world's most renowned sportsmen, having won a record 14 FIA Middle East Rally Championship titles, making him the most successful FIA title-holder in the world. His successful career includes 61 international outings in the European, African, Middle East and World Rally Championships. He has pioneered a number of educational and research initiatives in sport at undergraduate and postgraduate level in the Middle East. He was also one of the key promoters in establishing a Chair in Road Safety Management at Saint Joseph University, Lebanon. The University of Ulster awarded him an Honorary Doctor of Science degree in 2012 in recognition of his work in sport, charitable works and civic leadership.

Urmilla Bob is an Associate Professor in the Discipline of Geography (School of Environmental Sciences) at the University of KwaZulu-Natal, Durban. She completed her Masters and PhD in geography at West Virginia University, USA. She conducts research on urban and rural development issues, sustainable land use and natural resource management, as well as the socio-economic impacts of tourism (specifically ecotourism and sport events). Prof. Bob has published in these fields in both nationally and internationally recognized academic books and journals. She has been involved in collaborative research with national and international organizations and has been an invited speaker at conferences and applied workshops worldwide.

David Hassan (Co-editor) is a Senior Lecturer at the University of Ulster, Jordanstown. He is the Academic Editor of *Sport in Society*, an international, peer-reviewed journal published by Taylor & Francis. He is also joint Series Editor of *Foundations in Sport Management*, a discipline-defining Routledge collection examining contemporary issues in this expanding field of study. He has published extensively on the social, historical and political aspects of sport and has received numerous awards for the excellence of his scholarship over the last decade. He is Vice Chairman of the UAE-based Motorsport Knowledge Institute and is active on a range of academic projects in the UAE.

Ajmalul Hossain, QC is a practising Barrister and Queen's Counsel in England, Senior Advocate of the Supreme Court of Bangladesh and International Arbitrator. He is a member of the International Chamber of Commerce Commission on Arbitration, Paris, a Code of Conduct Commissioner of the International Cricket Council, Dubai and a member of the Statutes Review Commission of the Fédération Internationale de l'Automobile, Paris.

Conor Kilgallen obtained a BSc (Hons) degree in Psychology from NUI, Galway (Ireland) and a Masters degree in Sport Psychology from Liverpool John Moores University (UK) before working with clients at *Sport Psychology Ireland*. He also acted as the sport psychology consultant to *South Galway Special Olympics* club and provided workshops for trainee football coaches at *Dochas don Oige*, Galway. Conor joined ASPIRE Academy for Sports Excellence, Qatar in 2006. In the intervening years he has contributed to the development of ASPIRE's sport psychology unit and is currently involved in several multidisciplinary service teams for ASPIRE football and squash programmes.

Luke McCloskey is a Lecturer in Sports Studies at North West Regional College, Derry, Northern Ireland. Luke holds a BSc (Hons) degree in Health and Leisure from Stranmillis University College, Belfast and a PGCFHE from the University of Ulster. His research is focused around sports coaching and games development and he is a highly regarded sports practitioner in his own right.

Tadhg MacIntyre is Lecturer in Sport, Exercise and Performance Psychology at the University of Limerick, Ireland. He is an accredited sports psychologist with both the British Association of Sport and Exercise Sciences and the Irish Institute of Sport. He graduated from University College Dublin with a BA (Hons) in Psychology in 1993 and was supervised by Professor Aidan Moran during both his Masters research, completed in 1996, and PhD, successfully defended in 2007. He has published 15 refereed publications and several book chapters in his professional career to date. In the applied field, he has more than a decade's experience consulting with sports performers at all levels, including international athletes in a number of sports. He is a former world-class canoeist and has a proven track record of research in the Middle East region.

Sean O'Connor (Co-editor) has 30 years' experience in the marketing and management of international sport. In the early 1980s he pioneered the communication of the successful Marlboro motorsport programme in the Middle East and later the World Rally Championship (WRC). He was the co-founder and promoter of Rally Ireland, which generated the highest TV figures on its debut in the WRC series, in 2007. A former Senator, he has lectured at Dublin Institute of Technology, where he was awarded an MPhil in 2005. He holds an MA from Dublin City University in Political Communication and gained a PhD (by published works) in 2011 from the University of Ulster. He is a Director of the Automobile and Touring Club of the UAE and Chairman of the Motorsport Knowledge Institute based in the UAE.

Philip O'Kane is a member of the Faculty of Arts at the University of Ulster, Magee. Philip holds a BA (Hons) degree in History from Queens University Belfast, an MA in Modern History from the University of Ulster and an LLB, also from the University of Ulster. His research interests centre around culture and identity, with a particular emphasis on sport, and he has published extensively in a range of leading academic journals and books.

Ethan Strigas is an Associate Professor in Sport Management at Indiana State University. He received his PhD in Sport Management from Florida State University and his MBA degree from Indiana State University. Dr Strigas has been teaching sport marketing and finance courses for the last ten years, whilst his research interests focus on sport volunteerism, consumer behaviour in sport, and social marketing and entrepreneurship. For his work in sport volunteerism, Dr Strigas was named the Eli Lilly Research Fellow of the year, whilst much of his recent work has focused on the emerging markets of the Middle East region.

Kamilla Swart is an Associate Professor in the Faculty of Business and leads the Centre for Tourism Research in Africa, Cape Peninsula University of Technology, Cape Town. Her research interests include sport and event tourism, with a specific focus on the 2010 FIFA World Cup and event policies, strategies and evaluations. Prof. Swart has published on varied topics relating to the bidding for and impacts of sport tourism events in South Africa (in journals such as *Politikon*, *Urban Forum* and *The Sociological Review*) and has published several books during the course of a distinguished career. She was instrumental in developing the 2010 FIFA World Cup Research Agenda and served as the City of Cape Town's Research Coordinator for 2010.

Douglas Michele Turco is an Associate Professor at Drexel University (Philadelphia). He received his PhD from the University of New Mexico and Masters and Bachelors degrees from the University of Wisconsin at LaCrosse. Turco is also a Faculty member at the Rajiv Gandhi Indian Institute of Management, IMC FH-Krems (Austria) and at the National Taiwan Sport University. Turco teaches courses on sport and tourism marketing, sport tourism, globalization of sport and sport economics. He has authored over 40 peer-reviewed journal articles in *Sport Marketing Quarterly*, *International Journal of Sport Management*, *Journal of Travel Research*, *Journal of Sport and Tourism*, and others, and has published several books in the field of sport management during a highly regarded professional career.

Foreword

Abdul Rahman Mohammed Al Owais
Minister of Culture, Youth and Community Development, United Arab Emirates

The United Arab Emirates (UAE) is renowned throughout the world as being in the vanguard of sporting excellence. Internationally, in most leading sports – thoroughbred racing, motorsport, golf, rugby and association football – the country commands widespread respect for its progressive and enlightened approach to the management of sport. The same could be said of many other countries throughout the Gulf and the region, where the importance of sport is both recognized and revered.

Sport retains significance culturally, economically, socially and even politically. It provides a sense of national reflective pride when success is secured and assists communities in gaining a better appreciation of their collective identities. Economically, especially in the expanding field of sport tourism and the positive financial impact of hosting major sporting events, it's clear that sport represents an important aspect of many national economies throughout the developed world. We are no different in the UAE as the vibrancy of our country is reflected in our appetite for the further development of our global sporting identity. We aim to achieve this through the staging of major events and the enhancement of our very best athletes and teams, and in our investment in state-of-the-art sporting infrastructure throughout the country.

We take particular pride in our commitment to sport, therefore, as it is an instantly recognizable medium around the world. But it is important to continue to build on this success in the future and that is why I take great pleasure in welcoming the publication of this edited collection examining the management of sport throughout the region of the Middle East, including the UAE. Only by furthering our education and appreciation of this field can we enhance our reputation internationally for exemplary sport management. I am delighted that the editors of this book have brought together such an internationally revered collection of scholars as those who have contributed to this edited compendium.

I'm particularly pleased that the key cornerstones of sport management – bidding for and staging major sporting events, the identification and development of prodigious sporting talent, not to mention the domains of sport marketing, law and governance – are all addressed, and the further illumination of these fields by case studies from the Gulf and other countries across the region make for a quite superb production. The embellishment of this much awaited publication is secured by the use of some fascinating images, which, combined, serve as a further reminder of how much the region and, I'm bound to say, the UAE in particular, have to be proud of as a people.

I take tremendous pleasure and indeed pride, therefore, in penning this short foreword and wish to place on record my thanks to Mohammed and his co-editors for this long-overdue compendium, which I hope will be but the first of many similar books in the time ahead. I recommend it to scholars of sport management and business studies, political and civic leaders and indeed anyone with an interest in Middle East culture without reservation and thank the editors again for their foresight, dedication and scholarship in the production of this quite superb text.

The protection and enhancement of sport through responsible corporate governance

Mohammed Ben Sulayem

Overview

This chapter gives an initial overview of the career of Mohammed Ben Sulayem and his current role as President of the Automobile and Touring Club of the United Arab Emirates (ATCUAE) and that of the Vice President of the Fédération Internationale de L'Automobile (FIA). It introduces the reader to the power that sport exercises as a medium for building relationships in the Middle East and overcoming language, cultural and religious barriers wherever they emerge. The chapter examines how the process of effective governance plays an integral role in the delivery and organisation of modern sport and does so whilst profiling related governance matters which are manifest in the management of sport on a global scale. Issues of transparency, accountability and fairness are addressed within the chapter, and examples of the value of volunteerism, good governance, and the implications of politics and legislative matters are also provided. In this regard, a high-profile case study, dealing specifically with the issue sport governance, serves as a suitable opening to the chapter.

Case Study 1: FIA vs. Ferrari in 2010

The Fédération Internationale de L'Automobile (FIA) is the governing body that brings together 213 national motoring organisations from 125 countries. As the FIA's Vice President, the author has a responsibility to promote the sport to the general public, but ultimately to ensure motorsport remains devoid of what many may consider to be unethical behaviour. The FIA focuses upon a code of ethics established around democracy and transparency, which it uses as a starting point for its worldwide operations. The FIA has established a series of legally binding statutes that are rigorously enforced by those in positions of responsibility throughout the FIA. The relationship between governance and legality within the sporting movement is a particular area of concern as the world at large becomes seemingly evermore bound by various legal complexities and requirements. A relevant example of the pressures faced by sport organisations is profiled in the legal battle which took place between the FIA and the Ferrari team in 2010. In the controversy that broke following the issuing of so-called 'team orders' by Ferrari in relation to the actions of their drivers and the team as a whole, the author was called upon to perform a central role in the resolution of this dispute.

At the F1 German Grand Prix 2010, staged at the Hockenheim circuit, Ferrari's Felipe Massa (who had dominated the race from its beginning and was leading coming into the final laps) pulled aside and permitted his teammate Fernando Alonso to pass him in an unchallenged manner. Alonso had been leading the F1 Driver's Championship and it may have been considered by some to be in the best interests of the Ferrari team to secure a first and second place finish in the race, with Alonso of course claiming first prize. This act by Ferrari was thought to have constituted a 'team order', which is deemed illegal within the sport of F1 as it is seen to affect an unnatural outcome to an otherwise competitive race. The incident provoked a widespread backlash against Ferrari from other teams and indeed fans and commentators of the sport argued its actions had damaged the credibility of motorsport as an industry. Ferrari argued that this act did not constitute a 'team order', but nevertheless the stewards decided that it had contravened Article 39.1 of the sporting regulations, which states that 'team orders which interfere with a race result are prohibited' and article 151 (c) of the International Sporting Code, which outlaws 'any fraudulent conduct or any act prejudicial to the interests to any competition or the interests of motor sport generally'. The stewards at the race decided to impose a maximum fine of US $100,000 on Ferrari and also forwarded their decision to the World Motor Sport Council (WMSC), meaning that Ferrari could have faced further repercussions in the wake of the stewards' verdict at the event.

After the fine had been imposed on the team, and maintaining Ferrari's innocence, Team Director Stefano Domenicali stated: '...in the interests of sport, we have decided not to go through a procedure of appealing against it, confident that the World Council will know how to evaluate the overall facts correctly'. Felipe Massa, who pulled aside to let his teammate overtake him in the dying moments of the race, responded to critics by saying, 'In my opinion this was not a case of team orders: my engineer kept me constantly informed on what was going on behind me, especially when I was struggling a bit on the hard tyres; so I decided to do the best thing for the team, and a one-two finish is the best possible result'. The FIA decided that there was insufficient evidence to prove any guilt on Ferrari's part. However, it did decide to uphold the financial penalty placed upon the team, but also agreed that it (the FIA) would review the rules in relation to team orders from that point forward.

This was an interesting case in terms of governance issues within a modern sport organisation. Both Ferrari and the FIA had instructed legal teams to represent them at the hearing in Paris, whilst members of the FIA essentially constituted the jury throughout its hearing. Although conflicts of interest will inevitably arise in various situations relating to this style of governance, it is important that an organisation such as the FIA can regulate and enforce the rules of its sport in an independent manner, without the need for recourse to the wider legal or political communities. In order for an organisation to sustain such privileges, it is clear that the FIA and other major sports governing bodies must govern in a professional, democratic and completely impartial manner.

A boy's story

I, Mohammed Ben Sulayem, am a proud Emirati and from my birth in 1961 my ambition was always that one day I would become an internationally established rally driver. Growing up in the UAE, the event that was closest to my heart, and one which I most sought victory in, was the FIA Middle East Championship. By the close of my competitive career I was lucky enough to have won this series on numerous occasions and indeed to have competed in many other such events around the world. As Vice President of the FIA and President of the Automobile and Touring Club of the United Arab Emirates (ATCUAE), it is now my responsibility to oversee all motorsport events in the UAE, to influence similar practices across the region and to play a key leadership role in the sport globally. I view my election as a tremendous honour for my family and I whilst it is my ambition to see motorsport in the UAE, and indeed the Middle East, become a major factor in the lives of the general public living there.

As Vice President of the FIA I am also very proud to be a part of an organisation that strives to provide leadership and direction in how sport organisations should operate around matters of transparency, professionalism and corporate social responsibility. As an organisation, we were founded in 1904, with headquarters in Paris, France and, as we did then, we continue to operate on a not-for-profit basis. All revenue generated by the FIA is invested back into motorsport in order to further grow and expand the horizons of the sport. The FIA's jurisdiction encompasses 132 different countries and some 227 national motoring and sporting organisations situated on five continents. The scope of membership of the FIA extends not just to motorsport but also to casual motor car users and represents millions of people worldwide. As part of my responsibility as Vice President of the FIA I actively seek to protect the interests of the federation's membership base through various campaigns and initiatives orchestrated by the governing body.

Indeed, people, quite understandably it might be said, often overlook the non-sporting aspect of our organisation, but a significant proportion of the FIA's workforce focus on promoting our members' interests in respect to safety, mobility, the environment and consumer law at the United Nations, European Union and through other relevant international organisations. Currently the FIA performs a key role in promoting the UN 'Decade of Action' to reduce road accidents, via the FIA Foundation, which is a UK-based charity. However, the governance of motorsport throughout the world is also of utmost importance and is central to our daily operations. As part of this responsibility the FIA administer the rules and regulations for all four-wheel motorsport events, and of particular significance in this regard is the FIA Formula One World Championship, FIA World Rally Championship and FIA World Touring Car Championship (FIA, 2011). The FIA's governance structure is shown in Figure 1.1.

Governance structure of the FIA

As President of ATCUAE I am also very pleased to see how motorsport continues to develop and gain traction throughout the Middle East. In any type of business, it is always encouraging to be able to say that we are extremely active to the point that we now oversee approximately 140 events that constitute the UAE motorsport calendar, incorporating various forms of motorsport, including circuit racing, rallying, drag racing and motocross. With such a robust schedule, it is essential that we ensure all events are compliant with current FIA standards and that the issue of health and safety for competitors, spectators, media and the general public is afforded top priority. We are also active on a daily basis in the marketing of our events, drivers and other club activities. In my view, without a professional communications strategy and

1.1
Governance
structure of the FIA

Source: www.fia.
com/en-GB/the-fia/
governance/Pages/
governance.aspx

FIA General Assembly   FIA International Court
of Appeal (ICA)

FIA President

Secretariat

Deputy President   Deputy President
(Mobility & Automobile)   (Sport)

World Council for   FIA Senate   World
Automobile Mobility   Motor Sport
and Tourism   Council

Mobility & Automobile   Sporting
Commissions   Commissions

FIA Secretariat

trained managers in each of these areas, no modern sporting organisation can develop and grow in the way it needs to in order to keep pace with the demands of sport in its present form.

First established in 1965, ATCUAE has now evolved to the point where we have offices in Abu Dhabi, Dubai and the other Emirates. An important aspect of our activities, and one which I find to be of particular significance, is that we also partake in non-racing-related initiatives such as safety training for our volunteers and staff and commissioning research to assess how we might manage and retain our some 1,000+ volunteers. In this process we can avail ourselves of expert assistance and support via the FIA Institute, a specialist unit of the FIA designed to elevate standards in the areas of safety and sustainability. I strongly believe that volunteers are worth much more than the limited publicity and praise that they typically receive in the media. In the absence of the commitment and dedication of volunteerism, events such as the Abu Dhabi Formula One Grand Prix would simply not take place. In accordance with this, in 2009 I initiated an academic research program that would examine this very issue. The research findings strongly suggest that:

> Emiratis are driven by a sense of national pride and a moral obligation to serve and give back to their country when they answer the call for volunteers at major sporting events ... UAE nationals who came forward to work as marshals for the Formula One Etihad Airways Abu Dhabi Grand Prix (in 2010) also displayed a strong

desire to act as role models for youngsters by doing something they considered to be worthwhile. By comparison, the strongest motivation for expatriate volunteers was their great love of motorsport and a desire to be as close as possible to the Formula One action

(ATCUAE, 2010)

Case Study 2: driving motorsport forward together – FIA Middle East Strategy 2010–2014

Motorsport first began in the Middle East region at the beginning of the last century, when the Automobile and Touring Car Club of Lebanon (ATCL) was created in Lebanon in 1919. Under Italian rule, the Tripoli Grand Prix (GP) was held in 1925, as was the Moroccan GP, staged during the same year. The late King Hussain of Jordan adopted the sport in the 1950s and substantially contributed to its development, both in terms of its image and popularity, from that point forward.

The first formal International Motorsport series in the region was the Rothmans Gulf Challenge, which began in 1976 and was staged initially in Kuwait, Bahrain, Qatar and Oman. It was therefore a marketing initiative from its very inception, one that witnessed the sponsors introduce European organisational expertise and a public relations and promotional strategy for the series, which was designed to capture the interest of the public throughout the region.

Prior to the mid-1970s the FIA had chosen not to undertake research dealing with motorsport in the Middle East. This changed following the launch of this new event, with the aim being to establish a series of benchmarks around key performance indicators such as driver population, trained marshals and national events. The ultimate aspiration was to allow a National Governing Body (more appropriately referred to as an ASN within FIA parlance) to track its own organisational performance and provide the FIA with a clear picture of development in the Middle East region. It was also designed to assist in the development of an informed strategy for the future of motorsport in that part of the world, which had traditionally been somewhat behind regions elsewhere in this respect.

In more contemporary times it is a similar research-led approach that has served to inform the Middle East Strategy for 2010–2014, the key elements of which include:

- An acceptance that over 25 years of the FIA Middle East Rally Championship (MERC) has contributed substantially to the development of motorsport in the region, via the

creation of regional sporting heroes who in turn gave rise to considerable media and public interest
- The development of grass-roots motorsport is the main focus of all sporting clubs (ASNs)
- Karting has the most club-run events in the Middle East, followed by rallying and racing
- Clubs issue 60% of licences to timekeepers
- On-going research is needed at club and FIA level to monitor progress and trends
- The traditional motorsport management model operated on two levels – national and FIA. (Indeed it is planned to introduce a new Pan Middle East Club consultative process to pursue common goals and generate synergies where these exist)
- Indeed on this particular theme, research has revealed that new pan-regional competitions are needed to respond to the demands of the marketplace
- Support of all stakeholders, in particular the media, on a national and regional level will be key to future growth
- All future initiatives at any level must be driven by the needs of current and future motorsport fans in each market and not merely be technically or sporting led
- Government backing is required in the realms of material, logistics and financial support.

It is clear that we must establish a blend of qualified UAE sport managers and volunteers to take our sport to the next level. Furthermore sport – all sports – in the region must strive to become knowledge based, drawing upon the very best research and knowledge transfer that we can avail ourselves of and capitalise upon. To further facilitate this initiative, I established in 2011 the Motorsport Knowledge Institute (MKI) which will address this very issue on a local, regional and global basis across the Middle East. This Institute will also look at the practical application of sport sciences and introduce a series of research and training projects at home and abroad. The development of knowledge is one of the key areas within the FIA's Middle East Strategy for 2010–2014, which is itself a product of a research-based approach to policy generation and decision making (see Case study 2).

The power of sport: my life experiences

Throughout my sporting career as a rally driver I was fortunate to have been exposed to many different cultures, visited numerous places and countries and formed long-lasting friendships and partnerships. Without sport, none of this would have been possible and I can only assume my life would be unrecognizably different to what it is today. Sport possesses a special power to transcend and break down barriers of communication, culture, politics and even religious and spiritual beliefs. It is one of the few universal aspects of modern-day life that can bring people together from all over the world. The pain of defeat and the exhilaration of victory are feelings that each individual has experienced at some point in their lives. The full spectrum of human emotion is so clearly evident in the faces and actions of people involved in sport, and our ability to relate to each one of those emotions is what makes sport so unique, absorbing and ultimately enthralling.

We are often witness to the bitter rivalries that exist between sports teams from the same country, region and even locality. Yet, when that country's national team play on the world stage, those same fans, who may not even speak to each other because of their particular affiliations, stand side by side in support of their team and put their issues of rivalry aside, even if it is for just a short period of time. However, this aspect of sport merely confirms that, when we look at the bigger picture, we are all in fact linked by our common love, appreciation and affection for sport itself. There are no age restrictions, social class or other requirements to prevent people joining this movement. Young boys and girls kicking a football on the street, and professional people going for a run after work or playing team games on their lunch break are all bound by similar rules, feelings and experiences.

When parents decide it's time for their children to become involved in organised sport, whichever sport it may be, they are granting them access to the largest association and movement in the world and potentially opening up the door for some great experiences both on and off the playing fields or racing tracks. They will begin to compete against other young athletes from different localities, different regions and maybe even different countries and cultures. This is such an invaluable and vital piece of every child's education, and sport is the medium that allows this education process to exist. However, introducing children to sport not only forms bonds and friendships among the participants, it also gives parents, coaches, officials and spectators the opportunity to meet new people from different walks of life and share their experiences of life and sport in a common forum that all involved can understand. Every successful sports person must start at a certain point in their lives. My career did not start when I took part in my first competitive rally. It began at a much earlier age when I sampled my first game at home and then in the school yard. Sport teaches children about the importance of ethics, morals, hard work, determination and need for motivation. They also learn the importance of respect, honour and graciousness in defeat – all valuable life lessons that are afforded to children because of their involvement in sport. The karting circuit, the swimming club or the local football academy are the places where the athletes of tomorrow hone their sporting skills and develop their young minds to become key citizens in our society.

As sportspeople, our first experience in sport will typically play a formative role in how we develop our sporting lives. Our first coach, teammates, facility, or season will all play a significant part in our growth and development and, in some cases, as successful and professional sportsmen and women. When a local sports team wins a regional championship or an athlete wins a gold medal at the Olympic Games, it has a ripple effect throughout the nation and establishes a deep and meaningful community attachment, which is reflected throughout the country. I have enormous pride and honour in the role I am able to play in society in the Gulf and beyond as a result of my experiences as a Middle East Rally Champion. Throughout their sporting careers, people are fortunate enough to visit many different nations and meet people from all walks of life, bearing witness to various different cultures. Due to these experiences, lifelong friendships are formed amongst people from many different continents. It is clear there is no other activity that retains such potential to bring people together in friendship in comparison to sport.

It is not only sports people who bring a sense of pride and honour to a country. Sporting events such as the Olympic Games and the FIFA World Cup also allow a nation's people the opportunity to showcase their culture, professionalism, friendliness and pride. During the 2010 FIFA World Cup in South Africa it was clear how proud the country was to host some of the best national football teams in the world. When the South African team emerged onto the pitch to play its first competitive match of the tournament, scenes of jubilation, excitement and joy were broadcast all around the world to millions of people. The presence of the FIFA World Cup had clearly united the people of South Africa in celebration, but the power of the tournament's presence also stretched far beyond just unifying people. Local clubs, businesses, broadcasters and fans, often of opposing local teams, worked together to mark this special occasion and as a result enjoyed the financial benefits that are associated with an event that attracts as large an interest and viewership as the World Cup commands.

Hosting such a large sporting event requires astronomical investment in infrastructure – both sporting and non-sporting. The benefit of this investment is that this infrastructure will be in place for many years to come and the South African people, in this case, will be able to avail themselves of many new services and facilities that previously had not existed. The financial and infrastructural advantages of hosting an international sporting festival are clear to see. However, this is not the only major benefit of hosting such an event. Aside from these issues, an opportunity exists to showcase the country to a worldwide audience and even help change perceptions of the country that may have existed in the past. In 2009, I was immensely proud to witness Abu Dhabi, capital of the UAE, host the inaugural Abu Dhabi Formula One Grand Prix. Formula One is the world's largest annual sporting event and hundreds of millions of people all over the world will watch the UAE host this spectacular event for many years to come. The impact that this will have upon the world's interpretation and understanding of the UAE is beyond comprehension.

Having reflected upon some of my own personal observations around sport, and the impact it has waged upon my own life experiences, I want to take the opportunity to engage somewhat in a more detailed, objective analysis of the modern sport organisation, its governance and role in society. To do so I will embrace some of the academic literature in the field, which I have been engaging with in recent times as I grapple with the full magnitude of the challenge presented by modern society to the effective governance of sport.

The modern sport organisation

In the modern sporting environment, organisations interact with a number of different entities such as the state, local and regional agencies, commercial enterprises and media outlets. All of these stakeholders occupy multiple and diverging, often contradicting, interests in the organisation. Sport organisations' objectives and strategies can often become incoherent and increasingly difficult to define as a result. A number of issues such as misappropriated funds, highly precarious financial practices, internal political conflicts and general sport mismanagement have contributed to a body of more recent literature which serves to seriously question the effectiveness and efficacy of many sport organisations operating in these times. Even large international sport organisations, such as the International Olympic Committee, have not escaped scandal, as that federation came under considerable attention and pressure in 1999 (and periodically since) due to doping and corruption allegations, and was forced to adapt its rules and membership accordingly (Chappelet and Bayle, 2005).

The modern sport organisation's administration and ongoing management requires increasingly specific industrial knowledge. To sustain this development of sport, managers must be equipped with the necessary skills to lead these organisations in the future, and a more professional approach must be adopted, particularly at executive levels. Managers must familiarise themselves with the various management techniques required to perform well within the modern sporting environment, which often requires adaptation of existing techniques applied in traditional business practices. Sport management courses at undergraduate and postgraduate level have been available in Europe and the USA for many years and it is my hope that this region will follow suit at the earliest available opportunity. Education in the field of sport management is no longer an option for the people of the Middle East – it is a necessity.

Sport has evolved to encompass a role in education, healthcare, economic development, the labour market and various social issues. Sport is increasingly taking the form of a tool for development on an educational, social, economic, urban planning, and image level for nations throughout the world (Chappelet and Bayle, 2005). The way in which these organisations are

1.2
Lifelong bonds
of friendship and
respect develop via
sport

Source: rolfo

governed and managed is therefore required to differ from traditional organisational management. The principles, methods and conditions that exist within sport organisations must be analysed before senior management decide on the best style and management practice which suits their organisation.

The modern sport organisation can be compared to a mini government of sorts. Their responsibility to ensure fairness, legality and transparency plays an integral role in how these organisations are viewed, respected and tolerated, not only within the sporting environment but also amongst the public at large. The CEOs, board members and representatives of large sport organisations such as FIFA, the IOC and indeed, in my case within the FIA, have a similar role to play to that of government officials in promoting fairness and the rule of law amongst all our constituents, from the youngest football fan to the professional Olympic sprinter or Formula One driver. Many of these organisations have come to realise the importance of adopting new ways of thinking and managing their organisations and thus have implemented new governance structures to support these responsibilities. As sport continues to develop it also begins to play an increasingly more important role in society, and as such the profile of sports such as association football, Formula One and the Olympic Games has increased accordingly and resulted in more attention from the media, politicians and legislators than ever before. It is a result of this increase in attention and responsibility that a requirement exists upon the modern sport organisation to ensure it governs its affairs on the basis of democracy, transparency and fairness. If these governance principles are absent from any organisation, it runs the risk of attracting the attention of political and legislative entities that could potentially undermine the principles of self-regulation, which have spawned the development of these worldwide sport federations. If the sporting movement loses its reputation for fair play and open competition, it also risks losing its unique self-regulation and legal status.

Governance in sport

The modern sport organisation is faced with difficult pressures and challenges. The emergence of new facets, including commercial interests, which typically include media rights and multimillion-dollar sponsorship deals, are particularly significant. A case can often arise whereby the sport organisation may in fact prove to be a victim of its own success, if it fails to remain fully cognoscente of issues relating to politics, legalities and the operating environment within which it functions. In the modern sporting landscape, situations have arisen in which a number of national governing bodies of sport have been compromised and, with this scrutiny, erstwhile policies of free and independent governance have been foregrounded and challenged.

Therefore the role of the sport organisation in relation to governance is manifold and complex. The organisation is first and foremost responsible for the management of its sport and its activities within its governing area but it also typically acts as an entity responsible for ruling on disputes and enforcing those judgements. The various facets that exist in the sport organisation in relation to governance makes it a unique and often difficult issue for many sport governing bodies and, as a result, their experiences cannot be directly compared with organisations operating outside of the sporting sector. In the opinion of the author, one of the most skilful sports administrators in world sport at present is the President of the FEI (International Federation for Equestrian Sports), Princess Haya bin al-Hussein (see Figure 1.3). Her re-election to the highest office within equestrian sport is surely testimony to her outstanding attributes and evidence of what can be achieved through tireless dedication and commitment to one's sport.

However, in a lot of instances the use of the term 'governance' is not always clear and precise and it can often be related to a variety of issues that sport organisations face on a daily basis. The various definitions and explanations of what the term 'governance' encapsulates are often diverse, puzzling and even contradictory. As a result of this, the term has evolved to have many definitions and has been employed both as a normative and descriptive concept in both explaining the methods of which organisations are, or should be, governed and also by attempting to explain a certain type of practice that is required within an organisation. Essentially, the term governance can be broken down into three different strands relative to the sport organisation:

Steering – governance and steering become interrelated when a sport organisation begins to analyse plans around its ongoing strategic direction.

RH Princess Haya
Bint Al Hussein

Michael ST

1.3

Jordan's Princess,
and President
of FEI, Haya
bin al-Hussein
addresses the FEI
General Assembly
in Estoril, 15 April
2007

Source: ©AMMAR
ABD RABBO/AFP/
Getty Images

The governance of the modern sport organisation has evolved to be less about control and strict direction to increasingly become about the processes of facilitating and planning. This results in a focus on the dispersal of authority as opposed to the underpinning of a single, all-powerful entity. Consequently, actors from both internal and external sources have become engaged with the issue of governance in a manner rarely witnessed before within many modern sport organisations.

Networks – instead of a traditional hierarchical approach to the management of a sport organisation, modern governance is often conceptualised as a process of cooperation between various agencies and organisations that share common interests and goals. This method of governing sees policy emerge from coordination and partnership between multiple organisations, which is again in contrast to the existence of one single authoritative entity that may have proven to be the case in the past.

Ethics – the final strand to be considered under the governance 'umbrella' is the issue of ethical standards existing within many sporting organisations. The manner in which organisations relate, operate and coordinate with each other can be understood as constituting examples of either fundamentally 'good' or 'bad' acts of governance. While it may be difficult to establish a 'best way' of safeguarding good governance, the concept remains essentially normative,

13

focussing on a number of interrelated issues such as responsibility, transparency, stakeholder involvement and the presence of an unambiguous legal and ethical structure.

The evolution of governance in sport

The management and governance of sporting organisations has been a continual process of evolution dating back over many decades and these issues have attracted the attention of a host of academics working in the field (Auld and Godbey, 1998; Hoye and Auld, 2001; Hoye and Cuskelly, 2003a, 2003b; Inglis, 1997; Shilbury, 2001). The professional and bureaucratic approach that many sport organisations have adopted has not typically occurred in a planned or methodical manner; instead, these organisational styles have emerged following a more organic process of evolution, with different approaches and requirements being adopted to suit the specific needs of particular sporting organisations.

It is clear therefore that governance within contemporary sporting organisations has become more than just about protecting the daily operations and mechanical cogs that turn for the given organisation to execute its strategic objectives. Instead, Milton-Smith (1997), amongst others, claims that governance within the sport organisation has evolved into a process of setting high standards of responsibility for policy-makers in response, in turn, to the demands of the general public for a greater sense of transparency within such organisations. This argument is further acknowledged by Francis (2000), who claims that the term 'corporate governance' has become synonymous with accountability in both the non-moral and moral sense. From a non-moral perspective, the term corporate governance has evolved to take its place alongside important issues such as efficient policy-making, the appropriateness of resource allocation, and even an organisation's fundamental strategic objectives. In contrast to this, from a moral perspective, the term corporate governance has become synonymous with establishing an ethical operational climate amongst the workforce, ensuring due diligence and focussing upon individual directors' particular responsibilities.

As the terms corporate governance and ethics within sport organisations become ever more intertwined, the need for a proper distinction between the two is thought to be more important than ever (Driscoll, 2001). This issue becomes even more complex, as has been made clear, because governance itself can often be viewed in very different ways, and, with the further addition of ethical considerations placed, the need for clarity and understanding becomes paramount (Collier and Roberts, 2001).

As the general public and society at large increase their demands and expectations around the workings of major sport organisations, the result is an increased focus on the everyday practices of these entities as a means of establishing transparency and a reputable public image. Researchers such as Francis (2000) and Hopen (2002) argue that how a sport organisation undertakes its daily operations can often prove an effective indicator of its commitment to establishing an ethical approach around its business practice, and also will inevitably create a particular image of the organisation within the minds of the integral stakeholders. If an event or situation arises that causes stakeholders to acquire a negative or even neutral opinion of an organisation's ethics, this in turn will contribute to the detriment of good governance within that organisation. These situations convey the fact that there is an integral relationship between ethics and governance, and that they can only be safeguarded through the establishment of governance structures, such as the formation of a code of ethics, ethical management initiatives and organisational ethical programs that give rise to protection, development, control and integrity of the sport organisation in question (Wieland, 2001).

A further complex relationship exists between the presence of a governance structure operating within a sport organisation that satisfies management, and the need for one that respects and responds to the external, legal pressures that are placed on an organisation in the modern business climate. Dalton (1996) argues that, 'while there is a need for laws to protect society from those who are not ethically responsible, the reality is that ethical corporate practice is best controlled by the members of the board, in other words, by a responsible corporate culture' (p. 179). It is almost impossible for any legal system to dictate the ethical standards and corporate governance model that should operate within a particular sporting organisation, as legislation is restricted to providing basic forms of procedure and accountability; instead, corporate governance within the sport organisation requires additional accountability and certainly much more depth (Farrar, 2001).

Governance in the modern sport organisation

Thus, it is clear that the issue of governance has also been brought to the fore in recent times due to the change in the dynamics of the modern sport organisation from a mostly volunteer-led sector to one that is now becoming more professional and bureaucratic in its approach to its management and daily operations. Additionally, it has been stimulated by demands for the organisations to become more effective as many utlise public monies to support their practices. More to the point, it is clear that there should be less potential for powerful executives, perhaps with their own agendas, to potentially abuse the trust placed in them either by stakeholders or again by the public, needs to exist and concerns about stakeholder involvement and accountability of senior management within these unique organisations should be alleviated.

Indeed, stakeholders' important involvement and active participation in the operations of international sport federations and national governing bodies have in turn raised a number of salient questions and concerns around the ongoing interests of players, fans and volunteers. A consequence of this has been the emergence in certain settings of specific interest groups designed to highlight the concerns of their members, which in turn are having an impact on the evolution of modern governance within such organisations (Hindley, 2007). For example, when a wealthy American family, the Glazers, became a majority shareholder in Manchester United Football Club, a significant number of supporters came together to assume a substantial shareholding within the football club in an apparent act of defiance against what they considered to be unwanted, external involvement in their club. The establishment of interest groups, such as these, is seemingly becoming more commonplace and in fact illustrates how such groups can determine the style in which sport is managed, posing legitimate questions around regulation and control of the organisation and ultimately the balance of power that exists within the sport in question.

In 2001, the FIA and the European Olympic Committee organised an inaugural conference on sport governance in response to the growing number of concerns from sport organisations surrounding this issue. The result of this conference was the production of a statement of 'good governance in sport' in an attempt to allay stakeholder and public demand for a proper response to issues of transparency, accountability and democracy within such organisations. Up until this point a rather naive argument had been advanced, which broadly suggested that, as all sport is ideally based around fundamental principles of sound ethics and fairness, that this too will transfer over to the running, planning and overall governance of these organisations by those charged with safeguarding their welfare. The agreed statement on behalf of the FIA and the European Olympic Committee incorporated a guide to nine governance principles that all sports entities should avail themselves of in order to ensure that good governance exists within their organisations:

The role of the governing body	Democracy, elections and appointments	Conflicts of interest
Structure, responsibilities and accountability	Transparency and communication	Solidarity
Membership and size of the governing body	Decisions and appeals	Recognition of other interests

Table 1.1
Principles of good governance

Source: Governance in Sport Working Group (2001: 2)

These principles, set out by the 'Governance in Sport Working Group', concentrated on the systems and process of governance that sport organisations should ideally adopt and included the role of the governing body, transparency and accountability measures, and the distribution of revenue incomes throughout the organisations that they govern. It appears that, although these principles were not intended as a specific 'code of behaviour' for a particular governing body and its board members, they do indicate that all elections and appointment of board members should be conducted with democracy to the forefront, that all dealings with stakeholders should ensure the highest degree of transparency and that appropriate and adequate measures should exist to deal with conflicts of interest if and when they arise. The working group behind this statement argued that, if governing bodies were to adopt these principles and uphold them to the degree to which they were made apparent in the declaration, then a number of positive outcomes would become manifest, as illustrated in Table 1.2.

Table 1.2
Rewards of good
governance

The principles will provide a useful 'check list' for sporting bodies to ensure that they are behaving responsibly with respect to their members and to third parties with a legitimate interest in their activities	It should go a long way to providing a solid defence to any litigation, serving to demonstrate that all actions and decisions are properly motivated and subject to appropriate checks and balances	By demonstrating the virtues of self-regulation, it should assist in persuading legislators that there is no need to interfere further in the running of sports.

Source: Governance in Sport Working Group (2001: 3)

1.4
Tunisian swimmer
Ous Mellouli swims
in the Men's 200
Meter IM finals of
the Missouri Grand
Prix in 2010

Source: Getty
Images

Summary

Sport is one of the greatest resources that we are fortunate enough to have the ability to enjoy in modern nations throughout every part of the world. Its uniqueness links people, cultures and communities from right across the globe within one united movement. The type of language one uses, religion one practices, politics one supports and race one belongs to all fade in significance in the face of sporting endeavour that typically offers universal joy for all those who engage with it. The pillars that sport rests upon – the ideals of fair play, fair competition and fair treatment – must continue to be resolutely protected by all those in positions of power and influence.

The lifelong bonds of friendship and respect that develop with people from all walks of life through a mutual love for sport go far deeper than politics and diplomacy; they are about the formation of genuine and meaningful human relationships, and this is why the author is so passionate about its protection and dedicates so much time to helping bring young men and women into his sport, and indeed all sports. It is something the author will continue to dedicate his life to in all relevant sporting endeavours. If I can help more people to receive the opportunities to experience the thrill of competition, of winning, of losing, but most of all of participating in something that they will benefit from throughout their lives, then I am satisfied that I am fulfilling my personal ambitions to return something to a sport, which in turn has given me so much.

Amid all of this of course the context in which sport takes place and the manner in which it conducts its affairs, that is to say the existence of good governance within sport organisations, will be a vital component in the sustained and continued success of the sporting landscape as we know it today. Many sports administrators do not have the privilege of gaining a university degree and learning about sport management and governance from an academic perspective. Instead, they are forced to learn 'on the job', which provides challenges but also allows them to bring their own expertise and knowledge from their sporting careers to the fore. However, academic research is a crucial component when it comes to the field of sport management and governance and that is why I personally place such high importance on its funding and support. The sporting movement needs scholars, researchers and visionary administrators to continue to develop sport from the grass-roots level all the way up to senior executives and management. If sport organisations continue to foster the development of dynamic systems of planning, managing, communicating and governance, the sporting movement can in turn continue to be a precious aspect of modern-day life from which all people can continue to derive tremendous pleasure for many years to come.

References

ATCUAE (2010), *Motorsport Volunteerism in the UAE*, Research findings from the 2009 Etihad Airways Abu Dhabi Grand Prix, Automobile and Touring Club of the United Arab Emirates, Dubai.

Auld, C.J. and Godbey, G. (1998), 'Influence in Canadian national sport organizations: perceptions of professionals and volunteers', *Journal of Sport Management*, Vol. 12 No. 1, pp. 20–38.

Chappelet, J.-L. and Bayle, E. (2005), *Strategic and Performance Management of Olympic Sport Organisations*, Human Kinetics: Champaign, IL.

Collier, J. and Roberts, J. (2001), 'An ethic for corporate governance?', *Business Ethics Quarterly*, Vol. 11 No. 1, pp. 67–71.

Dalton, J.F. (1996), 'Boardroom ethics', in Woldring, K. (ed.), *Business Ethics in Australia and New Zealand: Essays and Cases*, Thomas Nelson Australia: South Melbourne, pp. 173–82.

Driscoll, D.-M. (2001), 'Ethics and corporate governance: lessons learned from a financial services model', *Business Ethics Quarterly*, Vol. 11 No. 1, pp. 145–58.

Farrar, J. (2001), *Corporate Governance in Australia and New Zealand*, Oxford University Press: South Melbourne.

Francis, R.D. (2000), *Ethics and Corporate Governance: An Australian Handbook*, UNSW Press: Sydney.

Governance in Sport Working Group (2001), *The Rules of the Game*, Conference Report: Brussels.

Hindley, D. (2007), *Resource Guide in Governance and Sport*, Hospitality, Leisure, Sport and Tourism Network: Nottingham Trent University.

Hopen, D. (2002), 'Guiding corporate behavior: a leadership obligation, not a choice', *The Journal for Quality and Participation*, Vol. 25 No. 4, pp. 15–19.

Hoye, R. and Auld, C.J. (2001), 'Measuring board performance in nonprofit sport organisations', *Australian Journal of Volunteering*, Vol. 6 No. 2, pp. 109–16.

Hoye, R. and Cuskelly, G. (2003a), 'Board power and performance within voluntary sport organisations', *European Sport Management Quarterly*, Vol. 3, pp. 109–19.

Hoye, R. and Cuskelly, G. (2003b), 'Board-executive relationships within voluntary sport organisations', *Sport Management Review*, Vol. 6, pp. 53-74.

Hoye, R. and Cuskelly, G. (2006). *Sport Governance,* Butterworth-Heinemann.

Inglis, S. (1997), 'Roles of the board in amateur sport organizations', *Journal of Sport Management*, Vol. 11, pp. 160–76.

Milton-Smith, J. (1997), 'Business ethics in Australia and New Zealand', *Journal of Business Ethics*, Vol. 16 No. 14, pp. 1485–97.

Shilbury, D. (2001), 'Examining board member roles, functions and influence: a study of Victorian sporting organizations', *International Journal of Sport Management*, Vol. 2, pp. 253–81.

Wieland, J. (2001), 'The ethics of governance', *Business Ethics Quarterly*, Vol. 11 No. 1, pp. 73–87.

2

Bidding for major international sporting events

Kamilla Swart, Urmilla Bob and Douglas Michele Turco

Overview

Sport is a multi-billion-dollar industry worldwide. Countries and cities aggressively compete against each other for the rights to hold sport events including the Olympic Games, FIFA World Cup, America's Cup and other such events primarily for economic development purposes. In some cases, the brand and image of a destination becomes inextricably linked to sport, e.g., Augusta, Georgia (Master's Golf); Athens, Greece (Olympic Games); and Melbourne, Australia (Australian Open).

This chapter identifies key aspects of securing sport events, including: the bidding process; operations management and sport event impacts (environmental, economic, social-cultural, etc.). Event strategies employed by sport governing bodies, tourism ministries, relevant government agencies and so forth are also critically analysed and discussed. This chapter and the subsequent analysis offered by Hassan in this compendium, dealing with the process of managing sport events, complement each other perfectly and reflect the importance of these major gatherings for our understanding of the Middle East as a global sport event destination.

There have been a number of high profile sport events in the Middle East and North Africa over the past two decades including the 2006 Asian Games in Doha, Qatar; Bahrain F1 Grand Prix; Dubai Desert Golf Classic, and the Dubai World Cup (horseracing), but none bigger than the forthcoming

2022 FIFA World Cup in Qatar. Qatar in particular indicated that the country has focused on "three pillars in developing and diversifying its economy: education, health and sports – and within sports, the biggest areas of focus are football, golf, tennis, cycling, fencing and table tennis" (Doha's 2020 Vision, 2008). It's timely therefore to profile Qatar's hosting of the 2006 Asian Games as an appropriate departure point in the context of a chapter examining the successful hosting of major sports events, including across the Middle East region.

Case Study 1: Doha 2006 Asian Games

Having gained a favourable reputation over the years, Qatar is promoting itself as a popular venue for international sport events. The wide range of sport facilities and business opportunities that it offers makes it a lucrative destination for international sport federations and athletes in search of new markets. Given the government-funded project, ASPIRE, the Academy of Sport Excellence which aims to develop the most talented student athletes in the region (see Kilgallon's dedicated chapter in this collection profiling this institution) and the search for 'national prestige' in international competitions through the naturalisation of elite athletes, it is not surprising that the Qatari government undertook to bid for the 15th Asian Games in Doha in 2006, as part of a broader modernisation strategy. Qatar was the first Arab Middle Eastern Country to host these Games, which emerged as the biggest ever, with 45 countries, 40 sports and 411 events represented. The Doha Asian Games can be considered a 'third-order mega-event'. The Doha Asian Games Organising Committee (DAGOC) was established by the Qatar National Olympic Committee to coordinate and organise the Games under the auspices of the Olympic Asian Council (OCA) who actually retain the rights of the Games. A significant investment of US $2.8 billion was established to underwrite the event. Five years of preparations included major investment in the development of appropriate sporting arenas (including 38 permanent and temporary sport venues) such as the impressive Khalifa Stadium; major road and building construction, and development throughout Doha to transport and accommodate the Games and its guests; branding and advertising campaigns, and a sustained publicity campaign. The Games Village included 814 flats for athletes, 48 flats for *chefs de mission* and 48 national Olympic offices. Following the Games, the village became part of the Ministry of Public Health buildings and the city's central medical complex. Some 10,000 athletes competed in the Games and 16,000 volunteers were targeted. A media contingent of 5,500 personnel covered the Games (3,000 press, 1,000 broadcasters and 1,500 host broadcaster staff). It is argued that the success of the 15th Asian Games not only put Doha on the world's sporting map but raised the profile of Qatar and the whole region (Amara, 2005 and RasGas Magazine, 2006/2007).

2.1
Saudi Arabia fires
the ball past Kuwait
during the Men's
Team Tournament
Preliminary Pool A
match during the
15th Asian Games,
Doha in 2006

Source: Getty
Images

Introduction

Sport events are a multi-billion-euro segment of the broader sport and tourism industries. Sport mega-events including the FIFA World Cup, Olympic Games and UEFA Euro Championships are highly coveted by countries and cities for their ability to attract sport tourists and additional economic development. Indeed, as Hassan makes clear in his own contribution to this discussion, contained within this collection, the actual process of measuring the economic impact of sport events, particularly large-scale sport events, has itself become a major industry.

Sport as business

Madichie (2009) argues persuasively that professional sports have evolved from mere entertainment for spectators to a range of service offerings including attendance levels, media viewership and broadcasting rights, merchandising, public and private sector investments, sponsorships and ownership of teams, leagues, associations, etc. The service offerings are often profit-making driven and the foundation for the 'sport-as-business' model that dominates modern sport events. Madichie (2009) asserts that, in the Middle East, especially in the United Arab Emirates (UAE), the main focus in terms of developing professional sports in areas such as association football, golf and motorsports is not in increasing the fan base in terms of viewership or spectators or securing broadcasting rights, but in massive government investments in the construction of sport facilities and sponsorships. Investment in sport goes beyond the national borders to include sponsorship of major regional events such as the Pan-Arab Games and other globalised international events such as the Emirates Dubai Rugby Sevens, sponsorship of the WTA (Women's Tennis Association) Tour, Dubai Duty Free (sponsor of the Dubai World Cup of horse racing) and Fly Emirates, official sponsor of recent FIFA World Cups in Germany (2006) and South Africa (2010) (Amara 2005). Indeed Hassan, in his subsequent analysis of sport event management in the UAE, examines both the Dubai World Cup and the Emirates Dubai Rugby Sevens tournament in some detail in a manner that confirms many of the points made here. Madichie (2009) further illustrates how these events are prominent in the UAE's ambition to become the world's sport capital and the implications of these investments in professional or elite sports. However Madichie (2009) highlights that critical questions remain, which include the sustainability of these developments and their meaningful impact within wider society.

While not for developmental purposes *per se*, infrastructural investments have been the cornerstone of positioning certain countries in the Middle East as sport event destinations. Ernst & Young (2008) assert that diversifying economies, of which sport events is a component, is a push for these countries to move away from heavy reliance on hydrocarbon production. This requires massive infrastructure development that is being achieved, according to Ernst & Young, by public–private partnerships. Table 2.1 presents the value of the infrastructural investments in 2007 in the Gulf Corporation Countries. These figures represent the largest investments in the Middle East region.

Country	Value, US $ billion
Saudi Arabia	102.2
United Arab Emirates	70.32
Qatar	21.85
Kuwait	9.4
Oman	1.9
Bahrain	0.66
Total	206.33

Table 2.1
Value of 2007
infrastructural
investment in the
Gulf Corporation
countries

Zawya Project Monitor cited in Ernst & Young (2008: 3)

The increase in investment in the global sport market space in Gulf Coast countries is also demonstrated by the rise in the number of sport channels there such as Art Sport, Al-Jazeera Sport, Abu Dhabi Sport, Dubai Sport and Saudi Sport all of whom compete to broadcast regional and international sport events (Amara, 2005).

Most of the research on sport in general and the limited research on mega-events in the Middle East have tended to focus on economic impacts linked to infrastructural development and destination profiling. There is very little attention to social and environmental aspects, some of which will be briefly discussed later in this chapter, in relation to issues and impacts. There is no research specifically on the impacts of mega-events on visitors and local residents, although they are regarded as key stakeholders in relation to the successful hosting of mega-events.

Sport mega-event lifecycle and the initial stages of the bidding process

Much of the attention on sport mega-events rests around the athletic contest and the decisive moments when a champion is crowned. Years of planning and preparation, and billions of dollars spent seemingly come down to a few short minutes of climax. The lifecycle of a sport mega-event begins at the drawing-board stage when a bid is initially contemplated. Is it feasible for the host city/country to host the event? This exploratory stage may take as long as two to three years. It can be considered as part of the pre-event phase, along with the bidding process and the detailed planning and preparation. The other two distinct phases include event implementation and post-event (Emery, 2003).

The Olympic Games is generally considered as a benchmark for other mega-events and, since it is likely to have lessons for the bidding processes of other events (Pomfret et al., 2009), case studies from the Games are drawn on extensively in this chapter. The Olympic Games lifecycle outlines what Emery identified as three event phases: bidding, foundation planning, operational planning, operational readiness planning. Games times and post-Games dissolution (see Figure 2.2). Legacy has been presented as

•~9 years
•The procedure for the host city election is applied, ending with its election by the IOC Session

Bidding phase

•~7 years
•Foundation planning and Games-wide organisation

Foundation planning

•~5.5 years
•Detailed plans for Games operations progressively evolve

Operational planning

•~3.5 years
•Organisers and stakeholders achieve full preparedness prior to commencement of Games operations

Operation readiness planning

•2.5 weeks
•Organisers host participants and the Games are delivered, including the transition period and Paralympic Games

Games time

•+1 year
•Post-Games activities occur before the Organising Committee is dissolved

Post Games dissolution

LEGACY

2.2

Olympic games lifecycle

Source: Adapted from IOC, 2009

a cross-cutting phase that occurs across all the stages of the event as it has become an integral aspect of event bidding, planning and implementation.

Pre-event phase

Once a decision is made to commit to a bid, the formal bidding process is undertaken. Bidding for a mega-event can be considered high risk as there is of course only one winner (Berridge and Quick, 2010). Some organising committees enter the race knowing that they may not be successful but nevertheless do so to gain experience and/or to achieve other objectives such as awareness. For example, in the failed Cape Town 2004 bid, a number of facilities were built in disadvantaged areas as part of the developmental approach to the bid. In order to reduce some of the risks, the International Olympic Committee (IOC) introduced a two-phase system of bidding, whereby cities respond to an IOC Questionnaire as part of the Applicant City Phase. (See Table 2.2 for the timelines and requirements for the Olympic bidding process). For the 2016 Games, it is interesting to note that Doha was the only city in the Gulf to express its interest as an Applicant City. The other cities were Baku (Azerbaijan), Chicago (USA), Madrid (Spain), Prague (Czech Republic), Rio de Janeiro (Brazil) and Tokyo (Japan) (IOC, 2010a). Cities are then shortlisted to advance to the next phase of the process, the Candidate City Phase. For the

2016 Olympic Games, four cities were shortlisted, namely Chicago, Madrid, Rio and Tokyo. It is interesting to note that all these cities have either hosted a Summer or Winter Olympics and/or have submitted previous bids to host the Games. Once the cities are shortlisted, detailed planning and preparation begins in earnest. To host the 2016 Summer Olympiad Rio beat Madrid by 66 votes to 32 votes in the final round of voting.

Applicant City Phase	
September 2007	National Olympic Committees to submit name of Applicant City.
October 2007	Payment of Candidature Acceptance Fee and signature of Candidature Acceptance Procedure. IOC information seminar for Applicant Cities.
October 2007–January 2008	Applicant Cities prepare and submit responses to IOC Questionnaire.
January–June 2008	Responses examined by IOC Candidature Acceptance Working Group. Presentation of Working Group Report to IOC Executive Board. Candidate Cities selected.
Candidate City Phase	
June 2008–February 2009	Candidate Cities prepare their Candidature Files.
July–November 2008	Payment of Candidature Fee and signature of Candidature Procedure document. Participation by Candidate Cities in Beijing 2008 Observer Programme and attendance at Beijing Debrief.
February–October 2009	Submission of Candidature files together with signed undertaking document and guarantees. Evaluation Commission visits Candidate Cities. Technical aspects of bid presented to IOC Members Briefing. Evaluation Commission Report released. Final presentation of Candidate Cities and voting by IOC members to elect host City.
October 2009	Host City Contract is signed.

Table 2.2
Timeline and requirements for Olympic bidding – a case study of the 2010 Olympic Games Process (Adapted from IOC, 2010a)

Source: Adapted from IOC (2010a)

The Candidature File represents the Master Plan for organising the Games (Westerbeek *et al.*, 2006). For the 2016 Olympic Games, Candidate Cities had to address questions relating to 17 themes (see Table 2.3). These themes can be applied generally to the bidding process around other mega-events as well. The themes reflect the complexity of a mega-event, as accessing the relevant information will require interactions with a range of stakeholders. Key strategies for successful bidding will be highlighted in the next section of this chapter.

Table 2.3

	Theme
1	Vision, legacy and communication
2	Overall concept of the Olympic Games
3	Political and economic climate and structure
4	Legal aspects
5	Customs and immigration formalities
6	Environment and meteorology
7	Finance
8	Marketing
9	Sport and venues
10	Paralympic Games
11	Olympic Village(s)
12	Medical services and doping control
13	Security
14	Accommodation
15	Transport
16	Technology
17	Media operations

Source: Adapted from IOC (2008)

It is clear that the timelines are non-flexible and demanding, with no room for extending deadlines arbitrarily. A critical path plan highlighting key milestones that need to be delivered will be required by any serious bidder for a major sporting event. Schedules for detailed planning, community consultation, design, construction, site preparations and test events must be drawn up to ensure timely delivery and that all parties involved also have a clear idea of roles and responsibilities (Maralack and Lloyd, 2005).

Event-implementation phase

As demonstrated in Figure 2.2, Games time or the event-implementation phase is very short in comparison to the other mega-event bidding phases. This phase is the culmination and justification of all the preparation undertaken to date. In order to ensure professional and sound execution, mega-event planning usually includes a series of test events prior to the actual mega-event. In the case of the FIFA World Cup, the test event is the Confederations Cup, which is hosted a year prior to the actual event. These test events are particularly useful within the context of the one-off nature of a mega-event and provide an opportunity to test all operational management aspects from accreditation to ticketing, etc. To ensure that the mega-event runs as planned, control centres are put in place in order to monitor performance against planned activities.

Post-event phase

This phase includes the dissolution of the mega-event, along with the organi-sational structure, which generally takes about a year to wind up. During this phase, close-out and evaluation reports are prepared. These reports also serve to highlight best practice for future mega-events. It is also important to highlight that, while evaluation forms part of the final phase of the mega-event lifecycle, commissioned research would have been planned in the pre-event phase, and research amongst stakeholders would have occurred during this phase as well as during the implementation and post-event phases. For example, the City of Cape Town conducted pre- and post-event research amongst residents and businesses, and visitors were surveyed throughout the 2010 FIFA World Cup.

Legacy

As indicated in Figure 2.2, legacy occurs across all phases of the mega-event lifecycle. Given the scale and complexity of mega-events, greater emphasis is being paid to the legacies that mega-events can leave for the host destinations and their people. The Olympic Games have been at the forefront of integrating legacy planning into Games planning and preparation. The IOC, through its Games Knowledge Management Service, makes various documents such as Olympic Games Impact Studies and technical reports available to cities so that they can learn from previous host cities and adapt to their own context (IOC, 2010b). In the case of the FIFA World Cup of 2010, legacy has also become an important issue. For example, a dedicated legacy manager was appointed, a move that was not demonstrated in the organisation of previous World Cups. Legacy planning is integral to the bid plan and requires strategic long-term planning in order to sustain positive impacts on the host destination long after the mega-event has taken place, especially given the massive investments that will be required.

Sport mega-event bidding strategies

What makes a bid successful? A range of factors come into play, and various attempts have been made to identify criteria for success. In 2002, Westerbeek *et al.* conducted interviews with 135 event experts and identified eight key success factors that emerged from their findings, which are illustrated in Table 2.4.

Success factors	Description
1 Accountability	Represents the reputation, legacy components, technical expertise and facilities of the host city, and includes the following: capacity that the bid team and the city have to deliver high-quality services to the event promoter and the community stakeholders; an established presence in the bidding marketplace; reputation as a city for hosting successful sport events; ability to showcase a variety of excellent facilities through the hosting of previous mega-events.

Table 2.4
Key success factors in bidding for sport mega-events

2 Political support	Represents stability and economic contribution, as well as government support. Government involvement (at all levels) enhances the value of the event to the event owner and increased government involvement in the process of bidding is increasingly evident. Government guarantees are required. The regulatory environment is important in relation to the legal aspects of hosting the event.
3 Relationship marketing	Represents key relationships, including political and event decision oriented ones, in support of the bid. The bid committee must be able to influence key decision makers. Effective lobbying is critical and is usually developed with previous experience at bidding and hosting; includes internal lobbying for positive public opinion as well as external lobbying to key decision-makers.
4 Ability	Represents the sport-specific technical expertise, equipment and event capabilities of the event team, and includes organisational and event management skills, including sport-specific technical skills and all the basic requirements to host an event. Budgeting and financing are critically important aspects, especially in relation to the huge public subsidies utilized to fund mega-events. A solid track record in hosting similar events is critical, as well an event concept that will give the bid an edge over others.
5 Infrastructure	Represents the accessibility, transport infrastructure and community support for the mega-event. The city must have the necessary infrastructure (general and sport-specific) to host a successful event; this includes the ability to deliver services, accommodation and transportation as well as community support. Safety and security and environmental considerations have also become increasingly important.
6 Bid team composition	Represents the level of support, mix of personnel and selling capacity of bid team officials. A mix of talent on the team is essential to the way the team is perceived by the key decision-makers as well as to the success of the operation. Corporate and private sector representatives are required.
7 Communication and exposure	Represents the City's capacity to develop media exposure opportunities and the necessary communication systems to support the bid. The strength of a city's brand image is critical to attracting tourists. A strong marketing and communication plan based on the bid concept is required, and communication and IT systems need to be place to ensure global coverage of the mega-event.
8 Existing facilities	Represents the current facilities available, construction dates and accommodation capacity. Existence of critical and quality event facilities at the time of the bid is advantageous and is generally built up from the hosting of previous mega-events.

Source: Adapted from Westerbeek *et al.* (2002: 313–319) and Westerbeek *et al.* (2006: 131–132)

It is evident that the criteria include both objective and subjective aspects of a bid. While most bidding cities are able to present technically competent bids in terms of the operational aspects of the proposed event, it is often the subjective criteria that provide the distinctive edge that cities require to be successful.

Communication is singled out by Mallen and Adams (2008) as an essential factor for bid success. Communication is important in almost every aspect of the bid process, from the bid book submission to the visit by the evaluation commission, as well as the final presentation when voting actually takes place. Communicating to internal and external stakeholders (which will be discussed further in the next section) is also important.

Sheng (2010) presents a bid model based on competition and cooperation, arguing that countries strategically interact with each other in the bidding process. In terms of cooperation, this usually occurs either in the form of joint bids or to leverage support for their bids from other countries or regions. Thus, while bidding is a process of competing, it increasingly has elements of cooperation embedded within it. For example, Korea and Japan jointly hosted the 2002 FIFA World Cup and joint bids were submitted by Spain and Portugal and Belgium and Holland, respectively for the 2018 FIFA World Cup. For the 2022 FIFA World Cup bid by Qatar, the bid had the support of the entire Gulf region and ultimately proved successful.

Indeed it is apparent that successful bidding requires significant time and energy, and financial and personnel resources (Westerbeek *et al.*, 2006). Meticulous attention should be given to the various phases of the bid, including the compilation of the bid team, the technical preparation of the bid, the presentation of the bid book according to the requirements stipulated by the event owner and the final presentation and associated lobbying. Furthermore, despite all the effort, there is no guarantee that it will be a winning bid, as other, perhaps tangential, factors may come into play. Often geopolitical decisions will be the final determining factor as to on which continent a mega-event will be held, and one cannot ignore this when planning to bid. For example, Athens was unsuccessful in its centennial Olympic Games bid, which was awarded to Atlanta in 1996. Consequently, Athens bid again for the 2004 Games, and many believed that Athens was awarded those Games to make amends for the IOC's alleged error in awarding the 1996 Games to a rival bidder. Similarly, there has been much discussion surrounding the recent awarding of the FIFA World Cup, with the 2018 and 2022 editions being awarded to Russia and Qatar, respectively. Since these events seem to be awarded to emerging markets or semi-peripheral states, more-developed countries contend that it will be challenging for them to succeed in the future, which may convince them not to engage in the bidding process at all. Berridge and Quick (2010) assert that event owners prefer to consider geographical spread when selecting mega-event destinations, so that diverse cities/countries may stand a better chance than countries that have previously hosted the event.

Mega-event stakeholders

Individuals and groups with a vested interest in a sport mega-event are considered stakeholders. Stakeholders for the Asian Games in Doha, for example, included athletes, sport federation(s), the event rights holder, local residents and businesses, media, sponsors, host government(s), and spectators. Sport stakeholders may have different wants, expectations and motivations for supporting a sport event, and perceive its outcomes differently. For example, a hotel owner hosting athletes and spectators benefits directly from an event and will likely perceive the event more positively than a hotel owner who does not host many event participants but who may be subject to displacement on account of the event taking place. Decisions on whose wants are addressed in the bid, and ultimately in the event production, are based on political, economic and social forces. The success of the bid (and ultimately the event) can be achieved through the way in which these wants and demands are balanced (Westerbeek et al., 2006). Stakeholder theory is an organisational and business ethics theory that addresses morals and values in managing an event and can be useful to understand the decisions by and affecting stakeholders.

A comprehensive network of partners is critical to the success of any event. The key relationship in the network is generally represented by the event bidder (for example Qatar 2022) and the event owner (in this instance FIFA). In terms of bidding, the administrative power rests primarily with the event owner (Westerbeek et al., 2006). In order to strengthen its position, the event bidder seeks to enter into other relationships with organisations to strengthen its resources and ties to benefit the bid. Technical expertise, political and community support, and relationships with the sport organisations, sponsors and the media become significant to the event bid network. A strong relationship amongst the network is important to ensure that all parties are fully supportive of the bid (Westerbeek et al., 2006).

Issues and impacts of sport mega-events

Mega-events are not a panacea for all that ails a developing country, and this should be a consideration for those considering a bid to host a major international sporting event. After all, consequences of ethnic, religious and tribal conflict, war, economic disparity, social inequities, food and water scarcity, and poor public health and education have festered for decades. It is unreasonable to expect a sport contest that occurs for a few days or weeks to cure a country of its problems. Pomfret et al. (2009) warn that the bidding for mega-events itself is a costly process, often requiring massive investments from the public sector. This is certainly the case in the Middle East where political support from government is strong and reinforced by infrastructural development to underpin the bid.

Political instability in the region

Political instability remains a serious concern in certain parts of the Middle East and has increased in the last year with the dramatic rise in political unrest in certain countries, notably Yemen and Bahrain. This raises safety and security concerns as well as issues around whether mega-events should support what are considered by some to be non-democratic states. The latter is a serious issue, and countries and mega-event organizations have been heavily criticized for appearing to turn a 'blind eye' to human rights violations in host countries, as was the case in the 2008 Beijing Olympics. In terms of safety and security it appears as if the federations are satisfied if plans are in place to ensure safety during the event. This was the case when South Africa hosted the 2010 FIFA World Cup where, in the run-up to the event, crime was undoubtedly a key concern. However, the event was successfully hosted, with very few incidents taking place to cause concern. Nevertheless, this can be extremely problematic, since temporary solutions are presented to major problems confronting host countries. In this regard, post-event research is urgently required to monitor if gains are to be maintained after the event or were measures staged specifically for the event.

Establishing a sport-for-all culture in Middle East countries

Very little information on sport-for-all in the Middle East seems to be widely available. However, by all accounts, the concept appears to be receiving increasing attention. For example, in the 2022 FIFA Bid Evaluation Report for Qatar (2010), focus is given to the development of non-elite and grass-roots football, including the establishment of structures, talent-scouting, facility development, and supporting football programmes in schools and refugee camps. Attention is also given to football development for people with special needs and opportunities, including for women, as discussed in more detail below. As with other mega-events that have been held to date, it remains to be seen how and to what extent mega-events actually influence the broader sport development agenda, given that the focus is on hosting a successful mega-event in compliance with the requirements of the event owner.

Inequitable opportunities for women and girls in society and sport

Gender issues are neglected areas of research in terms of mega-events. Women's involvement as participants in sport mega-events is typically limited to the Olympic Games and, as Bob and Swart (2010) indicate, it is often assumed that mega-events are male dominant. Furthermore, Edwards (2002) cited in Manzenreiter and Horne (2002: 16) asserts: 'The world of competitive sport is naturally and irreversibly first and foremost the domain of male and natural masculinity.' An illustrative example of this is that the FIFA World Cup refers to (and is trademarked as the male World Cup, despite both men and women playing soccer at a competitive level within FIFA-sponsored leagues and competitions. However, there is increasing evidence that women's interest in sport as spectators and followers is expanding dramatically, and this was borne out in the recent FIFA World Cups (Bob and Swart, 2010). In the Middle East, the culture is highly patriarchal, conforming often to Islamic norms and values. This has tended to create high levels of inequalities among men and women in terms of participation and spectatorship. However, there is a concerted effort to increase women's participation in sport and this can be seen by the addition of the ladies sport facilities to Qatar's ASPIRE Zone as well as increasing participation by women in the Asian Games, not only as athletes and volunteers, but also in their inclusion in managerial positions (Amara, 2005). The promotion of women's involvement in sport is based on the assumption that it will reduce gender inequality, promote empowerment, enhance health and well-being and address the male orientation of competitive sport in particular. In terms of the latter, this is worsened by the fact of the commercialisation of sport and the reliance on huge sponsorships and ability to attract viewership. However, the major sport events and competitive teams that are able to attract large sponsorships are male, and this tends to reinforce gender inequalities.

Environmental sustainability

Environmental sustainability has historically been a neglected component of the bidding for and hosting of mega-events. Only recently has the green agenda emerged as a component of ensuring environmental sustainability as well as securing bids, since ensuring environmental sustainability and reducing the carbon footprint of mega-events are criteria included to assess bids, especially of mega-events that can generate considerable negative environmental impacts if not managed correctly. The Doha Declaration emanating from the 9th World Conference on Sport and the Environment organised by the IOC and the United Nations Environment Programme on 30 April–2 May 2011 focused on the theme of 'Playing for a Greener Future' (United Nations, 2011). The main aspects in the Declaration dealt with promoting sustainable development (especially among youth), sharing best practices and ensuring sustainable mega-events and sporting events in general.

A critical issue emerging from the discussion is how mega-events influence (or at least are believed to influence) the (re)making of place. The aspect of nationalism and national pride linked to hosting a mega-event is also important to consider. Cornelissen and Maennig (2010) and Waitt (2003) argue that nation-building and national pride are major impacts of hosting mega-events associated with the 'feel-good' factors that characterise residents' reactions. In the Middle East, there are high levels of tensions and differences linked to historical processes and ongoing political instability in defined parts of the region. As witnessed in countries like Germany (the 2006 FIFA World

2.3

The Emir State of
Qatar H.H. Sheikh
Hamad bin Khalifa
Al-Thani and
Sheikha Mozah bint
Nasser Al Missned
are presented with
the World Cup
Trophy by FIFA
President Joseph
S. Blatter after
winning the bid for
2022

Source: Getty
Images

Cup) and South Africa (the 1995 Rugby World Cup and the 2010 FIFA World
Cup), sport can be a powerful vehicle to contribute towards building national
unity. Again, this is an issue discussed in more detail by Hassan later in this
collection.

Bidding for mega-events in the Middle East is not without its
problems. As implied, the region remains embroiled in political unrest and
there are strong concerns regarding safety and security in certain parts of the
Gulf. Additionally, as is the case with Qatar's 2022 FIFA World Cup bid, there
are allegations of corruption and bribery surrounding FIFA's handling of the
process. Indeed, despite the re-election of President Blatter in June 2011 to
the leadership of world soccer's governing body, the federation was almost
fatally damaged by allegations of widespread malpractice, and reform appears
inevitable. This issue is linked to general concerns regarding mega-event
bidding made public during the Salt Lake City Winter Olympics fiasco in which
members of the IOC accepted bribes from representatives of the organizing
committee in exchange for votes for their bid.

The evaluation of Qatar's bid by FIFA (2010) illustrates the shifts in
what mega-event organizers are looking for in bids and therefore the staging of
the event itself. It also shows how traditional formats of delivering an event are
no longer applicable, as innovation and uniqueness is increasingly being valued
by decision-makers. The report indicates that Qatar's bid was in line with the
country's national development strategy and presents a novel approach to
event operations and legacy, as outlined in the case study below.

The report also indicates other key aspects that FIFA considers,
such as government guarantees, minimum number of stadiums required,
the marketing plan, accommodation facilities and transport infrastructure, are
important components. This shows that the rhetoric of development and a
sustainable event is underscored in the bid. However, it is important to note

that all bids make similar promises and deciphering rhetoric from reality is far from a straightforward process. So, what makes one bid stand out from the others? The report further outlines that the Qatar bid presented FIFA with an opportunity to bring the World Cup to the Middle East. This desire to ensure that different regions host the event was also one of the main reasons why South Africa hosted the World Cup in 2010. This leads us to infer that the politics of bidding may be more important than the technical and physical requirements of being capable of hosting a mega-event in the first place.

Case Study 2: FIFA World Cup, Qatar 2022

In February 2009, Qatar expressed its interest in hosting the 2022 FIFA World Cup. Subsequent processes included a bid registration in March 2009, a formal bidding agreement in December 2009, submission of the Bid Book in May 2010, a FIFA Inspection Team visit in September 2010 and the announcement of the successful bid in December 2010. Qatar competed along with Australia, Japan and South Korea, and the USA for the 2022 event but ultimately proved victorious. Qatar will be the first country in the Middle East to host this 'first-order' mega-event. The bid had the support of the entire Middle East region and was also aimed at creating a greater understanding of the Middle East throughout the rest of the world. Amari reported in 2005 that €40 million was being injected into the development of Qatari football, foreign coaches and the signing of foreign players on behalf of domestic club sides. In terms of previous hosting experience, Qatar staged the 1995 U20 FIFA World Cup, the 2006 Asian Games and will also host the 2011 AFC Asian Cup. Qatar's bid concept was aligned to the national development strategy and presented novel approaches to event operations and legacy. The bid is strengthened by steadfast support from the Qatari government and links to the 'Qatar Natal Vision 2030' and the Qatar Master Plan for infrastructure, with the transportation systems in particular. An expenditure budget of US $645.5 million for Qatar 2022, including the Confederations Cup (considered as a test event in the year prior to the World Cup), was submitted, with a projection of nearly 2.87 million tickets being sold for the actual event itself. Sustainability is the main criterion of the bid and is to be achieved by offering a compact and bespoke World Cup. The proposed stadiums are each less than an hour apart by public transport and fans will be able to stay in the same accommodation throughout the event, thus reducing the event's carbon footprint. By 2022 Qatar will have almost 110,000 hotel rooms and serviced apartments, 90,000 of which have been guaranteed for FIFA's use. Groundbreaking low-climate-control technology will be used to mediate the heat in the stadia, training grounds and fan zones. All of the 12 stadia are located near national landmarks showcasing Qatar's Arabian heritage and ultra-modern facilities to visiting football tourists and teams. In terms of addressing the 'white elephant' status of many stadia after hosting a mega-event, Qatar has designed modular stadia that can be dismantled and used both in Qatar to develop children's sport as well as donated to developing countries, thus meeting FIFA's commitment to social development through football. The various technological breakthroughs are also considered legacies for the sport worldwide. However, the 2022 bid has been mired in allegations of corruption and bribery to 'win' votes, and FIFA has had its reputation adversely affected on account of its alleged central role in this process.

(Source: Amara, 2005; RasGas Magazine, 2010; Qatar 2022 Press Release, May 2010)

2.4
Major sailing events have been hosted in the Gulf region

Summary

The interest in the Middle East in terms of hosting mega-events is not surprising, given the role that sport has played and continues to play in the region. Mega-events are used by host destinations and international sport organisations to achieve a range of objectives. Bidding and hosting mega-events are extremely challenging and daunting tasks for even the most experienced bidder. The Olympic Games is considered a benchmark for all other such large-scale events, and case studies from the Games have been drawn on extensively throughout this chapter. Hosting a mega-event can take up to 15 years from inception to completion, and it is important to consider all aspects of the mega-event lifecycle before officially embarking on a bid. The first key consideration should thus be to consider its feasibility. The staging of mega-events involves significant levels of investment in sport facilities and supporting infrastructure and services such as transport, accommodation and telecommunications. Bidding for mega-events requires economic, social, political and environmental consideration, given that mega-events are usually driven by government agendas, with a consequent use of taxpayers' money. Due consideration should also be given to unique and innovative concepts and sustainable legacy outcomes for the sport as well as the host destination, amongst other key success factors for successful mega-event bidding. It is also imperative that the bid team understands what the event owner wants and is looking to get from the event. Strategic planning, wide-ranging expertise and effective stakeholder networks are required for successful bidding. However, it is also important to understand, given the increasing competition to bid that many bids will still fail. It may therefore be important to plan additional outcomes given the significant resources required for mega-events. In conclusion, it is important to underscore that mega-events are not a panacea to solve all societal problems; however, if planned and managed strategically, they could contribute to achieving broader developmental objectives and impacts. Indeed, it is to the management of these major events that this collection now turns.

References

Amara, M. (2005). Qatar Asian Games: A 'modernization' project from above? *Sport in Society*, 8(3): 493–514.

Berridge, G. and Quick, L. (2010). Bidding and securing an event. In D. Tassiopoulous (ed.) *Events Management*, 3rd ed. Cape Town: Juta.

Bob, U. and Swart, K. (2010). The 2010 FIFA World Cup and women's experiences in Fan Parks. *Agenda*, 85, 85–96.

Catherwood, D.W. and van Kirk, R.L. (1992). *The complete guide to special event management.* New York: John Wiley & Sons.

Cornelissen, S. (2009). A delicate balance: Major sport events and development. In R. Levermore and A. Beacom (eds) *Sport and international development*. UK: Palgrave, Macmillan.

Cornelissen, S. and Maennig, W. (2010). On the political economy of 'feel-good' effects at sport mega-events: Experiences from FIFA Germany 2006 and prospects for South Africa 2010. *Alternation*, 17(2), 96–120.

Doha's 2020 Vision (2008). News. *Qatarsport*, 4, 5–6.

Emery, P.R. (2003). Sport event management. In Trenberth, L. (ed.) *Managing the business of sport*. New Zealand: Dunmore Press.

Ernst & Young (2008). Bridging the gap: Private investment in Middle East infrastructure. Online. Available at www.ey.com/Publication/.../Bridging_the_gap/$File/Bridging_the_gap.pdf (accessed 10 May 2011).

FIFA (2010). 2022 FIFA World Cup Bid Evaluation Report: Qatar. Online. Available http://www.fifa.com/mm/document/tournament/competition/.../b9qate.pdf (accessed on 10 May 2011).

Hall, C.M. (1992). Hallmark tourist events. London: Belhaven Press.

IOC (2008). 2016 Candidate Procedure and Questionnaire. Online. Available http:// www.olympic.org/Documents/Reports/EN/en_report_1318.pdf (accessed on 17 May 2011).

IOC (2010a). 2016 Olympic Games bid procedure. Online. Available www. olympic.org/.../Reference.../2016_Olympic_Games_Bid_Procedure_QRef_ june2010.pdf (accessed on 17 May 2011).

IOC (2010b). Factsheet legacies of the Games update – January 2010. Online. Available www.olympic.org/Documents/Reference...Factsheets/Legacy. pdf (accessed on 17 May 2011)

Madichie, N.O. (2009). Professional sports: A new 'services' consumption mantra in the United Arab Emirates (UAE). *The Marketing Review*, 9(4), 301-318.

Mallen, C. and Adams, L.J. (2008). *Sport, recreation and tourism event management*. UK: Elsevier.

Manzenreiter, W. and Horne, J. (2002). Global governance in world sport and the 2002 World Cup Korea/Japan. In Horne, J. and Manzenreiter, W. (Eds.) *Japan, Korea and the 2002 World Cup*, London, Routledge.

Maralack, D. and Lloyd, N. (2005). Bidding for major events. In D. Tassiopoulous (ed.) *Events Management*, 2nd ed. Juta: Cape Town.

Pomfret, R., Wilson, J.K. and Lobmayr, B. (2009). Bidding for sport mega-events. Paper presented to the First European Conference in Sports Economics at the University Paris 1 held on the 6–8 August 2009.

Preuss, H. (2007). The conceptualisation and measurement of mega sport event legacies. *Journal of Sport and Tourism*, *12* (3/4), 207–227.

Qatar 2022. (2010). Bold technology for a cool, compact World Cup is highlighted in Qatar's historic bid. May 2014. Online. Available http:// www.qatarbidfiles.com/pr/en/Zurich%20Press%20Release%202.pdf (accessed 14 May 2011).

RasGas Magazine (2006/2007). Doha Asian Games 2006. Issue 17. Online. Available http://www.rasgas.com/files/17_english.pdf (accessed 17 May 2011).

RasGas Magazine (2010). Eyes on the prize. Issue 30. Online Available http:// www.rasgas.com/magazine_articles.cfm?news_id=1795 (accessed 20 April 2011).

Roche, M. (2000). Mega-events and modernity: Olympics and Expos in the Growth of Global Culture. London: Routledge.

Sheng, L. (2010). Competing or cooperating to host mega-events: A simple model. *Economic Modelling*, 27, 375–379.

United Nations. (2011). World Conference on Sport and the Environment The Doha Declaration. Available. Online http://www.un.org/wcm/webdav/site/ sport/shared/sport/pdfs/2011-05-03%20IOC%20Doha_Declaration_Final. pdf (accessed 29 May 2011)

Waitt, G. (2003). Social impacts of the Sydney Olympics. *Annals of Tourism Research*, 30(1), 194–215.

Westerbeek, H.M., Turner, P. and Ingerson, L. (2002). Key success factors in bidding for hallmark sporting events. *International Marketing Review*, 19(3): 303–322.

Westerbeek, H., Smith, A., Turner, P., Emery, P., Green, C. and van Leeuwen, L. (2006). *Managing sport facilities and major events*. London: Routledge.

3

The management and retention of sport volunteers

Lessons for the Middle East

Ethan Strigas

Overview

The spirit of volunteerism has contributed significantly to the advancement of societies all over the world. This is not only because it enhances and improves the lives of both the volunteers and the people they serve, but also because it contributes to the efficiency of organizations and social institutions in financial and social terms (Shin & Kleiner, 2003).

Volunteerism is synonymous with economic efficiency, innovation, and social cohesion. Volunteer labour is extremely valuable to an organization because it provides its administrators with the ability to sustain services, expand the quantity, quality and diversity of these services and at the same time keeps its budget within its pre-specified limits (Strigas & Jackson, 2004). For individuals associated with voluntary organizations, offering time, services and expertise helps them increase their self-esteem, develop new relation-ships, enhance skills and abilities, remain active, reduce depression levels, and build healthier attitudes about aging (Shin & Kleiner, 2003). However, one of the predominant benefits of volunteering has to do with social and community cohesion. Communities that face challenging problems rely heavily on this volunteer labour in order to overcome needs and difficulties, improve their public image, and promote social harmony, understanding, equality, and tolerance.

The growing use of volunteer labour in different facets of everyday life creates a compelling need for all such people who are involved with service organizations (like sport organizations), to review and re-evaluate the existing knowledge regarding volunteer activity. Recruiting and retaining volunteer labour are primary marketing problems (Green & Chalip, 1998; Herron, 1997; Kotler & Andreasen,1996). Understanding what motivates people to get involved in an organization providing free assistance, time and expertise is extremely important because agencies could use this knowledge to design their marketing efforts in a way that could appeal persuasively to this free labour during recruitment time (Cnaan & Goldberg-Glen, 1991).

The whole procedure of evaluating motivational theories and incentives in addition to designing the marketing tools for recruitment and retention of volunteer labour requires a very careful approach and proper consideration. Recruitment and selection processes of volunteers can be proved to be a very expensive endeavour in most cases (Cnaan & Goldberg-Glen, 1991). Limited knowledge of current trends in volunteerism or ignorance of the real needs and motives of volunteers can prove catastrophic for the expansion of volunteer human resources, the morale of the organization, or the execution of a special event.

Additionally, it is also important for the recruiters of volunteer labour to understand that, although the motives that initially influence people to offer free services to any organization may differ from the motives that keep them involved for a long time, it is to the benefit of the organization to detect and understand the initial motives of those who commit themselves for long time periods (Cnaan & Goldberg-Glen, 1991; Gidron, 1984). These are the kind of volunteers that recruiters would prefer to attract rather than short-term volunteers because they save the organization time and monetary resources. The best way to attract long-term commitment volunteers is "to appeal to their motives as long as such motives are known" (Cnaan & Goldberg-Glen, 1991, p. 270).

Despite the growing amount of literature about volunteers in western societies (U.S.A, Europe and Australia), very little is known about the different kinds of volunteer work in Middle Eastern countries and the motivational patterns underpinning them. Studies tend to homogenize categories of volunteers to create large aggregates that do not illuminate possible important differences in patterns of volunteering among various populations. Until it has been clearly described who volunteers and why, scholars cannot move on to more in-depth studies of other issues related to volunteers. As a result, a firmer foundation of knowledge about volunteering in Middle Eastern countries should be developed.

The motorsport mega-event

The inaugural Formula 1 Etihad Airways Abu Dhabi Grand Prix, which took place on 1 November 2009, was a watershed event for the world of motorsport. Most importantly, it was a major landmark event for Abu Dhabi, the United Arab Emirates (UAE) and the motorsport community in this region. While the UAE has been a regional leader in motorsport for over 30 years, the development of the Yas Marina Circuit and staging of the Formula 1 Grand Prix presented challenges in a number of areas for the Automobile and Touring Club of the UAE (ATCUAE), the national governing body of motorsport in that country. A major issue was the need to extrapolate from the country's traditional need for 150 trained officials for a major rally or race event, to more than 700 such individuals required for the first-ever F1 Grand Prix. Coupled with this, volunteerism in sport is a relatively new phenomenon in this country, particularly among the indigenous Emirati community. ATCUAE, therefore, embarked upon a formal research process to generate information concerning the motivation factors for UAE-based individuals to volunteer for the Grand Prix.

Background to this research

Recruitment, selection and training processes for volunteers can be a very expensive endeavour in many cases. Limited knowledge of current trends in volunteerism or ignorance of the real needs and motives of volunteers can undermine the expansion of volunteer human resources, not to mention, in this case, the morale of ATCUAE officials, or even the successful hosting of a special motorsport event.

Thus the purpose of a research project, undertaken by the author, was: a) to examine the primary motives that influence the decision of volunteers of motorsport events to offer their services, time and expertise at the event; b) to explore the major dimensions of volunteerism within motorsport more broadly; and c) to provide insight (motivational profiles) to assist ATCUAE in developing strategies and tactics to overcome the challenges associated with volunteer recruitment.

Methodology

In order to assess the motives of volunteers at the 2009 Grand Prix in Abu Dhabi, volunteers were classified based on their ethnic origin, i.e. expatriates and Emiratis.

Expatriates

The survey used for the purposes of this research was adapted from a scale of volunteerism deployed extensively throughout the USA to assess motivation levels amongst sport volunteers on duty at various sporting events. Several demographic questions addressing factors such as age, gender, marital status, employment status, household income and detailed ethnic background were added to help understand the demographic profile of the UAE expatriate population. The final draft of the instrument consisted of seven demographic-related questions and 35 motivational statements. Expatriates were asked to indicate to what extent each of the motives provided in the survey influenced their decision to volunteer at the Grand Prix event.

Emirati volunteers

An in-depth interview was utilized to assess volunteerism motives for the Emirati volunteers. Since, this was the very first research study of its type undertaken in UAE, the research team did not know beforehand what the Emirati considered to be strong motives for participating as volunteers at motorsport events.

Findings and discussion – expatriates

Identification of the primary motives

The Grand Prix volunteers were asked to indicate to what extent each motivational factor contributed to their decision to volunteer at this sport event. A 5-point Likert scale was used, from 1 (not an important motive at all) to 5 (an extremely important motive).

I. According to the answers given, the most significant motives in order of importance were:

(1) I wanted to be part of the history of hosting a Formula 1 Grand Prix for the very first time in UAE.
(2) I wanted to be close to the action of the race.
(3) I am a motorsport fan.
(4) It is fun to volunteer for the Abu Dhabi Grand Prix.
(5) Volunteering helps prove that the UAE can host major sporting events.

II. On the other hand, the least significant motives in order of importance were:

(1) My school/employer is going to give me an extra credit/bonus for volunteering my services.

(2) My school/employer expects their students/employees to provide community service in the form of volunteering.

(3) I wanted to receive complimentary items and free gifts.

(4) I wanted to be recognized for doing this volunteer work.

(5) Volunteering is in accordance with my religious beliefs.

Expatriate Volunteer Profile

In the main the expatriate volunteer is a devoted fan of motorsport and Formula 1 events, and a person who demonstrates great love for (and typically extensive knowledge of) the sport. The opportunity to be as close as possible to the object of his/her affection is a great motivational factor. That desire is further exploited by the fact that the 2009 Formula 1 Etihad Airways Abu Dhabi Grand Prix was taking place in the UAE for the very first time and being staged at a prestigious new venue, which has attracted the admiration of the sporting world for its progressive design and seemingly endless capabilities. Egoistic (self-serving), motorsport-specific and social interaction motives are the motivating forces behind his/her intentions to volunteer his/her time and services. On the contrary, issues such as complimentary items, recognition, or religious convictions did not play a serious role in his/her decision to volunteer.

Findings and discussions – Emirati volunteers

As mentioned above, for Emirati volunteers, a different data collection approach was deployed. Qualitative data derived from extensive individual interviews of a representative sample of volunteers were used to compare their views with those of the expatriates. Although there are similarities in the way that both groups address motivation for the 2009 Etihad Airlines Abu Dhabi Grand Prix, the Emirati group demonstrated a number of significant differences that need further clarification over the course of subsequent research studies. The following statements are a representative group of motives expressing their unique views. In our question, 'What motivated you to volunteer time, services and expertise for the racing event?', Emirati men and women reported the following distinct motives:

1 There was a sense of doing something that was worthwhile and the appealing idea of serving for a greater cause.

2 Volunteering for the event created a sense of personal accomplishment and an opportunity to express their personality in a meaningful way.

3 Although most of them were temporary fans of motorsports – and Formula 1 in particular – they found the opportunity to be involved

as volunteers a great entertainment option (feeling enjoyment and having fun).

4   Most of the Emiratis seized the opportunity to socialize with people from other cultures and nations, and exchange ideas and knowledge that ranged from social to business or even religious issues. Elements of culture shared were a) histories, legends and jokes; b) rituals, ceremonies and celebrations; c) beliefs and assumptions; d) attitudes; and e) rules, norms, ethical codes and values.

5   Young Emiratis welcomed the opportunity to socialize with people of the opposite sex – in a safe and acceptable way according to social norms – as a form of understanding gender differences and worldviews.

6   Older volunteers (particularly females with children) viewed volunteering as an opportunity to become a role model for the new generation of Emiratis. A mother of three said, in her own words, 'I wanted to set an example for my kids. I want my kids at this early age to learn how to help our neighbours and give back to their country; I want them to understand through my life stories the past and the future of their country, learn to think better than people from my generation.'

7   The event served as a boost to Emirati national identity. A sense of national pride was evident amongst all the Emiratis interviewed. The idea that their country was capable of organizing a sporting event of the Formula 1 Grand Prix generated a lot of enthusiasm and joy.

8   Emirati volunteers recognize that the UAE government had done great things to improve the quality of life of its citizens and expressed their moral obligation to give something back to their government and society as a whole.

9   Volunteerism of any form answers religious calls for compassion and altruism.

10 There was an implied obligation to serve visitors for the event in a way that makes that experience a memorable one for those visiting the Emirates for the race.

11 There was a desire to improve language and communication skills.

12 The nature and scope of the Formula 1 race (an international mega-event that attracted global attention for the UAE) was attractive.

Emirati volunteer profile

The obligation to serve and/or give back to their country and society, the strong desire to act as role models for younger people, doing something they considered to be worthwhile, their compliance with religious norms and sense of national pride are all indicators of the Emirati volunteers' desire to benefit, through their actions, the stated objectives of ATCUAE, contribute to the motorsport event and give back to the wider community. Their connection and support to motorsport is largely of a temporary nature (i.e. they demonstrate strong support while the sport is at the centre of the media attention, but go back to their previous engagement levels when the event is over). This is another major difference in comparison to their contemporaries amongst the expatriate community, who are rather devoted fans of motorsport and of Formula 1 racing specifically. The desire to socialize with people from different walks of life, cultural or ethnic backgrounds and, more importantly, with members of the opposite sex, has a special significance for the Emirati volunteer. Unlike the expatriate, who seeks social interactions for fun, the Emirati volunteer sees this interaction as a means of educating other people about the UAE culture and everyday life, as well as a golden opportunity to meet members of the opposite sex in a safe and socially acceptable environment, one that promotes mutual respect and collaboration.

3.1

Views of the Yas Marina Circuit the night before the inaugural Abu Dhabi Formula 1 Grand Prix, 2009

Source: Getty Images

Definition of volunteering

Volunteering, as defined by the National Centre for Volunteering in the United Kingdom, 'is any activity which involves spending time, unpaid, doing something which aims to benefit someone, individuals or groups, other than or in addition to close relatives or to benefit the environment including animals' (NCVO National Report, 1998).

3.2
Palestinian fans
cheer for their
national team
during the 2012
Olympic qualifying
football match
against Bahrain on
23 June 2011

Source: AFP/Getty
Images

In addition, the Australian Bureau of Statistics (ABS) Voluntary Work survey in 1995 included the following definition of a volunteer as:

> someone who willingly gives unpaid help, in the form of time, service or skills, through an organization or group. An organization or group is any body with a formal structure. It may be as large as a national charity or as small as a local book club. Informal and temporary gatherings of people do not constitute an organization.
>
> ABS Voluntary Work: Preliminary (1995)

This latter definition of volunteering currently includes three important concepts: a) the provision of a service to the community; b) freedom of choice to become involved; and c) non-payment for the service provided (except the reimbursement of expenses). Current Australian literature is also clear that volunteering is not about coercion to be involved, limitation of women's right to workforce participation, substitution of paid workers or provision of a cheaper, 'second-class' service.

Volunteers in sport settings

Any sport or voluntary organization, city council, or governmental agency that takes the initiative to stage a sport event, must plan, organize, coordinate and execute numerous activities concerning the event's organization and promotion in addition to controlling the competition and dealing with the athletes (Farrell *et al.* 1998).

Activities of organizers include, but are not limited to, promoting the event to sponsors and spectators prior to the games, providing venue support (ticketing and ushers) and dealing with parking, concessions and security needs. In major sport events, like World Championships or the Olympic

Games, these activities extend to include logistics, accreditation, media, VIP and sponsors' hospitality, merchandizing sales, medical support and volunteers' training and supervision, to name but a fraction of such demands.

To overcome the lack of skilled event employees and simultaneously address the operational cost of hosting the sport event in question, the organizers appeal to the local community, asking for volunteer workers to assume some of the tasks mentioned above. From this standpoint, volunteers 'enable administrators … to complement and enrich … current services and expand both the quantity and diversity of services without exhausting the agency's budget' (Cnaan and Goldberg-Glen, 1991, p. 270).

Today, volunteers are 'a core component of sport service delivery' (Green and Chalip, 1998, p. 14) and play a significant role in the overall success of many major sport competitions (Beamish, 1985; Berlonghi, 1994; Daly, 1991; McPherson, 1986). They serve sports as coaches, administrators, fund-raisers and staff members. They can be found assisting local sport programs (recreation leagues administered by city authorities), national (Special Olympics programs), or international sport events (FIFA World Cup). Hallmark events, such as the Olympic Games, would simply not succeed without the contribution of skills, time and commitment by the thousands of volunteers who respond to the organizing committee's call for support. At the 2000 Olympic Games in Sydney, Australia required up to 50,000 volunteers, whilst the number for the 2004 Games in Athens, Greece increased to 70,000 volunteers both for the Olympics and the Paralympics, which followed. Other local sporting events may need only several dozen volunteers to function; however, their impact and contribution to the efficient organization of minor sporting events should not be underestimated.

Is volunteering a 'leisure' activity?

Volunteering 'is frequently approached from a human resource perspective' (Green and Chalip, 1998, p. 14). In order to recruit volunteers, administrators write job descriptions, advertise through the media, undertake formal interviews, train and supervise in the same way they would do if hiring paid staff (Brudney, 1990; Green and Chalip, 1998; Lauffer and Gorodezky, 1977; McCurley, 1994). However, Tedrick and Henderson (1989) argue that volunteering is better conceptualized as a leisure choice – not an analogue to work. Volunteers are exchanging their time, effort and labour in order to get, not financial benefits, but rather psychological gains (Green and Chalip, 1998). That conclusion makes volunteering look, in many ways, similar to a leisure choice.

Other studies have also demonstrated that volunteering services, or participation in voluntary associations in general, is considered by many people as a form of leisure activity (Burdge, 1969; Crandall, 1980; Deffe, Schultz and Pasewark, 1974; Dennis and Zube, 1988; Noe, 1973; Stern and Noe, 1973). Beard and Ragheb (1983) in their study measuring leisure motivation proposed that, 'individuals are driven to engage in leisure activities for different reasons, and the study of these reasons, their origins and etiology is central to the understanding of leisure behavior' (Beard and Ragheb,1983, p. 227). Dennis and Zube (1988) and Green and Chalip (1998) have also stated that very little is known about the decision processes involved in adopting leisure activities and even less about the decision processes that lead to volunteer behaviour.

Benefits from volunteering

There are a number of benefits that people can derive from volunteering their time. Young volunteers are always excited with the opportunity to acquire new skills. Research around volunteerism confirms that the development of interpersonal skills (understanding and motivating people, the ability to handle crises and control large crowds) is one of the most desired benefits that volunteers seek from their involvement in sport organizations. In addition, the development of organizational and other managerial skills is a great motivation when people consider various volunteer opportunities. These skills can also be used as a CV-builder for young professionals seeking employment in the sport or entertainment industries.

With the advance of social media and its widespread use by sporting agencies, volunteering services in sport creates opportunities for social networking, for either leisure or professional purposes. Being part of a sporting event or a prestigious sport organization positions volunteers in prominent places to meet and collaborate with staff, clients and/or other volunteers – who often come from diverse backgrounds and possess various professional skills – and, as a result, to enhance the size and quality of their personal network faster and more effectively.

However, benefits that are often underestimated in terms of their importance are health-related ones associated with volunteering (Corporation of National and Community Service, 2008). Research work in many voluntary sectors of the economy has revealed the following remarkable outcomes:

1 *Volunteering services results in greater life satisfaction and reduces anxiety and depression levels*
Personal sense of purpose and accomplishment constitutes one of the most important motives for people seeking volunteer opportunities in sport and recreation (Farrell *et al.*, 1998). Numerous research papers in the field confirm that a well-designed volunteer experience enhances this sense of accomplishment and contribution to society and results in greater levels of life satisfaction and overall happiness (Greenfield and Marks, 2004). In a study conducted by Musick and Wilson (2003), volunteering was also positively associated with lower depression levels amongst older adults.

2 *Volunteering services and physical well-being are positively associated*
Longitudinal studies in the USA have positively associated volunteering with a person's physical well-being; volunteers tend to report higher levels of life

satisfaction, enhanced self-esteem, a sense of control over life and greater levels of physical and mental health than non-volunteers. Furthermore, people who report enhanced self-esteem, high levels of life satisfaction and satisfactory health levels are more likely to volunteer than people who do not (Thoits and Hewitt, 2001).

3 *Individuals who volunteer live longer*
There is strong evidence that people who volunteer services live considerably longer than those who do not – even when taking into consideration factors such as physical health, age, socio-economic status and gender (Musick *et al.*, 1999).

4 *Older volunteers are most likely to receive greater health benefits from volunteering*
Older adults who decide to become volunteers enjoy greater health benefits than those of a younger age. Volunteering is found to be an antidote to depression for older volunteers, who experience significant changes in their role in life and social relations as they grow older (Li and Ferraro, 2006).

It should be said, however, that the health benefits described above only accrue when people pass what is called the 'volunteering threshold'; that is, a considerable amount of volunteering, which can be defined as a) volunteering services with two or more organizations; and b) volunteering a significant amount of hours (at least 40 hours per year or more) for the organizations of choice (Lum and Lightfoot, 2005; Luoh and Herzog, 2002). Once the volunteering threshold is met, no additional health benefits are acquired by increasing the quantity of volunteering.

Barriers to volunteering
Volunteering services, time and expertise at sporting events is not derived without any personal costs being expended. Often, volunteers face a number of challenges in their attempt to serve the sport they love (Gaskin, 2008). Volunteer coordinators should understand that they deal with two distinct groups when they develop strategies to remove barriers to volunteering: a) short-term volunteers (people, who have demonstrated limited capacity to volunteer a substantial amount of hours; and b) non-volunteers. In both cases, the main barriers to volunteering can be summarized as follows:

1 *Time constraints:* A great number of people who decide to become short-term volunteers or abstain from volunteering altogether, mention time constraints that relate to either family or work-related commitments, as the principle reason for their decision. Families with young children, for example, may have difficulty in finding carers to supervise and/or look after their children while they spend time volunteering at a sport venue. Similarly,

people who work excessive hours in demanding jobs may feel overwhelmed and thereby cite a lack of rest time as a further barrier to offering their time and expertise to a sporting event. Volunteer coordinators should recognize the need to provide accommodation, such as day care facilities on site, or develop corporate volunteer programs that allow employees to volunteer their services while they enjoy certain benefits (like time release) from their employers. In both cases, the sport organization needs to recognize the urgent need to intervene with a well-planned solution that alleviates problems related to time constraints and allows volunteers to perform their tasks with the least possible personal cost.

2 *Personal health problems or disability:* Although older couples may not have children currently living in their household, or may have retired from their jobs, they are more likely to mention health problems or a physical disability as a barrier to volunteering. A health problem that requires only mild physical involvement or a physical disability that depends on fully accessible sporting facilities can prohibit older volunteers from seeking volunteer opportunities in sport. Volunteer coordinators need to match disabled and/or older volunteers with tasks that take health and disability issues into consideration. Positions that require limited movement in fully accessible parts of the facility need to be primarily reserved for volunteers who have special needs.

3 *Personality clashes:* Building a diverse workplace with tens or hundreds of volunteers can create an environment that is susceptible to personality clashes. Normally, volunteers are not selected on the basis of organizational or team suitability. In addition, due to the temporary character of their 'employment', volunteers tend to challenge more the organizational chain of command and be less tolerant of personality differences. Volunteer coordinators need to understand that building a team culture early on in the process is a decisive factor in the future success of that group of volunteer workers. Creating open communication channels (daily debriefs, group retreats, brainstorming sessions, etc.) can diffuse unpleasant situations attributed to personality differences and contribute to the success of that volunteer group.

4 *Organizational politics:* Volunteers often complain about the existence of internal politics and power games within the organization they have selected to serve. Situations like these are viewed very unfavourably and often force volunteers to quit prematurely. Volunteer coordinators and staff members need to understand that volunteer labour should be protected from these types of 'experiences' as much as possible. Clear-cut organizational policies and procedures, fairness and openness in all actions that involve volunteers (task assignments and volunteer recognition actions) and regular feedback from volunteers can minimize negative effects from organizational politics and boost the morale of volunteers and their support of the sport organization.

5 *Financial cost of volunteering:* A fact that often goes unnoticed is the overall financial cost of being a sport volunteer. Possible transportation and/or housing costs, meals and use of a personal vehicle can often build up to become a burden, especially to people with limited financial resources. Since sport organizations have a moral obligation to society to provide volunteer opportunities to all people, regardless of financial ability, volunteer coordinators should seriously consider all such factors that constitute a financial burden to volunteers. Whenever possible, attire, transportation and meals need to be covered free of charge or significantly subsidized by the sport organization.

6 *Dissatisfaction with a previous experience:* Dissatisfaction with a previous experience is one of the main reasons that current volunteers cease their involvement with a given sport organization. Although a lot of things can go wrong, volunteer coordinators should always seek alternative ways to establish the correct fit between the volunteer role and the person – given their skills, experience and confidence levels – as well as providing guidance to volunteers on how to perform their tasks well. Substantial effort should be made to develop resources (like orientation programs, volunteer manuals and training, recognition systems and awards, and internal social media) that support the functions discussed above.

7 *Lack of interest:* People will not pursue volunteer experiences that do not appeal to their personal motivations. Volunteer coordinators need to constantly access motives and measure volunteer satisfaction through research. The result of these actions should be job/task descriptions that are designed to improve volunteer skills, experiences and confidence levels. Unless a task is satisfying to some or most of the volunteers' motives then recruitment efforts – over the long run – are destined to fail.

8 *Lack of information on how to get involved:* People often complain that they have limited access to information related to volunteer opportunities. Volunteer recruiters need to understand that potential volunteers should be approached through a well-planned, integrated marketing effort. The use of social media can make this task a little bit easier, especially when dealing with young volunteers. In general, sport agencies need to develop promotional campaigns that specifically target each one of the demographic segments from which they wish to attract to their cadre of volunteers. These campaigns should take account of the unique needs, desires and characteristics of each of the population segments (e.g.. single young professionals, senior citizens, corporate workers, special interest groups, etc.) and tailor their message and distribution (through traditional media, social media, in-game promotions, corporate volunteer programs, etc.) in a way that reaches the targeted groups successfully.

9 *Belief that they have already given enough time to volunteerism:* In many instances, volunteers tend to believe that they have already given enough time offering their services and that they are not needed anymore. This false perception may lead some to cease prematurely their involvement with the sporting agency. During volunteer training and orientation, volunteer coordinators should explain in detail not only the job/task requirements and performance standards, but also the time required to accomplish the predetermined tasks. Unless volunteers have a clear understanding of all requirements, in terms of expected task performance and time commitment, they tend to trivialize and underestimate their contributions and, consequently, lose interest in volunteering in the first place.

10 *'No one asked':* Research repeatedly reveals that the single most important marketing action to attract volunteers is simply asking them to volunteer! Volunteer coordinators can start filling up their pool of volunteers by asking existing customers and fans of the sport organization to undertake volunteer positions within the organization.

Sport volunteers – rights and responsibilities

Volunteer rights

1 Volunteers should be provided with appropriate orientation and training.
2 Volunteer assignments should be clear and abide with the law of the given state.
3 Volunteers should have management's support and constant collaboration.
4 Volunteers should be recognized for their overall contributions to the sport organization.
5 Volunteers need to be respected by the sport organization's paid staff.
6 Volunteers' time needs to be respected as a valuable organizational resource and not be wasted.
7 Volunteers should work under safe, healthy and appropriate working conditions.

Volunteer responsibilities

1 Volunteers need to have full understanding of their role and responsibilities.
2 Volunteers need to be honest about their motives, skills and limitations.

3 Volunteers should accomplish in a professional manner the tasks they have accepted through their appointment.
4 Volunteers should cooperate with paid staff and other volunteers.
5 Volunteers need to be flexible and open-minded when providing services.
6 Volunteers should stay informed about developments that may affect their performance with the sporting agency.
7 Volunteers need to ask for help when they do not have a solution to a problem/crisis, or when they have no authority to act.

Sport agency's rights

1 The agency should expect volunteers' support for the program and its personnel.
2 The agency has the right to perform background checks for all volunteers.
3 The agency has the right to request references and conduct interviews with all prospective volunteers.
4 The agency has the right to require volunteers to attend all scheduled training and study operational manuals.
5 The agency should expect its volunteers to be (and act) responsibly while performing their duties.
6 The agency has the right to reassign sport volunteers if needed.

Sport agency's responsibilities

1 The agency should prepare and provide all volunteers with a written job description.
2 The agency should provide appropriate training that safeguards volunteers' safety and assist them in meeting performance standards.
3 The agency should provide appropriate supervision and task support.
4 The agency should establish open communication channels among paid staff and all volunteers.
5 The agency should not treat volunteers differently from paid staff.
6 The agency should inform volunteers about all special benefits associated with their volunteer status.
7 The agency should consider experienced and/or successful volunteers for leadership positions when they become available.
8 The agency should conduct an exit interview with all volunteers at the end of their commitment.

(Source: Herron, Green and Stepenuck (2009) *The Urban Institute*)

Volunteer trends and their implications

1 *Short-term or 'episodic' commitments*: Most new volunteers today seek assignments with a clear beginning, middle and end. One-time-only volunteering opportunities continue to expand. The good news in all this is that, after people have been engaged in a successful volunteer effort, they often enquire as to what further opportunities exist and what they can do next. Volunteer program managers should start thinking of 'retention' in terms of an ongoing sequence of short-term assignments.

2 *Singles as a target audience*: Connected to the popularity of one-day volunteer projects, there's a new awareness of an old fact: people who volunteer make friends with other volunteers who share their interests. In a world in which young people delay marriage and in which divorce hits half the couples in the USA, it isn't surprising that volunteering is being adopted as part of the so-called 'singles scene'. An increasing number of programs are targeting single volunteers, either as their only participants or for especially designated work shifts.

3 *Internet-based distance learning*: The number and quality of websites, listservs and newsgroups offering resources for volunteer program leaders continues to grow. Several exciting uses of this electronic medium, including complete books, are available at no charge online, increasing the use of audio and the introduction of 'streaming video' for distance learning options. Complete online courses in volunteer management are also available – with some institutions even giving academic credit – so now the challenge is to see how volunteer program managers can adapt the technology to train and update active volunteers.

4 *Family volunteering*: While offering well-intentioned commentary over the years, most agencies have not yet found meaningful ways to put family units to work as volunteers. Interest in this idea is increasing, as evidenced by new guidebooks, training materials and conference presentations. To make the idea work, they have to recognize the many variations that the word 'family' covers today. Intact nuclear families are increasingly in the minority. However, volunteer programs can tap into grandparents raising grandchildren, divorced parents and homes with adults who are each other's 'significant other'.

Motivating volunteers to serve and succeed

Clary *et al.* (1998), in their attempt to understand and assess the motivations of volunteers, adapted a functional approach to motivation as described in the classic theories of attitudes offered by Katz (1960) and Smith *et al.* (1956).

In their incentive (motives) typology, Clary *et al.* (1998) proposed a set of six motivational functions served by volunteerism. These factors (functions) were labelled:

1 VALUES: This motive involves opportunities for volunteers to 'express values related to altruistic and humanitarian concerns for others'.
2 UNDERSTANDING: This motive involves opportunities for volunteers to 'permit new learning experiences and the chance to exercise knowledge, skills and abilities'.
3 SOCIAL: This motive involves opportunities for volunteers 'to be with one's friends or to engage in an activity viewed favorably by important others'.
4 CAREER: This motive involves opportunities 'for career-related benefits that may be obtained from participation in volunteer work'.
5 PROTECTIVE: This motive involves processes associated with 'the functioning of ego, like addressing one's own personal problems'.
6 ENHANCEMENT: This motive involves opportunities for volunteers to 'obtain satisfactions related to personal growth and self-esteem'.

UAE

Strigas (2010) conducted a research study in the UAE in order to investigate the motivational patterns of volunteers for the 2009 Formula 1 Etihad Airways Abu Dhabi Grand Prix. This was one of the very few studies into sport volunteerism to have taken place in a Middle Eastern country. The results indicated a six-dimensional solution that clearly mirrors motivational functions of volunteers found in the literature. The definitions of these motivational dimensions (group of motives) include the following:

1 The first dimension was entitled *Egoistic Dimension* and involves motives (e.g. *I wanted to explore new interests*) related to the individual's needs for self-actualization, self-esteem and achievement. It expresses the volunteer's need to reflect and serve his/her own interests. This dimension also contains motives related to the individual's need to relax, engage with like-minded people and enjoy their surroundings.
2 The second dimension was labelled *Purposive Dimension* and involves motives (e.g. *Volunteering creates a better society*) related to the desire of the volunteers to benefit, through their actions, the stated goals of ATCUAE, the national governing body of motorsport in the UAE, and contribute to the Grand Prix event and thereby, in their minds at least, the community at large.
3 The third dimension was called *Social Interaction* and involves motives (e.g. *I wanted to develop friendships with other volunteers*)

related to the individual's needs for social interaction and interpersonal relationships.

4   The fourth dimension was named *External Influences* and assesses the extent to which motorsport volunteers are engaged in activities influenced by motives (e.g. *My friends are also volunteering at this sporting event*) related to factors outside their immediate control (e.g. family traditions, significant others and so forth).

5   The fifth dimension was labelled *Material Factor – Career Enhancement* and includes motives (e.g. *I wanted to make new contacts that might help my business or career*) that permit volunteers to carry out a rational calculus of expected utility gain (such as the career enhancement benefits of experience and networking) in exchange for their services.

6   The sixth dimension was called *Sport-specific* to indicate the importance of understanding sport-specific issues (likes rules and major athletes playing the game) when motivating people to volunteer at sporting events like the Formula 1 Grand Prix (e.g. *I'm a fanatical motorsports fan*).

A typology of volunteerism

Recent New Zealand research looking at existing, potential and lapsed volunteers identified six distinct types of sport volunteers. Note that sport volunteers 'differ primarily in relation to their attitudes and experiences rather than demographically' (Sport and Recreation New Zealand, 2008, p. 12).

Mutual beneficials – these are sport volunteers who understand that volunteering services, time and expertise creates a win/win situation for both the sporting agency and themselves. Through volunteering, people provide valuable services to their community and the sport they love, while – at the same time – reaping the benefits associated with their involvement (networking, social interactions, skill acquisition, status, reflected glory, etc.).

Investors – these are volunteers who impact the sport agency through their work contributions, but do not receive as much benefit as *mutual beneficials*. These are most likely older volunteers, people who are retired, with no children, or at least none living at their home. They have a selfless interest in their agency; they choose to volunteer for the love of the game or to express their altruistic support to the sport organization.

The cautious, but keen – these are sport volunteers who, while similar to *mutual beneficials* in terms of the benefits they are seeking (networking, skill acquisition, status), are not as engaged (they select carefully the areas of their involvement) and have certain concerns about the commitment levels (usually time commitment) required by the sporting agency.

Social norms – these are sport volunteers who are involved with a sporting agency because a significant other/family member has been/is involved. Their levels of emotional and time commitment to the agency – compared to all other volunteer types – are usually low; they are more likely to volunteer a minimal amount of hours and less likely to volunteer all year round. As the name implies, they volunteer because of external factors (family member, friends) and in order to satisfy an expectation of their social environment to be supportive.

The frustrated – these are sport volunteers who, while they understand, and probably have experienced in the past, the importance and positive aspects of volunteer involvement, feel that their commitment and contributions are not currently being appreciated or adequately recognized. They may have serious concerns in relation to clarity of roles and responsibilities, internal politics or personality clashes with other volunteers or staff members, as well as the time commitment required by the sporting agency.

The disengaged – these are sport volunteers who, it seems, cannot capitalize on the benefits of volunteering (personality issues, overall working environment, personality clashes, etc.) or have experienced some negative situations whilst involved in the past (unorganized volunteer program, internal politics, etc.).

(Source: Sport and Recreation New Zealand, 2008)

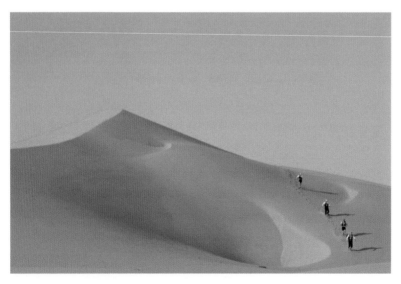

3.3
Extreme sports are growing in the region

Source: Getty Images

Volunteer recruitment

After identifying the sport organization's needs in relation to volunteers (in terms of tasks to be accomplished and number of people to be recruited), volunteer coordinators need to develop a recruitment plan. At the beginning of this process, the following set of questions – for each volunteer assignment – needs to be addressed (AAAT, 2001):

1   Who might be interested in the position?
    ACTION: Identify all such demographic groups that may express a high interest in the position.
2   Who will be qualified to fill this position?
    ACTION: Develop a list of targeted individuals or groups of people who most likely possess the abilities and qualifications required for the volunteer task.
3   Who will be able to meet time requirements for this position?
    ACTION: Calculate time requirements for the volunteer task at hand and clearly communicate these time commitment require-ments to possible volunteers.
4   Where will the agency find these people?
    ACTION: Locate places, sporting and other special events, rival service organizations, corporations, schools, religious and other venues, chat rooms, online environments, social media outlets, etc. where potential qualified volunteers may be found.
5   What motivates potential volunteers to serve?
    ACTION: Identify all motives that each volunteer assignment may satisfy (e.g. the need to socialize with people belonging to the same age group, opposite sex, etc.).
6   What is the best way (communication mix) to approach potential volunteers?
    ACTION: Develop a list with all communication actions (direct mail, word of mouth, social media campaigns, live presentations, etc.) to be used in order to advertise the position to potential volunteers. Note that specific messages appeal to specific audiences; there is not just one universal recruitment message that will successfully entice all potential volunteers.

Table 3.1

Information
on trends and
promising practices
with regard
to recruiting
volunteers

Most useful ways to find volunteers	
Word of mouth	71%
Internet recruitment services	37%
Live presentations to groups	33%
Events	29%
Newspaper ads	29%
Local volunteer centre	17%
Relationships with local corporations	15%
Direct mail	8%
Radio/TV ads	8%

Source: Smith and Feuer (2007)

When the volunteer assignment requires specialized training (e.g. operating a sophisticated ticket sales software), extensive time commitment (e.g. interning with a sport organization for a six-month period) and/or high level of expertise (e.g. a requirement for extensive experience in crowd control management), a targeted volunteer recruitment plan is the best approach for meeting the needs of the sport organization. When the volunteer assignment requires no special attention on behalf of the management team and/or a great number of people to fill volunteer positions, then a broad-based volunteer recruitment approach is recommended.

Targeted volunteer recruitment
Targeted recruitment is a specific and highly focused marketing campaign that addresses target audiences and/or individuals with the specialized skills, interests and time availability needed for the volunteer assignment. It requires greater effort on behalf of the management team because they have to outline, as clearly as possible, the person they are seeking to recruit for the assignment and the type of motivational message that will entice prospects to come forward.

Broad-based volunteer recruitment
For volunteer assignments that require minimal training, or for short-term sporting events where a large number of volunteers are needed, broad-based recruitment is the recommended option. The purpose of a broad-based recruitment plan is to keep the organization's needs for volunteer labour in the public eye through numerous communication strategies (Herron *et al.*, 2009). Some of these strategies are presented below:

1 Constantly keep your brand in the public eye, through newsworthy activities and collaboration; exposure builds name recognition and this can be helpful next time the organization is looking for qualified volunteers.
2 Use existing volunteer opportunity directories and referral services such as community or university volunteer centres.
3 Network with other community groups and leaders and collaborate in mutually beneficial local projects.
4 Encourage existing or past volunteers to share their success stories with other members of the local community; word of mouth is the best recruitment tool.

Tips for recruitment

1 Collaborate with other established groups in the community that have compatible interests (local sport clubs, school varsity teams, fitness clubs, etc.).

2   Do not start the recruitment process unless everything is in place for the volunteers.

3   Provide support in the form of formal training, training manuals, facilities and supervision.

4   Build a diverse volunteer workforce.

5   Develop partnerships with other service organizations and higher education institutions.

6   Share recruitment efforts and volunteers with other service organizations (schools, non-profit organizations, other sporting agencies, etc.).

7   Develop joint marketing and public relations campaigns (in order to attract volunteers) with other service organizations in the area.

Summary

Volunteerism is synonymous with economic efficiency, innovation and social cohesion. Volunteer labour is extremely valuable to an organization because it provides its administrators with the ability to sustain services, expand the quantity, quality and diversity of those services and at the same time maintain the budget within its prespecified limits (Strigas and Jackson, 2004). For individuals associated with voluntary organizations, offering time, services and expertise helps them increase their self-esteem, develop new relationships, enhance skills and abilities, remain active, reduce depression levels and build healthier attitudes concerning the aging process (Shin and Kleiner, 2003). However, one of the predominant benefits of volunteering has to do with social and community cohesion. Communities that face challenging problems rely heavily on this volunteer labour in order to overcome needs and difficulties, improve their public image and promote social harmony, understanding, equality and tolerance.

The process of evaluating motivational theories and incentives in addition to designing the marketing tools for recruitment and retention of volunteer labour requires a very careful approach and proper consideration. For example, when the volunteer assignment requires specialized training (e.g. operating a sophisticated ticket sales software) extensive time commitment (e.g. interning with a sport organization for a six-month period) and/or high level of expertise (e.g. requirement for extensive experience in crowd control management), a *targeted volunteer recruitment* plan is the best approach for meeting the needs of the sport organization. When the volunteer assignment requires no special attention on behalf of the management team and/or a great amount of people to fill in volunteer positions, then a *broad-based volunteer recruitment* approach is recommended.

Recruitment and selection processes for volunteers can prove to be a very expensive endeavour in a lot of cases (Cnaan and Goldberg-Glen, 1991). Limited knowledge of current trends in volunteerism or ignorance of the real needs and motives of volunteers can be proved catastrophic for the expansion of volunteer human resources, the morale of the organization in question or the execution of a special event, such as a Formula 1 Grand Prix.

References

American Association of American Theater (2001). *Volunteer recruitment*. Fort Worth, TX: Author. Retrieved June 20, 2011, from www.aact.org/running/VolunteerRecruitment.pdf.

Australian Bureau of Statistics (1995). *Voluntary work, Australia: Preliminary*. Canberra: Author.

Beamish, R. (1985). Sport executives and voluntary associations: A review of the literature and introduction to some theoretical issues. *Sociology of Sport Journal*, 2, 218–232.

Beard, J. and Ragheb, M. (1983). Measuring leisure satisfaction. *Journal of Leisure Research* 12(1), 20–23.

Berlonghi, A. (1994). *The special event risk management manual* (Rev. ed.). Dana Point, CA: Alexander Berlonghi.

Brudney, J. L. (1990). *Fostering volunteer programs in the public sector*. San Francisco: Jossey-Bass.

Burdge, R. J. (1969). Levels of occupational prestige and leisure activity. *Journal of Leisure Research* 1(3), 262–274.

Clary, E.G., Ridge, R.D., Stukas, A.A., Snyder, M., Copeland, J., Haugen, J. and Miene, P. (1998). Understanding and assessing the motivations of volunteers: A functional approach. *Journal of Personality and Social Psychology*, 74(6), 1516–1530.

Cnaan, R.A., and Goldberg-Glen, R.S. (1991). Measuring motivation to volunteer in human services. *Journal of Applied Behavioral Science*, 27, 269–284.

Crandall, R. (1980). Motivations for leisure. *Journal of Leisure Research*, 12(1), 45–54.

Daly, J. A. (1991). *Volunteers in South Australian sport: A study*. Canberra: Australian Sports Commission.

Deffe, J.F., Schultz, J.H. and Pasewark, R.A. (1974). Occupational level and organizational membership. *Journal of Leisure Research*, 6(1), 20–26.

Dennis, S., and Zube, E.H. (1988). Voluntary association membership of outdoor recreationists: An exploratory study. *Leisure Sciences*, 10, 229–245.

Farrell, J.M., Johnston, M.E., and Twynam D.G. (1998). Volunteer motivation, satisfaction, and management at an elite sporting competition. *Journal of Sport Management*, 12, 288–300.

Gaskin, K. (2008). *A winning team? The impacts of volunteers in sport*. The Institute for Volunteering Research and Volunteering England. Retrieved June 20, 2011, from http://www.ivr.org.uk/NR/rdonlyres/2D1DDC0B-0093-470A-93673BE120584532/0/ A_Winning_Team.pdf.

Gidron, B. (1984). *Rewards from sustained volunteer work: A study of volunteers in family health and mental health institutions*. Unpublished doctoral dissertation, University of Maryland, Baltimore Professional Schools.

Green B.C., and Chalip L. (1998). Sport volunteers: Research agenda and application. *Sport Marketing Quarterly*, 7(2),14–23.

Greenfield, E. and Marks, N. (2004). Formal volunteering as a protective factor for older adults' psychological well-being. *The Journals of Gerontology*, 59(5), S258–S264.

Hager, M. and Brudney, J. (2004). *Volunteer management practices and retention of volunteers*. Washington, DC: The Urban Institute. Retrieved June 20, 2011, from www.urban.org/uploadedPDF/411005_VolunteerManagement.pdf.

Herron, D.B. (1997). *Marketing nonprofit programs and services*. San Francisco: Jossey-Bass.

Herron, E., Green, L. and Stepenuck, K. (2009). *Volunteer management and support*. USDA National Facilitation of Cooperative State Research Education Extension Service (CSREES) Volunteer Monitoring Efforts. Retrieved June 20, 2011, from www.usawaterquality.org/volunteer.

Katz, D. (1960). The functional approach to the study of attitudes. *Public Opinion Quarterly*, 24, 163–204.

Kotler, P. and Andreasen, A. R. (1996). *Strategic marketing for nonprofit organizations* (5th ed.). Upper Saddle River, NJ: Prentice Hall.

Lauffer, A., and Gorodezky, S. (1977). *Volunteers*. Beverly Hills: Sage.

Li, Y., and Ferraro, K. (2006). Volunteering in middle and later life: Is health a benefit, barrier, or both? *Social Forces*, 85(1), 497–519.

Lum, T. and Lightfoot, E. (2005). The effects of volunteering on the physical and mental health of older people. *Research on Aging*, 27(1), 31–55.

Luoh, M. and Herzog, A. (2002). Individual consequences of volunteer and paid work in old age: Health and mortality. *Journal of Health and Social Behavior*, 43(4) 490–509.

McCurley, S. (1994). Recruiting and retaining volunteers. In R. D. Herman (Ed.), *The Jossey-Bass handbooks of non-profit leadership and management* (pp. 511–534). San Francisco: Jossey-Bass.

McPherson, B.D. (1986). Policy-oriented research in youth sport: An analysis of the process and product. In C.R. Rees and A.W. Miracle (Eds), *Sport and social theory* (pp. 255–287). Champaign, IL: Human Kinetics.

Musick, M. and Wilson, J. (2003). Volunteering and depression: The role of psychological and social resources in different age groups. *Social Science and Medicine*, 56(2), 259–269.

Musick, M., Herzog, A. and House (1999). Volunteering and mortality among older adults: Findings from a national sample. *Journal of Gerontology, Series B: Psychological Sciences and Social Sciences*, 54(3), S173–S180.

National Council for Voluntary Organizations (1998). *National Report*. London: Author.

Noe, F.P. (1973). The political ideology of the leisure class. *Journal of Leisure Research*, 5(3), 49–59.

Shin, S. and Kleiner, B. (2003). How to manage unpaid volunteers in organizations. *Management Research News*, 26(2–4), 63–71.

Smith, G. and Feuer, S. (2007). *Effective practices in recruiting and retaining volunteers: An adult literacy perspective.* White paper. Orlando, FL: The Florida Literacy Coalition. Retrieved November 18, 2012 from www.floridaliteracy.org/volrecretention.pdf.

Smith, M., Bruner, J. and White, R. (1956). *Opinions and Personality.* New York: Wiley.

Sport and Recreation New Zealand (2008). *Volunteers: The experiences and motivations of sport volunteers.* Wellington, New Zealand: Author. Retrieved November 20, 2012 from www.sportnz.org.nz/en-nz/Information-For/Volunteers.

Stern, S. and Noe, F. (1973). Affiliation-participation in voluntary associations: A factor in organized leisure activity. *Sociology and Social Research*, 57(4), 473–481.

Strigas, A. (2010). *Motorsport volunteerism in the UAE: Research findings from the 2009 Etihad Airways Abu Dhabi Grand Prix.* Automobile and Touring Club of the United Arab Emirates. Abu Dhabi: UAE.

Strigas, A. and Jackson, N. (2004). Assessment of motivational patterns and demographic characteristics for college student volunteers. *ICHPED-SD Journal*, 40(4), 60–63.

Tedrick, T. and Henderson, K. (1989). *Volunteers in leisure.* Reston, VA: American Association for Health, Physical Education, Recreation and Dance.

Thoits, P. and Hewitt, L. (2001). Volunteer work and well-being. *Journal of Health and Social Behavior*, 42(2), 115–131.

4

Sport marketing in the modern age

A case study of Etihad Airways' sponsorship of Manchester City Football Club

Hisham J. Al Masari and Sean O'Connor

Overview

Today almost everyone is exposed (albeit to varying degrees) to the activities of the sport industry, regardless of where they live in the world. Sport is watched on television, read about in the print media, listened to on the radio, viewed on the Internet and discussed amongst friends and family. People attend events, buy merchandise, play sports computer games, and are made aware of a wide range of promotional and marketing campaigns using sport or sports stars to sell goods (Mullin, Hardy, and Sutton, 2007; Graham *et al.*, 2001; Shank, 1999).

The Middle East markets, on an individual or collective basis, represent a unique challenge to those involved in the study and practice of sport marketing. The authors have been involved as marketing professionals across the region for almost three decades and bring their experiences to bear throughout this chapter. At present sport is benefiting from very significant investment in the region, especially in the Gulf Cooperation Council (GCC). While the FIFA World Cup project in Qatar must be regarded as the regional flagship in terms of sport marketing potential, equally, both of the United Arab Emirate's (UAE's) major airlines, Emirates and Etihad, have recently begun to increase their market profile by using sport as a key marketing tool. In light of this evolution, and indeed the broader growth of sport marketing across the Middle East, an appreciation of professional sport marketing strategies designed to ensure a return on objectives (ROO) and/or a return on investment (ROI) for the stakeholders involved is required.

According to Shank (1999), as the sport industry has flourished it has triggered the creation of more vocationally relevant jobs, and nowadays more students are becoming interested in careers in the sport industry than ever before. On a global scale, the role of Mark McCormack and his IMG sports and media group has been an important catalyst for such changes as are being witnessed in recent times, and indeed in the adoption of marketing by and through sport on the part of those who previously may not have considered this medium relevant to their prospective target markets. Founded in 1960, IMG enjoyed early success with both golf and tennis and today it has 3,000 employees working in 30 markets involved in providing a range of services including talent representation, media rights, sponsorship and consultancy to leading sports federations, leagues and competitions, and of course individual sports professionals.

In stark contrast to what is broadly accepted to be sport marketing in its most refined form, Saudi Arabia, a key market in the Middle East, only recently witnessed the formation of the country's first sport marketing agency. Since then, Sela Sport, a Jeddah-based company, has generated over 1.6 billion Saudi Riyals in new revenue for Saudi sport. However, many of the budgets associated with sport are still managed by traditional adverting agencies rather than by the specialised sport marketing providers, such as IMG, and thus the niche field of sport marketing has, for the most part, remained just that.

Murray and O'Driscoll (1999) confirm that the relationship between the theory and practice of marketing is an ongoing and evolving field. They suggest that the creation of knowledge capital in the marketplace arises following the integration of the practitioner *and* the researcher. This integration is one of the unique features of the Institute for Sport Research (ISR) in the UAE, founded in December 2010 as a result of collaboration between the Automobile and Touring Club of the UAE (ATCUAE) and the University of Ulster, UK. The ISR intends to help develop new knowledge in the area of sport management in the Middle East via research, knowledge transfer and education programmes and recently spawned a further dimension to its work through the creation of the Motorsport Knowledge Institute (MKI), which focuses specifically on work in the field of motorsport.

What is sport marketing?

Sport is broadly understood as a game, contest or competitive activity usually involving some level of physical exertion. In contrast, Kotler *et al.* (2008)

observe how different scholars have defined the process of marketing in a variety of different, often contradictory, ways. That said, he concludes that a synthesis of agreed definitions leads one to conclude that marketing is,

> the processes by which companies create value for customers and build strong customer relationships in order to capture value from customers in return.
>
> Kotler *et al.* (2008)

Mullin *et al.* (2007) claim that the publication *Advertising Age* first coined the term 'sport marketing' in 1978 to describe the activities of consumer, industrial product and service marketers which were increasingly using sport as a promotional vehicle. Not surprisingly, however, since its first use, the term 'sport marketing' has had many definitions and appears to be in a continual state of flux, albeit that adapting to the needs of the end-user is paramount and constant in this process.

Today, a useful, practical definition of sport marketing is provided by Shilbury *et al.* (2009), who parallel some of Kotler's earlier observations when claiming that 'sport marketing is a social and managerial process by which the sport manager seeks to obtain what sporting organisations need and want through creating and exchanging products and value with others' (p.13).

Evidence that the term and indeed the practice of sport marketing is a comparatively recent phenomenon (and since then an evolving one) is confirmed by the fact that Howell (1983), one of the foremost British sports administrators of the late twentieth century, makes no reference to the specific term 'sport marketing'. The Howell report, named after its Chairman, a former UK Minister of Sport, was developed by a committee of enquiry, set up in 1981 by the Central Council for Physical Recreation. The committee was to enquire into the rise in sports sponsorship and consider the effects of this for the integrity and well-being of sport as a social and cultural concept throughout the UK. Whilst in fact it did not refer to any analogous terms one might expect in a report of this type – sport management, sport marketing or event marketing – the report does describe marketing in the context of sport as 'an integrated and professionally planned and executed promotion of sport, event, programme or individual' (Howell, 1983, p.7). However, at the very same time that this report was being compiled, the authors of this chapter were engaged in the first ever professional sport marketing programme for the tobacco brand Marlboro on a Pan-Arab basis, underlining the fact that sport marketing in the contemporary sense was alive and well and, consequently, it could be accurately claimed, has been in existence throughout the region since the early 1980s.

The term 'event marketing' is employed by Graham *et al.* (2001) to help make a distinction between traditional and contemporary forms of marketing practice. The former is classified as the marketing of events by organisers, whilst the latter is reflective of a new strategy employed by companies and communities to reach target consumers beyond the traditional advertising mediums (Graham *et al.*, 2001). Support for the validity of this term can perhaps be derived from the industry itself. Philip Morris, who produced the Marlboro brand, was motor sports' largest 'non-trade' sponsor (Williams, 2001). The Event Marketing Department of Philip Morris managed all the Marlboro sponsorship programmes in Formula 1, the World Rally Championship and Grand Prix Motorbikes, including the Middle East Rally Championship and other sponsorships throughout the GCC in particular.

From an academic perspective, Shank (1999) positions 'sport marketing' as one of the key elements in the study of what is referred to as sports administration, an early form of what is more widely understood today as the practice of sport management. He describes sport marketing as a multidimensional field of study encompassing a wide variety of activities, some of which are difficult to discern or adequately describe. Nevertheless, Shank (1999) suggests an appropriate definition of sport marketing as, 'the specific application of marketing principles and processes to sports products and to the marketing of non sports products through association with sport' (p.2). A case could be made that Shank's (1999) definition lends to the division of the field into three stand-alone areas, namely:

1 the marketing of sport
2 the marketing of sports equipment
3 the marketing of non-sports products through sport.

In some cases, it could be argued persuasively that there exists a symbiotic relationship between these three disciplines, which are otherwise thought of as different. In fact, the recent publication, Driving Motorsport Forward

Together, the FIA Middle East strategy report, would seem to endorse such an approach (ATCUAE 2010) in the promotion and development of new forms of motorsport in the Middle East.

The above analysis further supports the existence of an 'exchange process' in the context of sport marketing (Kotler *et al.* 2008, Mullin *et al.* 2007, Shilbury *et al.* 2009). According to Shank (1999), the understanding of the exchange process is central to any successful marketing strategy. He sets out the general definition of this process as involving, 'a marketing transaction in which the buyer gives something of value to the seller in exchange for goods and services' (p.29).

Shank (1999) further suggests that, for such an exchange to take place, the following conditions must be satisfied:

1 There must be at least two parties.
2 Each party must have something of value to offer.
3 There must be a means of communication between the two parties.
4 Each party must be free to accept or decline an offer.
5 Each party must feel that it is desirable to deal with the other(s).

Another confusing element in the proper understanding of this domain is the use of sports (plural) rather than sport (singular) marketing. Mullin *et al.* (2007) contends that the plural form tends to imply the industry is a diverse and uncoordinated series of segments that have little commonality. Rather they believe that for standard practice to develop the industry needs to be treated as a homogeneous entity.

Mullin *et al.* (2007) further adapt a general definition of marketing to describe sport marketing as consisting of,

> all activities designed to meet the needs and wants of sport consumers through exchange process. Sport marketing has developed two major thrusts: the marketing of sports products and services directly to consumers, and marketing of consumer and industrial products or services through the use of sport promotions.
>
> (p.5)

Marketing practice in sport

In a study of the European sport industry, Rines (2001) is critical of its poor management, stating that,

> there is still a long way to go before the sports industry reaches the level of business maturity seen in other industries. So far, its revenues have been driven by television and by simply charging high admission rates to spectators.
>
> (p.2)

Eighteen years earlier, Howell (1983) made a similar observation when he highlighted the lack of expertise evident within many governing bodies controlling sport and the failure to recognise that all aspects of sport management, particularly the area of media relations, needed to be significantly improved. The authors would argue that this remains the case in many organisations in the Middle East today. Indeed, the very term 'Public Relations' is misunderstood as a profession in the Gulf region, where it is a title given to the person designated to generate visas in state organisations. This is a very different role from the board-level public relations profession employed by major sports organisations in other parts of the world.

4.2
Over 30 years ago, Saudia Airlines proved to be an innovative sponsor of the Williams Formula 1 team

Source: Getty Images

Marketing myopia

The term 'marketing myopia' was introduced over 50 years ago by Levitt (2004) to describe the practice of defining a business in terms of goods and services rather than in terms of the benefits that consumers seek. Shank (1999) reports that organisations that fail to recognise the link between sports and entertainment suffer from 'marketing myopia'. He further suggests that sports organisations can eliminate marketing myopia by focusing on the needs of consumers rather than on the production and selling of sports products.

Many Middle East sports organisations still believe that the only way to market their product is to secure success on the field of play. The flaw present in this theory, however, according to Bovinet (2004), is that it is impossible to achieve this on a consistent basis due to factors such as injuries and competition. Moreover, sport marketing is never wholly about instant return on investment and a long-term, strategic approach is both preferable and ultimately achieves greatest value for the client. The authors of this chapter, drawing upon a blend of professional marketing expertise and academic scholarship in the field of sport, would endorse this view.

Lamb (1991) offers his opinion of minor baseball league operators whilst exploring the problem of non-attendance at such games by potential consumers. He draws a contrast with fast-moving consumer goods (FMCG) companies such as Procter & Gamble and Nabisco, and their depth of knowledge with regard to their brands' consumers, and the comparable lack of such research by operators of minor league baseball. A later study by Derrick (1999) further examines this issue and concludes that sport in general must change its philosophy around how it is managed and become more consumer focused in order to remain competitive. This warning is equally relevant to all stakeholders of sport in the Middle East region to the present day.

Two case studies, dealing with rugby in New Zealand and cricket in Australia and selected from Gilson, *et al.* (2001), reveal that both sports were forced to adopt full-scale marketing orientation plans as a result of external factors/threats. Once they adopted these principles, however, the sports grew, and both consumer support and revenue increased (Gilson *et al.*, 2001). A case study of the marketing of the World Rally Championship (O'Connor 2005) underlines the difficulties that a promoter faces in moving a sport from being one that was primarily sporting led to one that is marketing led.

Today the sports apparel firm Reebok is, according to Santomier (2001), one of the best companies currently marketing through sport. He states that its objective is to become the number one sport/fitness brand in the athletic shoe market, which is currently valued at between US $12 and 15 billion, through a strategy which includes sponsorship and endorsements across a range of sporting platforms. In a marketplace that also includes Nike and Adidas, this is by no means a straightforward process. More recently the UAE airline Etihad has also proved itself adept at marketing through sport, as the case study detailed below serves to effectively illustrate.

Case Study: Etihad Airways – Manchester City Football Club

(Based on 2010 Arabian Sponsorship Awards submission)

Project details

Project Title (the name by which your entry will be referred to on all publicity material)	ETIHAD AIRWAYS, OFFICIAL CLUB SPONSOR AND SHIRT SPONSOR OF MANCHESTER CITY FOOTBALL CLUB
Name of Sponsor	Etihad Airways
Budget	£600,000 plus sales and marketing

Annual Rights Fee	Confidential due to agreement
Annual Exploitation Budget	£600,000 plus sales and marketing

In 2008, Etihad researched a sponsorship that would give the company global brand awareness and help expand its UK and UAE businesses. The goal was to reach a wider mass of consumers with special focus on those in the UAE and Manchester, UK.

The English Premier League (EPL) was identified as an ideal sponsorship platform to achieve these objectives, as association football is by far the most popular global sport and is particularly well developed in England. Somewhat fortuitously, Sheikh Mansour bin Zayed al Nahyan's acquisition of Manchester City Football Club (MCFC) provided Etihad with the opportunity to launch its UK and global business-to-consumer strategy through sport by engagement with a club that was now owned by one of the key figures in the UAE.

This sponsorship was expected to position Etihad as an industry leader in the global market and help build a strong consumer network in the UAE and the UK. Etihad also hoped to increase its revenue streams to and from Manchester through an increase in the number of people flying into the UAE. Previously, this sector had been underperforming as a route for the airline.

Sponsorship planning – rationale and objectives

The UAE is viewed as a 'travel' nation; flights to the UAE are popular for short sunshine breaks or as a connecting hub to eastern destinations such as Sydney, Bangkok and/or Singapore.

The UK is important commercially for Etihad; since 2003, the UK sales figures witnessed steady growth, but from 2007 the airline has been reviewing its strategy for a dramatic increase and expansion plans. Sponsorship, specifically its association with Manchester City FC, was a key component of this strategy.

Etihad believed that sponsoring an English Premier League (EPL) team offered:

- a great promotional and customer entertainment platform within the UK consumer/corporate markets;
- engagement of the Middle Eastern market in the sponsorship, serving to grow the business from the UAE;
- global promotion of the Etihad brand, particularly in Europe and Asia, to thereby widen its customer base.

Interestingly, in Q2 2008, as Chelsea FC's official airline, Etihad was in discussions with that club to replace the electronics and media firm Samsung as its shirt sponsor for the 2010–11 season. However, when HH Sheikh Mansour bin Zayed Al Nahyan purchased Manchester City FC, Etihad immediately adapted its strategy and opened discussions within two months of the club's purchase. It was self-evident that Abu Dhabi was to receive a heightened level of promotion and, as the de facto consumer brand of Abu Dhabi, Etihad represented the club's perfect commercial partner. Additionally, Etihad and Manchester City's values proved complementary; both had bold ambitions to be leaders in their field. At that time it was clear that Manchester City was going to command very prominent coverage in the global sporting media, and it made perfect sense that Etihad became the lead sponsor and thus capitalised upon this publicity for mutual gain.

Sponsorship objectives

- increase sales to and from the UAE, and to and from Manchester (individual, corporate and trade consumers);
- increase global brand and destination awareness amongst consumers;
- engage and interact with fan base, increasing brand awareness in local markets (the UK and the UAE) to gain new consumers;
- Etihad also wanted to create new fans for the club from the UAE/Arabian Gulf.

Sponsorship execution – fan engagement and brand awareness

Upgrade your seat initiative
A competition to win two hospitality seats and Etihad VIP treatment at each home game reflected Etihad's brand philosophy; winners were collected at home in the Etihad Gold taxis, greeted with a gift pack and experienced the game from the Etihad Golden Seats. Approximately 3,500 fans entered this competition over a seven-month period.

Soccer schools Abu Dhabi

- Manchester City FC's leading stars took part in coaching and media interviews in Abu Dhabi to further enhance the close link between the UAE and the club.
- Over 400 juniors participated in these soccer schools, proving their widespread popularity.

- This initiative alone generated over US $117,000 of local and international TV and print coverage.
- This increased the fan base of Manchester City FC in the UAE and highlighted the sponsorship link to Arabic consumers.

Big shirt promotion

In August 2010, thousands of Etihad consumers in the UAE signed and presented a giant shirt to Manchester City to recognise their return to the country, which they used as a base for their pre-season training. In a reciprocal move, the shirt was then signed by the team and other UK-based fans and was showcased at the club's home ground, Eastlands, during the 2010–11 season. Considerable public relations benefits and associated digital content in the UAE and Manchester documented the shirt's journey, thereby generating brand awareness to wider audiences/consumers.

Competition

- At the Manchester City versus Manchester United EPL game during the 2010–11 season, fans could win a holiday for four to any one of Etihad's many global destinations.
- Fans had to download online 'wacky' paper sunglasses two weeks before the game, choosing from four available designs. Each design symbolised the 'winter sun' destination they could fly to using Etihad Airways.
- To win, fans had to wear the sunglasses at half-time during the all-Manchester clash. Cameras would roam the crowds and one winner would be selected instantly and awarded the prize.
- On the night, a team of Etihad Airways-branded promotional girls distributed an additional 50,000 'winter break' sunglasses, increasing the overall power of the promotional initiative considerably.

'Coming home' competition

- This was also a competition to fly two fans 'home' to Eastlands for the aforementioned Manchester United game and included a chance to meet the club's star players, have their photograph taken on the pitch at half-time and have an all-expenses paid VIP day out at the club.
- Followers of the club from throughout the world submitted

a video explaining why they should win the prize. Fans then had to vote online for the best entry.

- This initiative had a tremendous viral effect on Facebook, Twitter and other social media platforms. Entrants appealed to their local media (i.e. Toronto, Sydney) to generate local support for votes.
- Some 7,900 entries were received from destinations across the world, including Abu Dhabi, Frankfurt, Cape Town, Toronto, Sydney, Melbourne and New York.

Player of the Month

Etihad decided to take the industry standard 'Player of the Month' competition one step further. Fans who participated in the vote to identify the club's player of the month were in turn placed in a prize draw to interview the player in person. The prize presentation was filmed, in turn creating excellent online content and achieving Etihad's objective of fan engagement and brand awareness.

Sales promotions

- Discounted fares for fans. This was a season-long campaign offered to Manchester City staff and season ticket holders, which promoted discounted fares for those who wished to avail themselves of these.
- Win a holiday with Etihad/MCFC fan holiday packages. Holiday packages were also offered to fans wishing to see the pre-season friendly game staged between Manchester City FC and the UAE national team. Packages started at £699, including accommodation, return flights and match day tickets for the game staged in the UAE. Packages for this particular promotion sold out in less than one month.
- Etihad holidays. A series of 'UAE/MCFC home game package holidays' were launched and were targeted at a wider fan base (Manchester United/Liverpool/Chelsea fans, etc.).

Public relations: global coverage

- There was a huge volume of MCFC news headlines and Etihad's shirt positioning, thereby benefitting Etihad's global brand exposure.
- Repucom Brand Analysis (RBA) media value translated to approximately £10 million and US $18 million (global) – $2

million (global) more and £6 million more than Carlsberg's media value from its shirt sponsorship activities (source: Repucom).

UAE mascot for Derby Day

- This was a competition staged on BBC Radio 2 to find the Manchester City mascot.
- Etihad flew the winner and his father to Manchester City for this once-in-a-lifetime experience. Sparky, the Radio 2 presenter, travelled with the mascot and captured his experience on camera to promote on Radio 2's Facebook and websites. This specific initiative served to further develop relationships with the wider Manchester community.
- Monthly competitions for tickets for Etihad's hospitality through local radio and print, i.e. Manchester Evening News (MEN) and Key 103 radio station continued with considerable success.

Media sponsorship

- Sponsorship of the MEN MCFC column in return for PR/branding opportunities in the business pages, designed to reach a wider consumer audience.

Digital

- This is a core component in promoting Etihad's competitions, brand awareness and interacting with wider fan base/consumers.
- MCFC's website generates approximately 800,000 unique users every month; Facebook page has approx 150,000 fans.
- Club's website, Facebook and Twitter pages were used to refer fans to www.etihadfootball.com, where they could enter other competitions and win flights/holidays.
- The website www.etihadfootball.com was the 'call to action' on all Etihad/MCFC advertising.

Advertising

- Photo shoot with six players used for bespoke MCFC advertising to promote flights/competitions/special fares in club and Manchester-based media. The shoot was also used to generate in-flight/viral content to spread Etihad's brand awareness even wider than the football fraternity. MCFC TVC produced content to be broadcast in Abu Dhabi and other GCC markets from November 2010.

Branding

- Stadium branding, hospitality branding, LED screens were used to promote special promotions, increasing awareness locally and internationally.

Corporate hospitality

- The box was completely redesigned to match the high quality of the Etihad First Class lounges, including VIP gifts and First Class spectator seats (sofa-style loungers with inbuilt heaters).
- The stadium was used to entertain trade partners from Australia, Ireland, Singapore, China, South Africa and Germany, the Chamber of Commerce, media, suppliers, internal stakeholders and fans – vital for direct business and spreading the brand's experience/service to consumers.

Etihad guest

- Etihad's award-winning customer rewards scheme ran monthly promotions for consumers worldwide to win tickets to MCFC matches and other prizes such as 'Be the Etihad MCFC Mascot'.

In-flight

- Etihad promoted their sponsorship with in-flight announcements around key matches, regular features in the in-flight magazine and the MCFC season highlights video.

Sponsorship evaluation

Since Etihad's sponsorship strategies execution, the airline witnessed a greater than 35% increase in the Manchester/Abu Dhabi route in 2009. Etihad's loyalty programme witnessed a 34% increase in members in 2009. The RBA media value translated to approximately £10 million and US $18 million (global).

4.3
Ford Abu Dhabi
World Rally Team
competing in the
Swedish Rally

Source: Getty
Images

According to Rines (2001), many companies marketing through sport fail to fully exploit the rights they have acquired through investment. He suggests that the northern European markets have a more sophisticated approach than the rest of Europe and that this is in line with that region's overall approach to marketing. Rines (2001) believes that the rest of Europe's shortfall is due to both poor research and the tendency to look at marketing as a solitary exercise designed to simply put the corporate logo in the way of the viewers, with a good day out in the hospitality area reserved for top management. He suggests that this is not the case in other areas of marketing and corporate practice where staff are trained and experienced professionals. The same argument can be strongly made for the marketing and communication of a wide range of sports properties in the Middle East today. Therefore, considerable potential exists for marketing professionals and future graduates to have a real impact in the marketplace and to ensure that both sport and consumers benefit as a result.

The evolution of sport marketing

Industry evolution takes on critical importance for the formulation of strategy (Porter, 1996). Murray and O'Driscoll (1999) report that the evolution of general marketing practice can be viewed through a number of phases, from product orientation, through sales and marketing orientation and, most recently, via market focus.

Kotler (1999) states that, 'marketing management today is a subject of growing interest in all sizes and types of organisations within and outside the business sector' (p.29). Shilbury *et al.* (2009) believe that an evolution of the marketing function has emerged with the professionalism of sport over the past 20–30 years, often in the face of strong internal resistance.

As implied, Shilbury explains the development of sport marketing in three stages, namely:

1 *Pre-sport marketing*: In this phase, the marketing function does not exist and volunteers, in the spirit of amateur participation, run the organisation. The predominant task of the organisation is to ensure the ongoing sporting operation.
2 *Transition to professional sport*: Here, a progression from administration to management takes place. The main role of management is to monitor the environmental trends and to plan future growth.
3 *Customer as the controlling function in sport marketing*: Together with the sporting elements, marketing is the organisation's primary ground for identifying and creating a competitive advantage.

The authors would argue that there is in fact an earlier phase of what might be termed 'pre-sport marketing'. In this phase, one individual coordinates all functions, including finance and sporting operations. This would be the case at the regional amateur level for many sports, including golf and motorsport, where budget constraints remain the largest barrier to sporting success and ironically the lack of marketing skills is the greatest barrier in turn to securing a proper budget.

Murray and O'Driscoll (1996) suggest the image of successful marketing orientation as akin to a pair of scissors in operation. One blade represents real market understanding and market orientation, the other represents the organisation's competence to do certain things well. This is relevant in the context of the present chapter, with one blade representing the marketing function, the other competence in the sporting domain. Working together, the two parts can represent a successful sport franchise.

Consumers of sport

Understanding your consumer or target audience is the key to success in the marketing of sport at a professional or even at an amateur level. This is particularly true in the Middle East, which as Stigras has already identified, has little research in the field, particularly that drawing upon academic sources and certainly in comparison to the developed EU and the US markets. This represents a substantial opportunity for both scholars and progressive practitioners in the time ahead.

Sport consumption in the Middle East is an important vehicle for social, economic and political change using modernisation agendas (Amara, 2005) and, with the personal and political support provided at the highest levels of government, it is increasingly used as an indicator of the state's stability and prestige. It is also diverse in terms of what sports citizens consume and indeed how they consume different sports. By the use of proprietary marketing data collected by TGI Arabia/ PARC, some inroads can be made into understanding the popularity of sports by market.

4.4
Manchester City's
Argentian defender
Pablo Zabaleta
celebrates with the
FA Cup trophy at
Wembley Stadium
in London, on 14
May 2011

Source: ©
ANDREW YATES/
AFP/Getty Images

TGI Arabia/ PARC research

The purpose of TGI-initiated research lies in identifying consumer trends across a broad spectrum, which includes 16 product-marketing categories using indices that include media usage, including newspapers, terrestrial and digital media, and product choice and brands, together with social attitudes and reference points using a standardised demographic index. This index includes education, income and home ownership, all factors indicating a disposable income which theoretically enables the respondent to be a sport consumer.

The data are derived from a quantitative and randomised survey using a structured questionnaire (Curwin and Slater, 2008) drawing a sample of 4,000–5,000 respondents within each nation-state, regardless of the population that represents the potential sample pool. The survey is conducted with individuals rather than households, and a point mechanism is used to achieve a potential score of 100, with education (university degree), car and computer ownership amongst those domains that achieve recognition under this system. Other points are awarded for ownership of a range of consumer goods, access to air travel and use of Internet, for example.

The consumption of sport in the region is very diverse (see Table 4.1).

Table 4.1
Sport consumption
by nation-state in
the Middle East

Top 10 sports by country (%)

UAE

Football	45.20
Cricket	35.23
Swimming	24.04
Basketball	20.15
Car racing	19.28
Boxing	18.52
Aerobics/keep fit	18.06
Athletics	17.63
Yoga	17.44
Tennis	15.73

Lebanon

Football	37.94
Basketball	34.85
Swimming	24.07
Car racing	17.21
Skating	13.44
Aerobics/keep fit	12.58
Boxing	12.30
Athletics	12.29
Tennis	10.58
Motor cycle racing	10.46

Saudi Arabia

Football	50.11
Swimming	23.42
Basketball	23.25

Car racing	23.24
Boxing	21.44
Athletics	20.60
Billiards	19.92
Horse-riding	17.20
Chess	15.84
Cycling	14.11

Jordan

Football	36.76
Basketball	17.62
Car racing	15.91
Swimming	15.70
Athletics	15.19
Horse riding	13.15
Aerobics/keep fit	12.33
Badminton	11.68
Boxing	11.29
Billiards	11.13

Syria

Football	42.87
Basketball	23.87
Swimming	23.84
Aerobics/keep fit	19.86
Athletics	17.48
Car racing	15.81
Chess	15.73
Boxing	15.56
Billiards	15.39
Cycling	13.72

Qatar

Football	49.09
Athletics	24.19
Swimming	23.90
Car racing	23.55
Basketball	21.18
Tennis	20.50
Jogging	19.85

Aerobics/keep fit	19.50
Volleyball	19.14
Table tennis	19.05

Egypt

Football	56.53
Boxing	13.01
Swimming	10.31
Car racing	6.55
Athletics	6.19
Basketball	4.80
Chess	4.28
Water skiing	3.66
Karate	3.41
Tennis	3.20

Bahrain

Football	51.37
Basketball	35.00
Car racing	26.40
Volleyball	26.25
Swimming	23.08
Water skiing	18.30
Athletics	18.20
Tennis	15.93
Billiards	15.53
Table tennis	14.76

Algeria

Football	41.98
Swimming	22.89
Basketball	22.30
Athletics	19.39
Boxing	18.44
Car racing	17.35
Skating	15.49
Aerobics/keep fit	15.01
Tennis	14.91
Volleyball	14.87

Kuwait

Football	51.27
Cricket	29.80
Swimming	28.92
Boxing	28.26
Basketball	27.99
Athletics	27.44
Horseracing	26.35
Car racing	26.22
Aerobics/keep fit	25.05
Cycling	25.03

Analysis

Football (soccer) is the most popular sport across the whole region, with highest ratings for Egypt (56.53%), Bahrain (52.37%) and Kuwait (51.27%); the second ranking sport is possibly more telling – *cricket* in the UAE and Kuwait, due to the high non-Arab, ex-pat consumers. In Lebanon, Jordan, Bahrain and Syria the most popular sport is basketball, and in Saudi Arabia (KSA) it is *swimming*. In Qatar athletics has the second highest consumption, and *boxing* in Egypt. Local and national factors help drive specifically identified sport such as *billiards* in Jordan and KSA. *Volleyball* is popular in Bahrain and Qatar as is *horse riding* in Jordan and KSA as a legacy of a national heritage. *Table tennis* is a cited sport in Qatar. *Aerobics*, *jogging* and *keep fit* are cited mid- to lower table in all the countries and can be construed as an aspect of the gendered nature of sport consumers (Walseth and Fasting, 2003).

Summary

Over the next decade, the Middle East represents a fertile area for the practice of professional sport marketing. Success in this area will depend on a number of key factors, including:

1 greater understanding of the value of effective sport marketing by regional stakeholders, particularly sports governing bodies and government;
2 more consumer research and the publication of findings;
3 the education of nationals at undergraduate and postgraduate level in both sport management and sport marketing;
4 evidence, via research, of the effectiveness of sport marketing initiatives;
5 increased competition between sports properties and brands.

It is also likely that other areas of specialist skills will be required to work in conjunction with sport marketing as governments continue to invest in the region. These specialist areas are already in the mainstream in developed markets and include sports tourism and political marketing. A career in sport marketing in the Middle East can be both challenging and rewarding. It is hoped that this chapter may serve to encourage the next generation to take the profession forward and to ensure a 'win/win situation' for all involved.

References

Amara, M. (2005). 2006 Qatar Asian Games: A 'Modernization' Project from Above? *Sport in Society* 8 (3): 493–514.

ATCUAE (2010). *Driving Motorsport Forward Together – FIA Middle East Strategy*. Retrieved from www.atcuae.ae/en/pdfs/fia-middle-east-strategy-english.pdf.

Bovinet, J. (2004). Marketing Sport Looking For Improvement Five Years Later. *Sport Marketing Quarterly* 8 (41). Retrieved from www.alliedacademies. org/public/proceedings/Proceedings14/pams-9-1-no04.pdf#page=14.

Curwin, J. and Slater, R. (2008). *Quantitative Methods for Business Decisions* (6th ed.). London: Thomson Learning.

Derrick, J. (1999). Marketing Orientation in Minor League Baseball. *The Cyber Journal of Marketing*. Retrieved from http://fulltext.ausport.gov.au/ fulltext/1997/cjsm/v1n3/derrick.htm.

Gilson, C., Pratt, M., Roberts, K. and Weymes, E. (2001). *Peak Performance*. London: Harper Collins Business.

Graham, S., Neirotti, L., and Goldblatt, J. (2001). *The Ultimate Guide to Sport Marketing*. (2nd ed.). New York: McGraw-Hill.

Howell, D. (1983). Committee of Enquiry into Sports Sponsorship. *The Central Council for Physical Recreation*. UK.

Kotler, P. (1999). *Kotler on Marketing: How to Create, Win, and Dominate Markets*. New York: Simon and Schuster.

Kotler, P., Armstrong, G., Wong, V., Saunders, T. (2008). *Principles of Marketing* (5th ed.). Harlow: Pearson Education.

Lamb, D. (1991). *Stolen Season: A Journey through America and Baseballs Minor Leagues* (1st ed.). New York: Random House.

Levitt, T. (2004). Marketing Myopia. *Harvard Business Review* July–August: 45–56.

Mullin. B., Hardy, S. and Sutton, W. (2007). *Sport Marketing*. Champaign, IL: Human Kinetics.

Murray, J.A. and O'Driscoll, A. (1996). A *Strategy and Process in Marketing*. Hertfordshire, UK; Prentice Hall.

Murray, J.A. and O'Driscoll, A. (1999). *Managing Marketing: Concepts and Irish Cases*. (2nd ed). Dublin: Gill & Macmillan.

O'Connor, Sean (2005). World Rally Championship Marketing Strategy – A Case Study. *International Journal of Sports Marketing & Sponsorship* 6 (4).

Porter, M. (1996).What is Strategy? *Harvard Business Review* (Nov/Dec 1996).

Rines, S. (2001). *Driving Business through Sport*. London: International Marketing Reports Ltd.

Santomier, J. (2001). *Sports Mega-brands: Case Studies in International Marketing*. Unpublished paper. Fairfield, CT: Sacred Heart University .

Shank, M. (1999). *Sport Marketing: A Strategic Perspective*. New Jersey: Prentice Hall.

Shilbury, D., Westerbeek, H., Quick, S. and Funk, D. (2009). *Strategic Sport Marketing* (3rd ed.) Sydney: Allen & Unwin.

Walseth, K. and Fasting, K. (2003). Islam's View on Physical Activity and Sport: Egyptian Women Interpreting Islam. *International Review for the Sociology of Sport* 38 (1): 45–60.

Williams, D. (2001, February 12). No Smoke. *Rally Sport*.

5

Sports law

Ajmalul Hossain, QC[1]

Overview

This chapter will detail how sports law is derived from several sources and that it operates at different levels according to the nature of the case under review. Sports law is used when referring to playing or participating in sport, when regulating the conduct of the participants and/or in ensuring discipline within the sport so that everybody abides by the 'rules of the game'.

Sports law determines the liability of the participants in a sport when they exceed the legal limits of that particular sport or if they somehow adversely affect the legal rights of others while participating in it. Sports law also deals with the different relationships that arise in the context of the sporting activity, its management and any associated commercial aspects.

The legal principles used in this chapter have been derived mainly from English law and to some extent from EU law. It is recognised and accepted that these principles may not be fully or even partially applicable in the Middle Eastern countries under the relevant domestic laws. However, the legal principles are derived from jurisdictions where the law has been active to give redress to those requiring justice and they are based on real life instances. It is hoped that these principles will aid the shaping of the law in the developing jurisdictions throughout the Middle East. At the very least, the reader will benefit from the legal developments in the field of sport and in sports law and be able to judge for themselves whether the extent to which the law is involved in sport is also necessary in Middle Eastern countries.

Case Study 1: Petr Korda

The initial case study in this chapter relates to a series of legal matters concerning Petr Korda, a tennis player. In 1998, Petr Korda made an application to the All England Lawn Tennis and Croquet Club to compete at the Wimbledon Championships, one of the foremost tennis tournaments in the world. In his application he accepted that the Rules of Tennis ('Rules') approved by the International Tennis Federation ('ITF') would govern the event in question. These included the ITF's anti-doping and drug-testing programme. After losing in the round of 16 (the round immediately prior to the quarter-finals), Korda was required to provide and did offer a urine sample for testing. The sample was tested and it was found to contain a prohibited drug.

The initial decision

The matter was referred to the Independent Anti-Doping Review Board ('Board') and it held that Korda was guilty of breaching the ITF's Anti-Doping Programme. The Board imposed the mandatory penalty of one year's suspension and forfeiture of all rankings and prize money earned at the Wimbledon tournament.

Appeal

Korda appealed to the ITF's Appeals Committee ('Committee') against the imposition of the suspension and argued that there were 'exceptional circumstances' for the presence of the drug in his urine sample. The Committee accepted Korda's submission and set aside the ban. The ITF subsequently lodged an appeal to the Court of Arbitration for Sport ('CAS').

English High Court

Korda then applied to the English High Court (Korda v ITF Ltd.[2]) for an injunction to restrain the ITF from pursuing its appeal to the CAS. He relied upon two grounds: i) that he was not bound by any contract to comply with the Rules; and ii) in any event, the Rules did not provide for an appeal to the CAS. The High Court decided that a contract could be inferred from Korda's conduct although there was no written or oral contract in existence and refused the injunction. The conduct relied upon was: i) submission of the urine sample for testing; ii) his appeal to the Committee against the initial decision of the Board; and iii) his choice to exercise a right of appeal to the CAS if the Committee decided his case against him. Korda then appealed to the English Court of Appeal.

Court of Appeal

The Court of Appeal (Korda v ITF Ltd.[3]) upheld the decision of the English High Court that it had correctly found the contractual relationship between the parties. Further, the Court of Appeal construed the ITF Anti-Doping Programme to include a right to appeal for a full rehearing where there was a dispute between the parties. Since there was a dispute around the meaning of 'exceptional circumstances' and on the penalty, ITF had the right of appeal to the CAS.

CAS

The CAS (ITF Ltd. v K[4]) held that Korda was unable to prove 'exceptional circumstances' in this case. Therefore, the CAS reinstated the original penalties that were imposed upon Korda by the Board.

Analysis

The several cases concerning Korda arising out of the factual matrix set out above demonstrates a number of points about sports law:

1 Korda wanted to establish his right to play the game, asserting that the suspension was wrongly imposed, while the ITF was contending for the suspension to remain in place to enforce discipline in the sport.
2 The relationship between the player (Korda) and the governing body (ITF) was based on a contract that was inferred by the court from the conduct of the parties although there was no written or oral contract in existence.
3 The ITF Rules were incorporated into that contract.
4 The rights and duties of players and governing bodies contained in the 'rules of the game' (here, the ITF Rules of Tennis) applied at all times to those who, like Korda, had consented to play the game according to them.
5 In seeking a urine sample, analysing it and imposing the penalty on Korda, ITF was attempting to ensure compliance with the 'rules of the game' by all players and maintain the integrity of the sport.
6 Dispute resolution procedures are normally agreed in the 'rules of the game' and they must be adhered to.
7 The national courts intervene in appropriate sporting situations to enforce contractual rights and to maintain discipline in the sport.
8 Players and governing bodies take their respective rights seriously and will take legal steps to abide by the 'rules of the game' or to exclude them depending upon what is most beneficial.

5.1
The national courts intervene in appropriate situations to enforce contractual rights and to maintain discipline in the sport

Source: Getty Images

Definition of sports law

Sports law

> is a combination of the law and legal theory found in … different sources. It is the interaction of sport and the law, it is the law, legal principles and legal procedures that resolve sports disputes and it can be seen in action by the impact that it has had on how sport is currently administered, participated in and consumed.
>
> (James, 2010: 21)

The law and jurisprudence in England is comparatively more developed in this field than in most countries across the Middle East. There have been several cases brought to the English courts to resolve disputes relating to sports during the latter part of the twentieth century. For example, speedway teams were banned from racing at a venue because of the noise generated during race meetings (Stretch v Romford Football Club[5]); compensation was awarded to a householder for damage caused by cricket balls from a neighbouring cricket ground (Miller v Jackson[6]); compensation was claimed for injuries received by a participant in contact sports (Condon v Basi[7]); a claim was made against match officials for their failures to apply the safety rules (Whitworth v Nolan[8]) and the process followed by disciplinary tribunals were faulty as they were not applying the rules of natural justice in cases decided by them (Jones v Welsh Rugby Union[9]). However, the very first reported case concerning the ability to 'buy' and 'sell' an employee player of the club was heard nearly 100 years ago (Kingsby v Aston Villa Football Club[10]). Legal history reveals that the legal profession in England has been resorting to the local courts to resolve disputes arising out of sporting activities for some time. The decided cases also demonstrate the nexus between 'sports and the law', namely, the national law applicable in England.

In contrast, sports law seeks to look at law that is specifically referable to sports, starting with the 'rules of the game', the disciplinary rules and their application, the control and regulation of the sport by national and international bodies and how the sporting activities are used to generate money for the players and those involved in the management of sport.

The European Court of Justice (ECJ) has identified the concept of 'specificity of sport' to put sport on a different footing from other forms of activity in allowing it to regulate itself rather than imposing regulation upon sport (Meca-Medina and Majcen v Commission (C-519/048)[11]). It may be this aspect that demonstrates that sports law and sports disputes are recognised as existing in a separate category from other areas of the law and should therefore be treated as such. The English cases have also followed a similar approach, for example, in effectively exempting fighting sports from criminal liability (Attorney-General's Reference (No. 6 of 1980)[12]; R v Brown[13]).

There are several sources of sports law. Each law derived from these different sources operate at different levels and sometimes in combination with each other. As will be outlined later, resolving sports disputes could involve laws derived from each of the different sources.

As indicated, the initial point of reference is the rules of the game or the sport itself: these set out how the game is to be played or how each participant should take part in the sport, the qualifications required to participate, the clothes that should be worn, the equipment or apparatus that should be used, what constitutes a legitimate method of play or participation, what should be done when there is an illegal or illegitimate move, who should adjudicate on any breaches of the rules and how disputes should be resolved and penalties imposed. As an example, the Queensberry rules in boxing may be referred to in order to illustrate some of these points.

The Queensberry rules came into existence and were formalised when the game or sport in question was initially invented or developed. As time unfolded, these rules were recognised and sometimes reformulated by national (e.g., Rules of the English Premier League for football) and international sporting bodies (e.g., International Cricket Council (ICC) Rules for cricket) or federations (e.g., Fédération Internationale de l'Automobile (FIA) statutes for motor sports) for the relevant game or sporting activity. The rules are based on one or more agreements or contracts between the players/participants and the national and international sporting organisations.

The English Courts considered the status of several sporting organizations in relation to its members in several cases: for example, the Jockey Club was held to be a private body and its relationship with its members was based on consensual relationships, and that it was outside the reach of the public law (R v Disciplinary Committee of the Jockey Club, ex parte Aga

Khan[14]); the court decided that there was a contract between a club and the Welsh Rugby union consisting of its constitution and the bye-laws (Aberavon and Port Talbot Rugby Club v Welsh Rugby Union Ltd[15]) whilst the court implied a contract between the sportsperson and the governing body for athletes (Modahl v British Athletic Federation Ltd[16]). These rules, having their origins in contract, are recognised and given effect under national and international law, although they do not in actuality form part of any national or international law. The management of the sport is in fact generally based on self-regulation, without any interference imposed by national or international law.

Disputes often arise between players or contestants or between players and the governing bodies. Internal domestic tribunals generally resolve these sporting disputes in accordance with the agreed rules. The tribunals make decisions and orders penalties by the imposition of fines or by banning the player or participant from taking part in the sport for a period of time. These decisions are enforced by the national or international sporting organisations. Some breaches of the 'rules of the game' are justifiable in the national courts by actions brought by a party to the contract on the basis of breach of contract.

Another source of sports law is the national law of a state and decisions of the national courts. In this situation, the national law is used to resolve a dispute arising out of a sporting activity through the courts or another agreed or nominated forum for the resolution of the dispute, for example, mediation or arbitration. These disputes may arise from the way a disciplinary tribunal acted when considering a breach of the rules of the game or in imposing a sanction against a guilty party.

From time to time the English Courts have judicially reviewed the decision-making processes followed by the sports tribunals, ostensibly under the courts' inherent supervisory jurisdiction (Nagle v Fielden[17]). The principle that is followed by the national courts is that it will review decisions of these tribunals where it is shown that the governing body exercises a high degree of control over a substantial part of the sport and the decision has adversely affected the sportsman's ability to earn a living. The national courts impose an obligation upon the tribunal to act within its rules and the law and also to act fairly in resolving the dispute. If it fails to do so, the courts will set the decision aside. However, the courts are not concerned with whether the decision made by the tribunal is correct or not. Any issues relating to the merits of the dispute will have to be resolved by any agreed disciplinary rules and its appeals procedure and not by the courts.

The national courts are also concerned with other aspects of sport. These often relate to commercial contracts arising out of the sport, for example, relating to advertising or television rights pertinent to the sport. There may also be claims arising in tort for compensation for loss and damage caused to someone by another person connected with the sport; for example, where a spectator is injured due to insufficient safety at the stadium or racetrack. In some situations, the criminal law is involved where bodily injury or death occurs as a result of some sporting activity where excessive force or illegal manoeuvres are used.

International law is also another source of sports law. Different states enter into bilateral or multilateral treaties and agreements to deal with different aspects of sports (e.g., Treaty of Amsterdam, 1997, Declaration 29; Treaty on the Functioning of the European Union, Art. 165; The Council of Europe's Anti-Doping Convention 1989; The World Anti-Doping Code 2011). In particular, the establishment by the International Olympics Committee (IOC) and acceptance of the Court of Arbitration for Sport (CAS) is an example of co-operation between states, international and national sporting bodies, players and others to set up an international body to resolve sports disputes. Decisions of the CAS are now recognised as a source of sports law. The IOC anti-doping regime shows the desire to resolve some sports issues on an international level (Rule 45, Olympic Charter). EU law and decisions of the ECJ is another example of international law being a source of sports law. Sporting relationships have been held by the ECJ to be subject to EU law when they constitute 'economic activity' (Walrave and Koch v Association union Cycliste Internationale (36/74)[18]; Union Royal Belge des Societe de Football Association ASBL v Jean-Marc Bosman (C-415/93)[19]). However, where the rules of any international sporting body is concerned with matters of 'purely sporting interests' or those rules are necessary for the proper functioning of the sport, EU law would not apply even where those rules affect personal interests.

Breaches of sports law

An important aspect of sports law is discipline during competition. The general idea of discipline in sport is to maintain a 'level playing field'. This would ensure that no one player is given or receives an unfair advantage over a competitor and so that each has the opportunity to participate according to the 'rules of the game' and to win using his or her skill, expertise, physical and mental abilities. Maintaining the integrity of the sport is a fundamental issue for sports law.

Sadly, as is ever present in every aspect of modern life, cheating is also a very common occurrence in sports. These take various forms: the taking of drugs to enhance performance or using certain forms of sports apparel that are not approved, again according to the 'rules of the game'. Apart from these situations, allegations of 'match fixing' and other forms of corruption are often brought and established by governing bodies. All these are but examples of a party seeking to take an unfair advantage, thereby completely ignoring and, indeed on occasions, deliberately breaking the fundamental 'rules of the game'.

These unnecessary challenges to the 'rules of the game' have placed a heavy burden on sports regulators to monitor conduct on a regular basis and introduce compulsory or random testing of the individual participants and the sporting gear or apparatus in use. The governing bodies have imposed counter measures on national and international levels to deal with these threats to the expectation of the fans that all sport should be fair at all times.

To monitor the conduct of the competitors and to ensure discipline, the 'rules of the game' provide for referees, umpires, stewards or marshals, all of whom act as independent supervisors, to make decisions on the field about whether the rules are being followed and whether an individual is seeking to attain an unfair advantage. These decisions are made today with the assistance of modern technology in recording and playing back the actual event several times and in slow motion to observe correctly what had happened during the game. The inclusion of the Third Umpire in games of cricket is an example of this in practice. Today, this does not depend upon the 'live' observation of individuals and their analysis based simply upon recollection, which, it is generally accepted, represents a positive step forward.

Developments in forensic science in analysing urine and blood samples to establish or exclude the possibility of performance-enhancing drugs is also intended to and does help to establish a 'level playing field'. The challenges to conduct outside the 'rules of the game' can come from the competitor or from the independent supervisor on the field. Interestingly the supervisor's decision is on occasion also subject to challenge and review. However, once the decision is made to subject a participant to a penalty, the right to 'due process' of the person who has been subjected to the penalty is triggered. He/she then has a right to have a fair determination of the allegation made against him/her. Essentially, this means that they have a right to be heard by a fair process. More often than not, the hearing will take place before their peers, who will be other or senior members connected with the same sport and who have no direct or other conflict of interest in deciding the allegations in question. In certain situations, the hearing will take place before a panel of lawyers acting as judges or arbitrators.

The process to determine the liability of the alleged wrongdoer, contained in the disciplinary rules of the sport, will involve stating the allegations against him/her in writing and informing him/her of the consequences that may follow if the allegations are admitted by him/her or proved against him/her. The process will also allow him/her sufficient time to state his/her case. S/he may both agree the breach and submit to a penalty or s/he may contest the allegation. If s/he chooses to contest the allegation, s/he would normally be afforded a personal hearing. At that hearing, s/he will have a right to challenge the witnesses called against him/her and to call witnesses in support of his/her case. Normally, these days a right of representation by legal advisors is almost universal in most disciplinary rules.

Once a decision is made on the allegations finding them proved, s/he will be notified of the decision against him/her and the penalty that has been imposed. At the same time, s/he would be advised on any right of appeal that s/he has under the relevant rules and of any time limit within which such appeal has to be brought. At the appeal stage as well, s/he will have the right to a hearing and legal representation.

As long as the sporting body follows the correct procedures and acts in accordance with the applicable rules and the national law, the national courts will not normally interfere with the decision, even if the court may disagree with such a decision. Issues of proportionality and restraint of trade will be relevant for the body deciding on the issue of the breach of the rules and also by any appellate body hearing any appeals from the original decision.

The doctrine of proportionality is very important in dealing with breaches of sports law. The consequence of imposing a penalty for a breach must be in proportion to the mischief found proven by the tribunal. In other words, the consequence of the breach, namely, the penalty, must be a reasonable response to the wrongdoing, i.e., if the breach is relatively minor, the penalty must also be minor, and *vice versa*. This doctrine is very relevant in the context of penalties imposed for doping offences. Since most regimes for dealing with these offences may impose the ultimate sanction of a lifetime ban on the sports person concerned, courts considering the effect of such a restrictive rule would require the governing body to prove that the sanction is required and also that it is proportionate to adjudge it lawful. If the penalty imposed is within the range of reasonable responses, the decision will not be interfered with either on appeal or by the national courts.

Restraint of trade is a concept that seeks to ensure that that no one is barred by any decision from earning his/her living (Nordenfelt v Maxim Nordenfelt)[20]. The person imposing the restraint has to demonstrate that it is reasonable and proportionate to protect his/her interests. The person on whom the restraint is imposed has to show that the restraint has in fact affected his/her earnings and that the restraint is not in the public interest. The working or professional life of a sportsman can be relatively short compared to other professions. This is due to the fact that everyone ages naturally and with aging the body also starts to fail and performance becomes restricted. Therefore, in dealing with even major breaches of any applicable rules, e.g., doping or corruption offences, the 'rules of the game' and national and international law take account of this concept. It is recognised that it would be wrong in principle to stop a professional sports person from earning a living by imposing a lifetime ban from professional activity except in the most extreme of circumstances. Whilst the sports regulator retains a right to disbar temporarily or totally exclude a wrongdoer from the sporting activity permanently, the concepts of proportionality and restraint of trade require the interests of the sports person to be taken into account before any extreme action is taken.

Where athlete Sandra Gasser was banned for four years for a doping offence, the ban was considered to be necessary and a proportionate means of protecting athletes from drug taking and the public by protecting the integrity of the sport (Gasser v Stinson)[21]. However, a challenge to the Football Association's transfer rules was successful as a restraint of trade since no evidence was presented to show why the player should be prevented from taking up new employment (Eastham v Newcastle United FC and the Football

Association[22]). The principle was again applied to the Football Association of Wales when it made a rule that any clubs playing in the English League would be unable to play in the Welsh League. The rule was struck down as being unreasonable and disproportionate (Newport County FC v Football Association of Wales Ltd.[23])

Liabilities from sporting activities

This field is applicable not just in the case of what is regarded as 'dangerous' or 'fighting' sports, but in all types of sports. Mainly, the focus is on liability that results from injuries, which may be caused to participants themselves, their competitors and to spectators who have come to view the sport in question. Different types of liability may arise when any person is injured or any property is damaged as a result of any sporting activity. The liability may be civil, giving rise to a claim for compensation, or it may be criminal, leading to a prosecution under the criminal law and the imposition of punishment on the wrongdoer.

Dealing first with civil liability, the injured person may be a participant in the sport, match official, spectator, passerby or neighbour of the venue where the sport is taking place. The injury may be bodily injury to his/her person or to his/her property or to both.

Whenever injury occurs, the obvious question that arises is whether the victim can achieve any reparation in the form of compensation, indemnity for medical expenses, restoration or replacement of damaged property. The further question that arises in this context is who should be liable to make reparation for the injury, loss or damage suffered by the victim. The answers to these questions are to be found in the domestic law that is applicable where the injury takes place. If the injury takes place in England, the remedy must be sought under English law. If the injury takes place in Egypt, then the remedy can only be available under Egyptian law. In this context, the 'rules of the game' are also relevant and any rules of any national or international governing body of the sport will be applied in deciding whether there has been any breach of any aspect of sports law.

The person who is the most likely candidate to be put in the frame for making good any loss or injury is the person who causes the actual injury. However, the person who causes the injury may be impecunious and not have any financial resources to pay compensation to the victim. In this situation, it would not be worthwhile pursuing him or her through the courts. Therefore, the victim will look at others to sue who are worth suing. The possible other defendants to a claim will include physical education teachers and trainers, coaches, instructors, supervisors, match officials, national and international governing bodies, owners of sporting venues and medical and other staff and organisations who have provided support to the victim.

Initially all claims for sports injuries were directed against physical education instructors and teachers and their employers. In one of the first reported cases, a teacher was held liable when he failed to assist his student to land safely after vaulting over a horse in the gym. As the student was not sufficiently trained to vault and land safely, a duty was imposed on the teacher to ensure a safe landing procedure. The teacher and his employer were under a liability to compensate the student for his injuries (Gibbs v Barking Corporation[24]). Liability similarly extended to coaches and the school when picking players in a rugby match where injury followed a tackle performed on the schoolboy victim by an older and a much larger opponent. Here, the obligation upon the coach was to ensure that the groupings should match in size and age and anyone not in the same group should not be picked to play (Mountford v Newlands School[25]).

Claims have been brought successfully against a referee in a rugby match where the player was injured by the mismanagement of the scrum that collapsed. The match official had failed to impose the safety rules in place for preventing the collapse of a scrum (Smoldon v Whitworth and Nolan[26]). Governing bodies and international federations are also not immune from claims. The organiser, the national governing body and the international federation were sued where a participant in a 'track day' at a motor racing circuit was fatally injured when he lost control and crashed into a tyre wall. Allegations were made that the track was not designed properly and the Royal Automobile Club (RAC) and the FIA were responsible. The court held that the RAC was liable but the FIA was not as it had lawfully delegated its responsibilities for track safety to the RAC (Wattleworth v Goodwood Road Racing Company and RAC and FIA[27]). Finally, medical support staff and practitioners could potentially be liable for injuries caused or aggravated by their actions in extracting and conveying, or medically or surgically assisting an injured participant (Bolam v Friern Hospital management Committee[28]; Bolitho v City and Hackney Health Authority[29]). However, it should be noted that the liability would normally be incurred to the injured sportsman and not to his employer club although the latter has made the referral and may even be paying the fees and expenses for the medical care (West Bromwich Albion FC v El-Safty[30]).

In order to establish civil liability against a wrongdoer, it would be necessary to consider whether there is any contract between him/her or any of the other potential defendants and the victim. There can be many instances where there would in fact be a contract, for example, where the person making the claim is a spectator who had paid to come into the venue or has leased or hired equipment that has failed during a sporting event. If there was a contract, then a claim for breach of contract could be brought. In order to establish a claim in tort, the injured person will need to establish whether there is a cause of action or legal ground for bringing a claim against the potential defendants and whether the injury or loss has been caused by any of them.

If the answers to these questions are in the affirmative, then the victim will be put in the position that they would have been in without the injury. In other words, they would get compensation assessed to put them back in the position immediately before the injury. He/she would be able to claim compensation for the pain and suffering, medical and rehabilitation expenses, loss of income and any other losses actually suffered by him/her. Normally the cause of action relied upon to bring a claim in tort is negligence. The victim will have to show that there was negligence on the part of the wrongdoer. To establish negligence, the victim must show that the wrongdoer owed him a duty of care. In other words, the injured person has to show that the wrongdoer owed him a duty to take care not to injure him. Analysis of decided cases shows that, in the case of a sporting activity, a sport-specific duty of care must be proved (Caldwell v Maguire and Fitzgerald[31]). Reasonable and competent actions or measures are required under the duty to take care. The person in charge, whether a teacher, coach or medical professional, has to act at the relevant time with the skill and competence reasonably expected of him/her by reason of his/her training, qualifications and experience. The duty is not to ensure a risk-free environment but to ensure that expected risks do not occur, causing foreseeable injury.

In addition to establishing a sport-specific duty of care, the victim will have to establish that the defendant failed to take the appropriate level of care and breached that duty. It must also be shown that the injury to the victim was caused by that breach of the duty of care. Causation is an important aspect of establishing liability. The test for establishing causation is what is known as the 'but for' test. In other words, would the injury have occurred 'but for' (i.e. were it not for) the breach of the duty of care. If so, liability will be established and the defendant would be liable? It follows that, in order to claim compensation, the claimant must prove a breach of duty of care and an injury resulting from it.

The other cause of action for injury in the course of sporting activity is trespass to the person in the form of the tort of battery. This involves causing actual bodily harm to the person of the victim. If battery is established, then compensation will also be awarded. The courts have distinguished between a 'rough' tackle or 'foul' play where there will not be any liability since these are part of the culture of sport and a breach of any safety rule of the game or a prohibited move, where liability will attach.

In both claims arising out of contract or tort, the employer of the person causing the injury may be liable on the principle of vicarious liability. This happens when the wrongdoer was in employment with his employer and the wrongdoer was acting in the course of his employment, for example, in the context of sport, where a footballer employed by a club to play football injures another player on the other side. The employer club can be held responsible for the injury if it is caused while the players were playing on the field, i.e. in the course of the employment of the player (McCord v Cornforth and Swansea City AFC[32]).

There are some defences that are available to wrongdoers for claims relating to sports. These are based upon consent of the victim or that the action was taken in self-defence. Apart from civil wrongs, sporting activities may give rise to criminal proceedings being taken against a contestant. This is generally where there is violence in sports and, in particular, in the 'fighting' sports. If there is serious injury that would not normally happen or death is caused by the sport, there may be criminal sanctions. In the case of 'fighting' sport the courts seem to allow these to take place on the grounds of public policy that the public wish to enjoy participating and watching the sport (AG's Reference No. 8 of 1980[33]; R v Brown[34]). However, there have been situations where the criminal law has been applied and convictions and sentences were imposed by the courts. A football player was convicted of manslaughter where he charged the deceased from behind, throwing him on the goalkeeper's knee and causing death (R v Moore[35]).

For the sake of completeness, dangerous premises and events are considered. Here, civil liability may attach to organisers and participants, and the victims may be spectators, neighbours of venues or even those passing by. This type of liability will arise, for example, when balls leave the playing area and injure persons or property inside or outside the venue or where the venue is defective. Examples of the latter may be that the playing areas and safety equipment are not in accordance with the specifications set by the national of international governing bodies, or the layout and exit routes from stadiums are inadequate, causing injury to spectators.

5.2

Passing the winning post at the newly built Meydan Stadium in Dubai, UAE.

Source: Getty Images

Relationships arising out of sport

Discussions thus far reveal that sport has many dimensions and that there are players who actually do not play any game but are nonetheless involved with the sport. Most relationships arising in sport do so out of contract, although some can arise out of the law or out of treaties connected with sports. The primary category of sports contracts would be made with and involve the sportsperson as the main contracting party. This would include contracts with a club or team, the suppliers of the sports gear, apparel or apparatus. Contracts with agents or managers, the national and international governing bodies would also be part of this category. When a sportsperson changes their club or team or the sports gear that they will use, another series of contracts have to be entered into, replacing the earlier relationships.

Case Study 2: Iestyn Harris and player transfer

The second case study in this chapter also relates to an actual instance concerning a sportsman who wished to transfer from one club to another (Leeds Rugby Ltd. v Harris and Bradford Holdings Ltd.[36]).

Facts

The sportsman involved was Iestyn Harris and the sport in question was rugby union. Harris wanted to move from playing in the rugby league for the Leeds Rhinos to rugby union for Cardiff Blues and Wales. To permit this move, four separate but linked agreements were required to be entered into by Leeds, Cardiff, the Welsh Rugby Union (WRU) and Harris.

Agreements

By the first agreement, Leeds and Harris entered into an agreement to release him from playing for Leeds. This agreement contained an option in favour of Leeds to employ Harris if he returned to play in rugby league again (i.e. at some point in the future).

By the second contract, Harris was employed by Cardiff as a rugby union player for four years. Harris had the right in this contract to terminate it at his choice after three years. The third contract was between three parties: WRU, Cardiff and Leeds regarding the payment of the transfer fee.

The fourth contract was between the WRU and Harris and it contained the terms on which Harris would play for Wales if he were selected to do so.

Harris terminated the first contract after three years and began instead to play rugby league for another team, Bradford Bulls. Leeds exercised the option in the second contract but Harris did not play for them. Leeds brought an action and asserted that Harris was bound to play for it (the club) for a further one-year period. Harris claimed that this was a restraint of trade and restricted his ability to earn a living.

The court decided that all four contracts were validly entered into and were enforceable. The court also held that, although the first contract restricted Harris's choice who he played for, it was not unreasonable and not a restraint of trade. Therefore, Harris was in breach in not playing for Leeds and had to compensate Leeds for his breach of contract.

Analysis

The case shows the following:

1 There can be several contracts dealing with one sportsman but making legal relationships with different parties.
2 Each contract may be independent and self-standing but be related to each other.
3 The contracts must be read together to give a complete understanding of the transaction and the parties' respective intentions.
4 They require consideration individually and collectively to determine their true meaning.
5 Sports contracts have become quite complex. Therefore, all parties require specialist advice and assistance from lawyers to negotiate and draft these agreements.

With the increased use of electronic and print media, sport has become internationalised, with followers in most countries in the world. It has also become very commercial in nature. As a result, several other types of contracts come into existence. Media and advertising rights require separate contracts with media and advertising agents. In turn, there are separate and independent contracts with each media and advertising company.

Likewise, merchandising has now become a big part of sport. Clubs, national and international governing bodies license the production and sale of sports clothing and other sports paraphernalia to make money from them. As a result, further contracts and more relationships connected with sport come into existence.

Summary

Sports law has come about in response to the needs of those involved in any sporting activity. It deals with the sport itself and those participating in it. Sports law deals with the supervision and regulation of the sport by national and international governing bodies and ensures discipline in sport to maintain its integrity.

Beyond the field, sports law is involved in adjusting liability between someone who has received bodily harm or suffered damage to property as a result of being associated with any sporting activity, whether as a participant, spectator, match official, passerby or neighbour to a sporting venue. Sports law also establishes relationships between parties to enable the commercialisation of sport and has made it international. Finally, there is national and international co-operation between nations in respect of sport and sports law.

References

James, M. (2010) *Sports Law* (1st ed.) (Basingstoke: Palgrave Macmillan).

Notes

1   Ajmalul Hossain, QC is a practising Barrister and Queen's Counsel in England, Senior Advocate of the Supreme Court of Bangladesh and International Arbitrator. He is a member of the International Chamber of Commerce Commission on Arbitration, Paris, a Code of Conduct Commissioner of the International Cricket Council, Dubai, UAE, and a member of Statutes Review Commission of the Fédération Internationale de l'Automobile, Paris.
2   29 January 1999, unreported, High Court, Chancery Division.
3   25 March 1999, unreported, Court of Appeal Civil.
4   CAS 99/A/223.
5   (1971) 115 Sol Journal 741.
6   [1977] QB 966.
7   [1985] 1 WLR 866.
8   [1997] ELR 249.
9   [1998] The Times, 6 January.
10 [1912] The Times, 28 March.
11 [2006] ECR 1–6991.
12 [1981] QB 715.
13 [1994] 1 AC 212.
14 [1993] 1 WLR 909.
15 [2003] EWCA Civ 584.
16 [2001] EWCA Civ 1447.
17 [1966] 2 QB 633.
18 [1974] ECR 1405.
19 [1995] ECR 1–4921.
20 [1894] AC 535.
21 15 June 1988, unreported, High Court (QBD).
22 [1964] Ch 413.
23 12 April 1995, unreported, High Court (QBD)
24 [1936] All E R 115.
25 [2007] EWCA Civ 21.
26 [1997] ELR 249.
27 [2004] EWHC 140.
28 [1957] 1 WLR 582.
29 [1998] AC 232.
30 [2006] EWCA Civ 1299.
31 [2001] EWCA Civ 1054.
32 11 February [1997] The Times, 11 February.
33 [1981] QB 719.
34 [1994] AC 212.
35 (1898) 15 TLR 229.
36 [2005] EWHC 1591 (QBD).

6

Sport event management in the Gulf

A focus on strategy and promotion

David Hassan

Overview

In an overarching sense this chapter examines the central themes of sport event management and specifically their application to the Gulf region. Indeed, in the latter part of this chapter these issues are examined in the context of the favourable international profile currently being experienced by the United Arab Emirates (UAE) in the field of sport. This chapter is not intended to be a comprehensive guide to event management, nor a step-by-step approach to successfully hosting a major sporting event. Rather it draws the reader's attention to a fundamental need to understand the different types of sporting events that exist, the strategic value they offer, in both economic and sporting terms, and how the wider global profiling of a specific country or city may be enhanced through its effective engagement with certain sport events. The latter part of the chapter details a series of events that take place on an annual basis in the UAE and explains how by doing so they serve an important role in embellishing that country's image as an evolving international business, tourist and leisure destination.

Key aspects of sport event management

When examining the nature of sport events it is important to appreciate how they can differ in terms of size, scale and importance (Allen *et al.*, 2002). Some events are organised on a global scale, whilst others are staged nationally or even on a regional, and thereby comparatively local, level. Certain events are open to athletes or teams of all abilities, others only to those with certain disabilities, whereas issues of gender, ethnicity or age may dictate the nature and profile of entrants for some other tournaments. Moreover, certain types of sport events are designed principally to be broadcast on various multimedia formats (primarily television) whilst, in the main, most others tend to attract spectators to a stadium or a venue to see the action unfold 'live' (Getz, 1997). Thus, the majority of sporting events, certainly those organised on a national or international level, are simultaneously spectator-led and media broadcast and it is self-evident that event organisers should make proper provision for both components to ensure the event, in an overall sense, is successful. Most sporting events that take place in the Gulf region, and indeed across the Middle East, are what scholars writing in this field refer to as 'mega', 'major' or 'hallmark' events (Getz, 1997, Goldblatt, 1997). However, there is something of a definitional discrepancy in the use of these terms, with the descriptor 'hallmark' being reserved by some authors for sporting events that become synonymous with a particular city or country, e.g. the Dubai Desert Classic or the Etihad Airways F1 Abu Dhabi Grand Prix. In contrast, the 2020 FIFA World Cup, also to be staged in the Gulf, is more appropriately referred to as a 'mega' event in both scale and impact whilst also recognising that the tournament is a comparative 'one-off' for its host country of Qatar and may not return to the region for some time following its staging in the Summer of 2022.

Getz (1997) further draws the reader's attention to other aspects of 'mega' events which have significance for students of sport management. In this case, the measurement of these events, be this the impact they have economically for the host country or city (the 'economic impact' of sporting events), the effect they exercise upon inward investment (again, this could be in the form of business or tourism spend) or even the impact of a major sporting event in transforming the international image of a country are all worthy of attention. For example, the effect of the decision taken by the International Olympic Committee (IOC) to award the 1992 Summer Olympic Games to Barcelona, Spain was experienced almost immediately after this announcement was made public in the mid-1980s. The overall market value of businesses based in Catalonia and across Spain rose significantly, and indeed the event in 1992 is typically cited as an example of the impact hosting a 'mega' sport event can have upon a host city. Likewise, the staging of the 2008 Summer Olympic Games in Beijing, China served to transform the image of that country in the eyes of some observers, many of whom either lacked full knowledge of it or were sceptical about its record around a range of critical governance issues (Weed and Bull, 2009). Such is the central importance of these factors to the overall event management process in the Gulf that the discussion will return to this field of investigation later in this chapter.

Viewed in its entirety, however, the literature reveals a lack of consensus around the use of language and terminology in the hosting of sport events (Goldblatt, 1997). Consequently, for the purposes of this chapter, 'mega events' will be a term used to describe an event that takes place only once in a generation within any given national setting (e.g. the Olympic Games or FIFA World Cup), whereas a 'major' sporting event refers to those events that attract large attendances, command a notable degree of prestige and are likely to exercise legacy effects, such as tourism or direct foreign investment. Thus major sport events, in contrast to 'mega-events', may take place regularly in a given country and indeed, as will become evident later in this chapter, the hosting of such events often forms an important component of certain countries' expansionist plans or, at the local level, 'city marketing' strategies (Weed and Bull, 2009). Consequently, the overwhelming majority of sporting events in the Gulf are accurately referred to as 'major' in form as they take place routinely throughout the year, are staged on an annual basis and thus realise financial benefits on a cyclical and sustained level. This compares with 'mega' events that may promote such advantages in a similar, perhaps even significant, fashion but lack the more strategic, long-term benefits of repeat trade provided for by the staging of 'major' events (Andrews, 2004). Finally 'minor' sporting events notionally only retain the interest of a small 'real' or 'virtual' (i.e. multimedia) audience and may be staged routinely (e.g. every year in the same city) or periodically (e.g. the same event taking place in different cities within the same country).

Of course this paradigm is by no means static and instead remains very fluid in nature, e.g. a comparatively small sporting event may in fact attract a niche audience that exercises a disproportionate economic impact upon a host city (Hall, 1992). A good example of this, and one explained in more detail later in this chapter, is the Volvo Ocean Race, which docked in Abu Dhabi for the very first time in 2011. Whilst the overall spectator number remained modest, certainly compared with the F1 Grand Prix staged each year at the Yas Marina circuit, the per capita spend of those who choose to patronise the round-the-world ocean race event can in fact prove to be greater. Consequently it is important to consider each event on its own merits, even if the categorisation of these events, along the lines detailed here, serves only as a useful starting point in establishing some level of uniformity for students of sport event management situated throughout disparate parts of the world.

Governance of sport events

The 'ownership' of major sporting events has come to dominate much of the discourse concerning their significance and impact, particularly over the last two decades. Prior to the early 1990s sporting events were organised, for the most part, solely to create sporting outcomes (Toohey and Veal, 2000). Thus, a successful tournament was one that reflected sporting achievement and participation levels, or even satisfied certain inclusion criteria. The exponential commercialisation of sport in the intervening period has changed, some would argue distorted, these erstwhile sporting ambitions. Not all forms of commercialisation, however, are bad and in fact where the purpose of investment in sport has been to achieve greater spectator satisfaction or embellish the sporting spectacle, there is little doubt that it has been to the overall benefit of the sport in question (Andrews, 2004). Thus, an appropriate balance to sport event management needs to be struck, and many of the Gulf states have to date achieved this very effectively by. respecting the integrity of the sport in question whilst simultaneously improving the overall attractiveness of a specific event through innovation, enterprise and strategic investment.

Again, the extant literature in the field of sport management draws the reader's attention to the various categories of owners or promoters involved in staging major or mega sport events (Weed and Bull, 2009). Domestic tournaments are also 'owned' (often by local authorities or regional governments) but the extent of their impact or broader significance is comparatively restricted by virtue of their scale. Instead it is possible to loosely categorise sport event promoters as belonging to one of the following categories: municipal or local government authorities; national or international governing bodies of sport; or private/corporate sponsors (Tarlow, 2002). In the latter case, major corporations, such as banks or other international conglomerates, privately promote a major sporting event for the purposes of casting their organisation in a positive light or entertaining important clients, including potential investors. A good example of this, again dealt with in more detail later, is the Emirates Airlines-sponsored Dubai rugby sevens tournament, which attracts a host of major 'blue chip' sponsors, including HSBC bank.

Thus, reflecting on this typology, which is by no means universally established or even (in some cases) appropriate, it is clear that those staging or managing sport events do so for a range of different reasons. Moreover, depending upon the purposes of the sporting event in question and/or the aspirations of those managing it, the actual event may itself be designed to increase the probability of other desirable outcomes (Jackson, Grainger and Batty, 2004). For instance, if an event's overall image is enhanced by the likelihood that it will attract a greater television audience should that particular sport's leading exponents compete in its latter stages, then the event itself may be designed to achieve this preferred objective. Whilst these principles will vary according to the sport in question, and indeed the particular level under consideration, the need for event organisers to prove adept at scheduling the tournament according to the strategic demands of television, the confines of a wider tour calendar or other extraneous factors, such as prevailing climatic conditions, are critical factors in its successful staging (Tarlow, 2002). Thus, event managers need to consider the nature of the tournament/event in question, the demands of key stakeholders and a range of additional, impingent factors when devising the schedule of their particular event. It is by no means a straightforward undertaking and requires the input of all internal and external stakeholders, as well as expert modelling, detailing all possible outcomes, to safeguard a satisfactory outcome (Hoye *et al.*, 2006).

At the internal level there are clearly a range of stakeholders that the event manager must liaise with and in turn respond to their needs. Foremost amongst these are the actual competitors/athletes, who can vary from professionals to amateurs, be established in teams or perform alone and may represent a particular nation or simply themselves. Entering into a dialogue with participants, their representatives and sponsors is a critical early part of effective event management (Tarlow, 2002). They may have a series of demands conditional upon their participation in the event or, even if they do not, most will expect a level of organisation that takes proper account of their status and desire to succeed during the event in question. Moreover, participants, if there is prize money available for the event, will expect to be properly reimbursed relative to their success in the tournament, to be made aware of any expectations the event organisers may have of them (e.g. media or sponsor commitments) and be accommodated close to where the event is being staged (Tarlow, 2002). Naturally, depending on the type of event being considered, the demands of the competitors can and do vary, but proper engagement with these individuals prior to the tournament will ensure smooth hosting of the event on the part of the organisers.

Beyond the actual participants of an event, its advocates must also consider the expectations of other significant stakeholders, both internal and external to the organisation, in a manner that up until that point they may not have had to do. This is because the context in which sport events now take place has changed, virtually beyond all recognition (Hoye *et al.*, 2006). External stakeholders have come to exercise a considerable – some might argue disproportionate – impact upon the nature and organisation of modern events. In this case, media platforms, sponsors, professional staff who are required to perform duties at the event and of course the paying public all affect the dynamic and nature of the event in question. Thus, advance planning and considered provision of the needs of each of these stakeholders remains a critical aspect of proper event management (Jackson *et al.*, 2004). For example, if the event is one that is likely to attract high levels of spectator demand for tickets, then event managers must devise an appropriate strategy for the release of these tickets and their pricing policy, while matters such as the wishes of corporate investors, who clearly demand additional value on account of their typically increased levels of financial outlay at the event, and the possibility that certain aspects of the event (e.g. days 1 and 2 of a major golf tournament) may not be as popular as other elements of the event – leading to the need to consider concessions to patrons to encourage them to attend these less attractive aspects – all require careful consideration. In summary, a multiplicity of factors may combine to make the job of the event manager a demanding and stressful one, confirming that proper levels of advance planning combined with open and informed lines of communication remain vital for the successful event manager (Hoye *et al.*, 2006).

The value of events for host cities

Reflection on what appear to be ever-increasing demands placed upon event organisers may lead some cities to question the overall wisdom of hosting major sports tournaments in the first place. The considerable levels of government investment, the concessions that are typically offered to competitors, not to mention accommodating the wishes of a typically demanding international media corps, may lead to the conclusion that the benefits accrued by a city or country, be they in the form of business, tourism or merely image-enhancement, are simply not worth the levels of investment required to achieve such dividends (Weed and Bull, 2009). Nevertheless, if there has been a defining feature of sport event management over recent decades, it has indeed been its incorporation into the wider marketing portfolio of cities, regions and nations (Van den Berg *et al.*, 2000). It appears that sport events, be they mega, hallmark or major in form, have increasingly been recruited as a platform for the justification of wider economic, social and even political agendas and, with these, a commensurate level of often scarce investment. A very good example of this is the critical role of sport in the achievement of the much vaunted Abu Dhabi 2030 vision, designed to position the city as one of the world's leading destinations for business investment, tourism and leisure.

Thus, it appears that sporting events are becoming more popular as a reason to visit a city or a country compared to more traditional tourist attractions, such as existing physical features or historical legacies. It seems therefore that the strategic use of sporting events by those countries and cities wishing to profile themselves internationally has become commonplace. Sport is used in this way to deliver on a variety of desirable outcomes, foremost amongst these being its almost unrivalled capacity to attract tourists to a destination, one that they may not otherwise have considered visiting (Dwyer *et al.*, 2000). Notwithstanding the well-established arguments around the so-called 'displacement effect' of hosting mega or even major sport events (the suggestion that people who otherwise would have visited a city choose not to do so as they are discouraged due to the perceived ill-effects of the presence of a major sporting event), there is little question that the consequences of hosting sport events are, for the most part, positive in nature (*Brown et al.*, 2002).

One of these factors, as briefly outlined earlier, is evidently the economic benefit accrued by the host city/nation from hosting a major sporting event. This effect can be more pronounced should the event 'fit' with other such sporting events in promoting the city or country in question; thus the strategic targeting of events that complement each other (e.g. tennis, rugby, motor sport and thoroughbred horseracing) have a multiplying effect when viewed alongside one another compared to any of these taking place in isolation. Whilst there has been some criticism of the accuracy of certain studies designed to measure the economic impact of particular events, this has mostly been as a result of flawed methodologies or grossly overoptimistic assessments of the event's true effect on the host economy (Weed and Bull, 2009). Instead, when proponents deploy a conservative approach to under-taking an economic impact study, choose if anything to underestimate its perceived impact and exclude otherwise tangential expenditure, there clearly is a very effective role for the commissioning of an economic impact assessment study. It serves to inform investors of the full effect of their investment, is a very useful adjunct to a city's tourism strategy and offers a quantifiable outcome from an event that otherwise may be predicated upon a less reliable, subjective assessment in order to justify continued federal support.

This is not to suggest, however, that such benefit as is accrued by a host city is somehow equally distributed within the indigenous economy. Instead, the reality of mega and major sport events has been that small and medium-sized enterprises have often been 'squeezed' by major interna-tional conglomerates, which in return for their financial support of an event require exclusivity in retail, service provision and overall market share. Often, therefore, major sporting events provide little or no succour for that society's most disadvantaged citizens and, indeed, it could be argued that, by diverting public funds away from everyday services to a one-off mega event, a society is actually guilty of increasing the levels of deprivation experienced by those most marginalised in society (Mules, 1998). Yet, this is where the continued quandary around the overall benefits of hosting large sport events is to be found, and it points to issues that only national and regional authorities can satisfactorily address.

Challip (2004) examined the so-called financial 'leverage effect' of sport events and concluded that there are in fact two, albeit interrelated, aspects to this process. These he understood to be 'immediate leverageable elements' and 'long-term leverageable' impacts deriving from the event under review. In essence, such a dichotomy is somewhat misleading because the former merely reflects a well established aspiration on the part of host nations to not only attract 'event tourists', but to maximise their presence in the country/city, whilst the latter is aimed at a process of transformation and enlightenment around the 'brand image' of a certain destination and is designed to entice visitors there over a much longer period of time. As such, it is more accurate to suggest that what exists is one, rather elongated, continuum of impact, from the immediate to the long term. It is a truism that hosting a global sporting event does confer a degree of legitimacy upon a host city, rendering it 'public' in a way that perhaps it may not have been prior to an event taking place there. It raises the destination's presence in the consciousness of the viewing public, poses questions about its apparent marginalisation in the tourist/ business psyche up until that point and challenges conventional wisdom about what represents 'viable destinations' for the modern tourist. Indeed, it often succeeds in delivering these outcomes in a manner that arguably no other medium can achieve as effectively (Weed and Bull, 2009).

Clearly the immediate economic impact of a sport event is achieved by facilitating visitors to spend their money on goods and services in the host city/country (Challip, 2004). The retention of visitor expenditure can be hampered when, as is increasingly the case with 'mega' sport events, money is actually being spent on products and services offered by 'off-shore' companies that are only temporarily present in the country for the duration of an event, leading in fact to any such expenditure having a net negative impact upon the host economy. It is on this level that those advocates of attracting major sporting events to certain countries require proper circumspection, otherwise, far from benefitting from staging a global sporting event, they may unwittingly facilitate the expanding profits of international non-governmental organisations like FIFA and/or deprive their host economy of the displaced expenditure they otherwise would have achieved had the event not taken place at all. The imperative, therefore, for effective event managers is to harness as much economic expenditure for the host region/country as possible and to ensure negotatiations with any respective rights owners are conducted with this intention at the forefront of their mind. Instead, smaller or marginalised nations may consider the desire to attract a major sporting event to their country as being of such importance that they end up achieving this at a net loss, saddling the country with a legacy of debt and compromising levels of spending for some years to follow.

Where increased expenditure can be leveraged on the part of the host economy, it is often at a distance from the stadium or venue where the event itself is taking place. Thus, event organisers should seek to engage service providers located in city centres or comparatively distanced from the centre of activity and encourage them to deploy a co-ordinated strategy – perhaps in the form of interrelated marketing approaches – to maximise the leveraged impact of the event in question (Tarlow, 2002). This requires the event organiser to draw upon a range of tangential skills, often beyond that which they at first considered relevant to the task at hand, but which, when combined, serve to maximise revenue for the host economy, encourage reinvestment in regard to future events and satisfy the local political classes who occasionally adopt a somewhat sceptical view of investment in non-essential public services like sport (Challip, 2004).

As attractive as it is to be able to state almost immediately what the impact of a particular event may have been upon a city, the reality is that much greater effect can be experienced by proper, long-term approaches to leveraging positive event legacies. In this regard, the event manager often relies upon expert strategic planning, especially around engagement with the media, to ensure the full effect of the host city/country is experienced for some time after the event itself has concluded and the sporting 'circus' has moved on to its next destination. For this, the event organisers require detailed profiling of those attending the event, the views of significant external stakeholders (e.g. in this case the importance of 'media management') and a confidence in the capacity of the host city to facilitate and meet the expectations of future visitors drawn there by their consumption of media images around the sport event in question. In essence, what is being considered here is a holistic assessment of where any single sporting event, be it large or small, exists within a portfolio of other sporting (and non-sporting) events that any such country may choose to host. Clearly, as has been implied, there must be coherency around these events, and an established rationale as to why the event somehow creates a positive 'fit' for the host country also needs to exist. Any incongruence between the event, the host city and the overall event portfolio of that country or city may lead to a confused or mixed message being created and, with that, commensurate damage to the profile of the city as a destination of choice for potential tourists. By the same token, on a more positive note, the skilful assessment of a city's event portfolio can serve to enhance its overall image for a defined target market (e.g. visitors from a country/continent that may currently be under-represented there), and cross-leveraging between events, in which the success of one event can create a cross-pollinating effect for others, and vice versa, leads to a mutually beneficial outcome for all concerned.

Sport events in the UAE

There are few countries in the world that use or indeed manage sport as effectively as the UAE. Whilst there is clearly prestige in being able to attract some of the leading sport events in the world to the UAE it also places considerable demands upon event organisers to retain the standard of excellence that has become the hallmark of sport in the Gulf's most revered sports destination. Yet, as has been made clear over the course of this chapter, the use of sport in this regard, indeed the choice of sport events, is as a result of careful strategic planning and not some randomised or opportunistic approach, reflective only of personal preferences, as has often been portrayed outside the Gulf. For the most part, the Emirates of Dubai and Abu Dhabi have been the destinations of choice for major sport events, and both cities have established themselves internationally as being in the vanguard of event management and sporting innovation.

Whether it is golf, rugby, tennis or a host of other sports, the Emirate of Dubai has arguably a disproportionate number of world class events taking place there every year. It clearly has established itself as a destination without compare for some of sport's leading governing bodies, attracted to the city by a combination of outstanding event management, favourable climatic conditions and the allure of the Dubai 'brand' that evidently conveys unparalleled levels of service and quality and has proved consistently enticing for corporate sponsors. A good example of this is the Dubai World Championship: the finale of golf's PGA European Tour calendar and internationally regarded as one of the preeminent golf tournaments in the world. The event, which is only in its third year, has a remarkable affect upon the local economy, driven by the lucrative field of golf tourism but embellished still further by a golf industry that recognises the effect of an expertly staged and globally broadcast showcase upon its sport. Consequently, the so-called 'Race to Dubai' has become embedded in the psyche of the golfing fraternity worldwide. This tournament has managed to attract all the leading European golfers in recent years, including golfing superstars such as 2011 US Open winner Rory McIlroy. Indeed, McIlroy is a particularly popular figure in the UAE on account of his commercial sponsorship from Jumeirah Hotels and Resorts, which has a very strong profile in Dubai and right around the world.

6.1

Rory McIlroy of Northern Ireland poses with the trophy after his eight-stroke victory on the 18th green during the 111th US Open at Congressional Country Club on 19 June 2011

Source: Getty Images

Indeed, golf is a sport that has a very strong tourism effect; it encourages casual golfers to a destination to play the courses on which such major tournaments, like the Dubai World Championship, are staged, and the additional expenditure this creates, in the form of hotel occupancy or leisure expenditure, all generates further revenue for the local economy. More to the point, the professional players, including Ireland's four-times Major winner, Padraig Harrington, consider the playing conditions in Dubai to be amongst the very best in the world. 'When they build these golf courses in the desert they really have a blank canvas so they really are in fantastic condition. You're guaranteed the prefect conditions for golf, its warm every day, a little breeze. So it's ideal' (www.bbc.co.uk/new/business; accessed 11 December 2010).

Perhaps the most internationally renowned sport event of all those staged in Dubai is the Dubai World Cup meeting, hosted by the Dubai Racing Club. Conceived of by HH Sheikh Mohammed bin Rashid Al Maktoum, the event is universally regarded as the most financially lucrative horseracing festival in the world by owners, trainers and the public alike. Indeed the Arab presence within international thoroughbred racing is itself world renowned, not only by virtue of successes throughout the USA, Europe and the Far East, but also following the establishment of the UAE, in particular, as a site for horseracing and breeding of the optimum kind. The event has grown annually following generous financial investment from the UAE government and is broadcast worldwide to a viewing public that has come to recognise the event, traditionally staged at the end of March each year, as beyond compare in regards to its standing and import within the field of thoroughbred racing. The meeting, now worth an estimated US $26.25 million, is embellished still further by the famous Meydan arena in which it is staged, again regarded as a race venue without comparison. It is here that the Dubai World Cup race, alone worth some US $10 million, takes place over one mile and two furlongs on a tapeta surface. Supporting races, including the US $5 million Dubai Duty Free and the US $5 million Dubai Sheema Classic, which together are the two richest races run on turf anywhere in the world, complete a race card that is the envy of all others. Indeed, the Dubai World Cup fits perfectly with the global branding of the Emirate of Dubai in particular, which is regarded as one of the leading cities in the world for business, leisure, tourism and investment. Thus, this symbiotic relationship, between Emirate and sporting event, is reaffirmed and their interdependency underscores the value of continued investment in major sport events and, of course, their successful management.

Dubai also hosts the world famous rugby sevens tournament, which is one of the UAE's longest running events, having been in continual existence for over 40 years. On peak days the event can attract over 45,000 spectators, which, alongside ticket revenue, also generates considerable profits in the field of hospitality, services and accommodation. The Emirates Airlines Dubai Rugby Sevens, to give the tournament its full title, demonstrates the positive mutually beneficial relationship that can be forged between a commercial sponsor and

6.2
Dubai ruler Sheikh
Mohammed Bin
Rashid Al Maktoum
hugs his son
Sheikh Rashid Bin
Mohammed al
Makhtoum who
finished first in
the equestrian
endurance
competition during
the 15th Asian
Games in the
desert outside
Doha, in 2006

Source: AFP/Getty
Images

a successful sport event. Emirates Airlines, which has been involved in the event since 1987, has worked alongside the organisers to make the tournament the success it is today. Interestingly, a key aspect of the Emirates strategic engagement with the Dubai event has been to drive global television, and indeed multimedia, coverage of the event, increasing its so-called 'global footprint' and making it the most widely televised rugby sevens tournament in the world. The Emirates-Dubai Rugby Sevens relationship is an appropriate, if only further, reminder of the positive symbiotic benefits that can be accrued by fully engaging the expertise of a company which, alongside its financial investment, can drive supplementary revenue streams through emphasising positive media relations and expanding the sporting public's appreciation of the event. On this theme, the corporate hospitality element of the Dubai Sevens is amongst its most distinctive features, with many of the world's leading multi-nationals using the annual event as an opportunity to invite important business clients and potential partners to enjoy their hospitality and to secure future business contracts. The other main benefit of the Dubai Sevens, particularly its attraction to various arms of the media, is its capacity to increase global participation in rugby and forge new markets for the sport in parts of the world where the game remains comparatively marginalised. A good example of this is the expansion of the game into North America, specifically the USA, which has seen growing numbers of rugby players and fans emerge, attracted by the concise nature of the rugby sevens format (games are seven minutes per half) as opposed to the more established, if somewhat elongated, traditional style of the game.

6.3

England celebrate
winning the Dubai
Rugby Sevens
Cup Final at The
Sevens ground on
4 December 2010
in Dubai

Source: Getty
Images

Sport events in Abu Dhabi

Abu Dhabi has also established itself internationally as one of the world's leading destinations for sporting events, foremost amongst these being the Etihad Airways Formula 1 Abu Dhabi Grand Prix. It is the only 'day-night' Grand Prix in the world, a decision taken to reflect the needs of a global television audience, but also to showcase the city as a tourist destination, a strategy that has proved remarkably successful. Equally noteworthy has been the speed at which the Yas Island site was transformed to accommodate the circuit, which evolved over a period of less than three years, from a barren, desert site into the location of the world's leading motor sport venue, five-star hotels, an 18-hole golf links and even a man-made marina to allow yachts to moor throughout the year. The circuit itself was the product of very clear strategic planning on behalf of the city of Abu Dhabi, as part of the Abu Dhabi 2030 plan, in which sport, leisure and tourism represent critical components. In 2010 the Grand Prix attracted over 20,000 international tourists, representing a 100 per cent increase on the previous year. HE Mubarak Al Muhairi, the Abu Dhabi Tourism Authority (ADTA) Director General (Abu Dhabi) remarked:

> The Grand Prix PR value is really huge. In Abu Dhabi we look at the media value, the PR value and not just the direct Grand Prix value …. We (ADTA) are really serious about tourism and this (the Grand Prix) is a milestone event.
> (www.bbc.co.uk/1/hi/programmes; accessed 15 November 2010)

The long-term aim is to establish Abu Dhabi as a global centre for culture, sport and tourism. Alongside the successful sporting developments, Abu Dhabi is also soon to become home to new satellite centres for both the Louvre and Guggenheim museums. According to James Hogan, CEO, Etihad Airways,

> Any event that's held in the Gulf is good for the region. The more you spotlight the Gulf as a destination, as a business centre, as centres of excellence in education and medical care (it) is good for all of us. Whether it be the Grand Prix, whether it be the golf, whether it be tennis, whether it be on the back of the Louvre or the Guggenheim opening up, Abu Dhabi becomes more of a centre of excellence and people want to come here and spend more time here, be it in business or leisure … [again it] is good for us all.
> (www.bbc.co.uk/1/hi/programmes; accessed 15 November 2010)

In conclusion, it is clear that major sporting events, including motor racing, are an extremely effective means of promoting tourism in various destinations around the world, but especially in the Gulf.

In this respect, one of the most famous motor racing brand names in the world, the Abu Dhabi Desert Challenge (ADDC), has undergone a remarkable revival under the direction of ATCUAE President Mohammed Ben Sulayem, a co-editor of this collection. The event, which takes place in the sand dunes of north west UAE, is regarded as one of the leading cross-country rallies in the world and is noteworthy because of its global appeal to competitors (in 2011 entrants came from as far afield as Australia), its visual impact (Eurosport provided mutli-platform coverage of the race for the first time in 2011) and its expert event management. The ADDC captures the spirit of exploration and intrigue often absent in some more sanitised sport events worldwide and instead offers viewers an accurate and revealing insight into the UAE, its multi-faceted nature and unrivalled appeal.

This concept was affirmed still further in December 2011 with the arrival of the Volvo Ocean race into Abu Dhabi for the first time. The flotilla of racing yachts included the Abu Dhabi Ocean Racing team, competing in the 63,000-km, nine-month race, universally regarded as the most dangerous round-the-world sailing event of them all. The addition of Abu Dhabi as a destination for the Volvo Ocean Race served only to embellish the image of the city as a progressive, international location, whilst the sport of sailing itself retains the attention of a certain cross-section of society who typically have higher levels of disposable income and are inclined to spend larger sums of money in the city and stay longer, thereby benefitting the city in a much greater sense than other visitors and confirming Abu Dhabi as an international tourism destination of considerable regard.

Summary

Long before other countries throughout the world recognised the potential use of sport as a key part of their promotional strategies, to attract foreign investors, to enhance their image for overseas tourists and to portray themselves as vibrant, progressive locations, the Gulf states, primarily the UAE, had already made considerable strides in this direction. The portfolio of impressive, world-class sport events that now take place, primarily in the Emirates of Abu Dhabi and Dubai, were not compiled by chance. Rather, each was carefully selected to embellish a broader image of the country, and of each respective Emirate therein, which when viewed in their entirety portrayed a desirable and coherent image to the world. Yet it was not only the promotional value of such events that drew the attention of the UAE. They also had economic value in their own right, both by exercising direct, immediate benefits through spectator and competitor expenditure on accommodation and hospitality, but also by leveraging so-called 'legacy' spending from businesses and individuals who are drawn to a given destination as a result of intrigue, heightened awareness of a country that they may not previously have frequented, or because the 'brand image' of the country in question is something they can relate to. Thus, effective event management in the future will call upon certain key attributes, foremost amongst these being an understanding of the wider 'fit' of a specific sport event, an appreciation of its immediate and legacy impacts and an awareness of the need to continually review and, if needs be, evolve the nature of such events to safeguard their ongoing relevancy and appeal.

References

Allen, J., O'Toole, W., McDonnell, I. and Harris, R. (2002) *Festival and Special Event Management*, 2nd edn (Queensland: John Wiley & Sons).

Andrews, D.L. (2004) Sport in the Late Capitalist Moment. In Slack, T. *The Commercialisation of Sport* (London: Routledge), pp. 3–28.

Brown, G., Chalip, L., Jago, L. and Mules, T. (2002) Events and Branding. In Morgan, N., Pritchard, A. and Pride, R. (Eds) *Destination Branding: Developing a Destination Position* (Oxford: Butterworth-Heinemann).

Challip, L. (2004) Brand Impact: A General Model for Sport Event Leverage. In Ritchie, B.W. and Daryl Adair (eds) *Sport Tourism Interrelationships, Impacts and Issues* (Clevedon: Channel View Publications); pp. 226–252.

Dwyer, L., Mellor, R., Mistilis, N. and Mules, T. (2000), A Framework for Assessing 'Tangible' and 'Intangible' Impacts of Events and Conventions, *Event Management*, vol. 6, pp. 175–189.

Getz, D. (1997) *Event Management and Tourism* (New York: Cognizant).

Goldblatt, J. (1997) *Special Events: Best Practices in Modern Event Management* (New York: John Wiley & Sons).

Hall, C.M. (1992) *Hallmark Tourist Events – Impacts, Management and Planning* (London: Bellhaven Press).

Hoye, R., Smith, A., Westerbeek, H., Stewart, B. and Nicholson, M. (2006) *Sport Management* (Oxford: Elsevier).

Jackson, S., Grainger, A. and Batty, R. (2004) Media Sport, Globalisation and the Challenges to Commercialisation: Sport Advertising and Cultural Resistance in Aotearoa/New Zealand. In Slack, T. *The Commercialisation of Sport* (London: Routledge), pp. 207–225.

Tarlow, P. (2002) *Event Risk Management and Safety* (New York: John Wiley & Sons, Inc.)

Toohey, K. and Veal, A. (2000) *The Olympic Games: A Social Science Perspective* (Oxford: CABI).

Van den Berg, L., Braun, E. and Otgaar, A.H.J. (2000) *Sports and City Marketing in European Cities* (Rotterdam: Euricur).

Weed, M. and Bull, C. (2009) *Sports Tourism* (Oxford: Elsevier).

7

Sport science

A roadmap for talent identification and expertise development

Tadhg MacIntyre

Overview

Sport science, in both application and research, has traditionally been a neglected area of investigation when examining sports performance in the Middle East. Similarly, within motor sport, a limited knowledge base exists in either the physiological or psychological aspects of performance. For instance, fewer than ten articles on motor sport have been published in the major sport science journals, which are routinely used by scholars working in this field. However, as we navigate this territory it will become evident that, in the UAE and in Qatar, (see Chapter 10), sport science has been recognised as a key component in achieving excellence in elite sports performance. This new avenue has the potential not only to illuminate the processes for identifying and nurturing talent, but, as we will see, it also has ramifications for our understanding of exercise, health and psychological well-being in contemporary Middle Eastern society. Let us first outline the genesis of sport science within the Middle Eastern context.

Sport science in the Middle East can be said to have a long past, but a short history. Over 2,000 years ago Greek physicians assisted in the preparation of Olympians with advice on both nutrition and training. Centuries later these ideas become formalised in the works of Galen. In the Arab World, Hunayn bin Ishaq (809–873 AD) translated this early work (Tschanz, 2003), penned nine treatises of his own and articulated ideas which later permeated into European medicine. Furthermore, Muhammad bin Zakariya al-Razi (865–925 AD) created influential treatises on an array of topics including medicine, philosophy and ethics. He conveyed a healthy scientific scepticism, which is integral to the philosophy of science to this day, by expressing the idea that *truth* in medicine was an unattainable goal (see Colgan, 2003). The theses of both polymaths, bin Ishaq and al-Razi, demonstrate that medical science has evolved from traditions in the Arab world. This was, in effect, part of the pre-history of sport science, which evolved in the last three decades. Sport science in turn evolved from a confluence of ideas from sports medicine, exercise physiology, sport and exercise psychology and allied disciplines (see Berryman and Park, 1992). Before we explore in further detail the discipline of sport science, let us first see where our journey will take us.

First, the author shall introduce the field of sport science and the rationale for studying this domain. The implications of research in sport science on the ontogenesis of new paradigms are also discussed. In the second section, the author shall explore the mental side of sport – paying special attention to the knowledge nexus – or the way that research informs practice and, conversely, how application can inform research. In the third section, the author shall briefly review accounts of expertise development and consequently highlight the theory of deliberate practice. The fourth part of the chapter will focus on the application of the expertise paradigm in a case study – a multi-disciplinary approach to talent identification in motor sport. Included here will be a discussion of three key questions: What are the task demands of motor sport? Which sport science disciplines can contribute to developing

7.1

Iraqi children play soccer on the dusty streets of the Sadr City district of eastern Baghdad

Source: ©ALI AL-SAADI/AFP/ Getty Images

appropriate tests for talent identification? Can these tests inform a model of expert performance in motor sport? Finally, the author shall summarise the key arguments for the reader to conclude the chapter.

Sport science: status, approaches and implications

We will attempt to answer three questions. First: What is sport science? Next, we will ask which sub-disciplines contribute to the parent discipline of sport science. And third, we will question the current approaches in sport science. From the above synthesis, the implications of contemporary sport science should become clear. In the broadest sense, sport science is an interdisciplinary domain in which the disciplines of exercise physiology, sport and exercise psychology, nutrition and biomechanics contribute to a common mission. The common mission of sport scientists is 'to optimise the mental and physical preparation, performance and overall experience of competitive sports participants' (Thatcher *et al.*, 2009, p.1). Sport science has traditionally been concerned with issues such as physiological adaptations to training, body composition, fatigue, injury onset, injury recovery, doping, psychological skills and talent identification (e.g. Garrett and Kirkendall, 2000; Rogozkin and Maughan, 1996). Interestingly, rather like the mythical Greek hydra creature, this early conceptualisation of sport science has become multi-faceted. In 2009, in the introduction to the Olympic Textbook of Science in Sport, Jacques Rogge states that the aim of sport science is 'the enhancement of the health and welfare of athletes at all levels of competition in all parts of the world' (quoted in Maughan, 2009, p.ix). This quote succinctly conveys the shift from a performance-enhancement focus for sport science, to a broader role, which now includes areas such as athlete welfare. This change in direction is also evident by comparing the contents of the aforementioned textbook (Maughan, 2009) with its predecessors (Garrett and Kirkendall, 2000; Rogozkin and Maughan, 1996). In the latest text, the topics of exercise, health, and psychological well-being are now key aspects of sport science. Some researchers differentiate between sport science and exercise science, which is concerned with optimising physical activity levels, experiences and benefits in the general population (Thatcher *et al.*, 2009, p.1). For the purposes of this chapter we shall use the term sport science, but one should be mindful that the research domains overlap and that new fields have developed with specific paradigms for evolving research questions. For instance, a new field of physical activity has developed as a sustainable interdisciplinary area of research. Based on the aforementioned evidence, one development is obvious. There is a growing trend of scientific interest in sport, exercise and physical activity (see Lippi, *et al.*, 2008).

Moreover, novel approaches in scientific enquiry have emerged from questions that initially captivated sport scientists. For instance, researchers in the sport sciences were fascinated with the age-old question of whether *imagery could enhance performance*. Over a century ago, the proto-psychologist William James wrote that 'anything you may hold firmly in your imagination can be yours' (James, 1890). The term *imagery* is worthy of further scrutiny. In order to illustrate what imagery is, we shall turn to the poem Markings, by the Irish Nobel Laureate, Seamus Heaney.

> We marked the pitch: four jackets for four goalposts,
> … Youngsters shouting their heads off in a field
> As the light died they kept on playing
> Because by then they were playing in their heads.
>
> Heaney (1993)

In this poem, from the collection Seeing Things, we witness a description of football, both real and imaginary. Heaney alludes to the concept of people playing football in their heads or engaging in imagery. Imagery is commonly referred to as visualisation or the capacity to represent in the mind experiences that are not physically present (Moran, 2012). In poetry, the written or spoken word can obviously evoke imagery but, in this above example, the poem alludes to the experience of imagery by the participants. Within Nabati poetry, a traditional form of Arabic poetry, an example parallel to Heaneys's exists. In the poem, I Pictured the Dreams – Rashid and Hamdan, His Highness Sheikh Mohammed bin Rashid Al Maktoum describes his own imagery in the lucid description of a dream world. The concept of the mind's eye is evident in both the title of the poem and in the following excerpt: 'Saw them, in my mind, whilst still in cradle.'

The above examples are illustrative of the complex nature of imagery. Imagery may refer to either the phenomological experience – one can possess an image (e.g. of winning a trophy) or it can refer to imagery as a cognitive skill (e.g. an individual's ability to engage in imagery). Although predominantly visual in nature, we experience imagery for each of our sense modalities (e.g. we can imagine the sound of an engine, the smell of oil, the touch of the steering wheel, sight of the track, etc.). As a consequence, researchers prefer the term *imagery*, rather than *visualization* because it puts less emphasis on the visual nature of imagery and accounts for the multi-modal nature (see Moran and MacIntyre, 1998). Dreaming is said to be a distinctive form of imagery, and sport imagery researchers are more interested in imagery in which the individual has conscious control. A particular type of imagery, called mental practice, which involves trying to see and feel oneself repeatedly performing a specific skill (e.g. getting off the start line) has been the main topic of study for researchers, even though imagery has other roles, including enhancing confidence, focusing attention and enabling creativity (see MacIntyre and Moran, 2007).

In the mental practice paradigm, a typical pre-test-post-test experimental design is employed to examine participants' ability (usually novice-level athletes) to acquire a novel motor skill (e.g. basketball free throw: Vandell *et* al., 1943). Mental practice studies usually comprise four groups: 1) a physical practice group (PP); 2) a mental practice group (MP); 3) a combined practice group (PP and MP); and (4) a control group. While this question preoccupied researchers for more than half a century, the mental practice paradigm was to provide a firm conclusion. Hundreds of studies conducted over several decades culminated in a number of meta-analytic reviews (meta-analysis is a method of statistically combining independent studies). The most recent of these reviews by Driskell et al. (1994) reported a result that can be succinctly expressed in the equation:

$$PP + MP > PP$$

In other words, physical practice and mental practice combined groups (PP and MP) outperform not only the control group, but also the physical practice group in experiments. Consequently, Driskell et al. (1994) concluded that mental practice has a significant (i.e. statistically robust) positive effect on performance. Over 15 years later, and imagery is now an effective intervention strategy in stroke rehabilitation (Daprati et al., 2010), recovery from developmental coordination disorder (Wilson et al., 2002), the training of surgeons (Arora et al., 2011) and in-flight training (Carretta, 1987).

Given that the aforementioned research has shown imagery to be effective, at least in the case of *mental practice* of a motor skill, what are the implications of this finding for sport science and other domains? As we will now see, the legacy of the *mental practice effect* goes far beyond the realm of sport psychology and sport science and, arguably, this finding has helped spawn two new fields of research, namely: motor cognition and social cognition. Over two decades ago, Jean Decety and Marc Jeannerod were among the most prolific scientists investigating the role of imagery in skill acquisition (see Jeannerod, 1995; MacIntyre, 2012). One of their key findings was the discovery of the *mental travel effect* (Decety et al., 1989). The *mental travel effect* is the congruence between the duration of actual and imagined time for an action, and subsequent research has indicated a high correspondence between the two durations for experts (Guillot and Collet, 2005). We shall return to this *mental travel effect* in our discussion of the mental skills of motor racers. A second key development by these two researchers was the finding that imagining an action or actually performing that action share similar neural circuits, and these brain areas are activated when one observes, imitates or imagines actions performed by other individuals (see Decety and Grezes, 2006). The ramification of this finding is that our action representation system is integral to our understanding of others. Consequently, the field of social cognition, or the study of how people make sense out of themselves and others, prospered. Marc Jeannerod focused his efforts on the role of mental practice as an action-simulation process. He sought to explore imagery as a window into the representation of action. Imagery was thus viewed as a part of the action representation continuum, rather than a unique epiphenomenon. In other words, this approach postulates that the difference between imagery (i.e. simulating a movement), motor preparation (e.g. planning a movement) and motor execution (e.g. actually moving your limbs) is one of degree, not of kind. This formulation led to the development of a theory of action and subsequent treatises (see Jeannerod, 1994; 2001; 2006). Thus, a new field of motor cognition emerged, a research domain that is concerned with understanding the representation of action and the associated processes (see Jeannerod, 2006). We have seen in this section that an applied research question (i.e. can imagery enhance performance?) ultimately led to the development of two new interdisciplinary fields, social cognition and motor cognition. Now we turn to the divergent approaches within sport science and, subsequently, we will explore the consequences of sport scientists' different motives for pursuing research endeavours.

Traditionally sport scientists were preoccupied with an applied approach (i.e. performance enhancement for its own sake), but recent approaches use sport as a *natural laboratory* to explore fundamental research questions utilising 'expert' participants in unique contexts. As Ron Maughan argues, 'it is also true, of course, that a significant number of exercise physiologists have little interest in sport. Rather they use exercise as a tool to study normal (2009, p.2). Similarly, within the field of psychology, Moran (2009a) has advocated that 'the domain of sport offers cognitive researchers a rich and dynamic natural laboratory in which to study how the mind works' (p.420). In fact, a paradigm shift has occurred within cognitive sport psychology. Specifically, whereas researchers in this latter field initially studied mental processes by investigating deficits in cognitive performance among clinical populations (e.g. patients with brain damage), they are now beginning to explore the neural substrates of cognition in action by focusing on highly skilled athletes (e.g. Yarrow *et al.*, 2009). This shift from a 'deficit-based' approach to a 'strength-based' approach to certain aspects of thinking (e.g. mental imagery; see Moran and MacIntyre, 2008) has led to an upsurge of brain-imaging studies of athletic expertise by cognitive neuroscientists. As a consequence of the above issues which have influenced the conceptualisation of the interdisciplinary field of sport science, its boundaries are now more permeable than previously thought. Furthermore, the overlap with allied disciplines of research, including physical activity and cognitive neuroscience, enables it now to answer questions relating to both basic and applied research. Contemporary sport science, as Maughan (2009) succinctly put it, is 'different things to different people' (p.4).

Sport (and exercise) psychology: knowledge and application

Now that we have seen that sport and psychology is at the interface of sport science and the allied fields of physical activity (i.e. exercise psychology) and cognitive neuroscience (i.e. motor cognition and social cognition), we will

7.2
Belgian former
cyclist Eddy
Merckx cycles with
children in Muscat,
in February 2011
before the start of
the Tour of Oman

Source: © PASCAL
GUYOT/AFP/Getty
Images

attempt to define what sport and exercise psychology is. And, furthermore, how this discipline can influence applied practice and the knowledge base in sport science. This next section briefly outlines how sport and exercise psychology has evolved into a field of research and practice that influences sports performance. Moreover, it will also evaluate how sport and exercise psychology expands our horizons in understanding, explaining and predicting behaviour, emotions and thoughts.

Most sports performers would agree that the mental side of sport is an important part of performance (Moran, 2012). Indeed, when reporting on outstanding performance – for instance, Formula One champion Sebastian Vettel (see Harwood, 2011) or Olympic Champion and 16-times grand slam winner, Roger Federer (see Foster-Wallace, 2006) – comebacks against the odds (e.g. Manchester United vs Bayern Munich, Champions League Final 1999, see Robinson, 2008) or catastrophic drops in performance (e.g. Rory McIlroy at the 2011 US Masters, see Syed, 2011), managers and journalists often refer to topics such as 'kinaesthetic intelligence', 'mental toughness' and 'choking'. Sport psychology is concerned with these issues, in several ways. First, there is the applied role which centres on the following question – How do we enhance human performance most effectively? And, second, researchers in the field are interested in understanding the processes underlying the behaviours, thoughts and emotions of sport participants, to help explain and understand human behaviour in general.

The sport psychology discipline is typically defined in terms of the wider field of sport *and exercise* psychology. The broader view of the discipline is a relatively recent artefact. To explain, the leading journal in the field, *The Journal of Sport and Exercise Psychology*, only included the term *exercise* in the journal title in 1988, to account for the proliferation of research in non-sport contexts. Furthermore, these two facets of the discipline, sport and exercise, share a knowledge base, disseminate information together and have a singular route for professional training. In summary, sport and exercise psychology is concerned with understanding the behaviour, mental processes, and well-being of people who are involved in sport and exercise. Other areas of psychology which are related to sport psychology include positive psychology (see Seligman and Fowler, 2011), organisational psychology (Fletcher and Wagstaff, 2009) and clinical psychology (Brown and Kogan, 2006). As we have noted previously, sport psychology involves much more than a *performance enhancement role*; however, it is this applied role that is most commonly recognised and most readily understood by stakeholders in sport (e.g. Lavallee *et al.*, 2005). Practitioners aim to promote performance enhancement and personal development. On the other hand, researchers' primary goal is to advance the knowledge base through investigations, conceptual development and theorising. However, these two groups, practitioners and researchers, are not mutually exclusive. To explain, many consultants contribute to research as they are often employed in educational institutions, where research is integral to their function. In fact, the interrelationship is more complex than one may first assume. In 1949, a conference on clinical psychology in the city of Boulder, Colorado, USA, led to the creation of a science practice model for applied domains of psychology. Known as the 'Boulder Model', it advocates that *practice* should be informed by evidence from scientific enquiry (research and relevant theory). Indeed, it would be deemed unethical to employ techniques or strategies which are not grounded in scientific research. So, while there may be an *art* of coaching, there should only ever be a *science* of sport psychology. But can we deny practitioners their *nous*, which they derive from applied work? The aforementioned al-Razi stated many centuries ago that books alone were beneath the knowledge of an experienced and thoughtful physician. Thankfully, practice-based evidence is the channel by which the field can learn from case studies. In summary, researchers contribute knowledge through scientific enquiry (both quantitative and qualitative) and this is disseminated through numerous outputs (i.e. publications, conference papers and books) and ultimately leads to evidence-based practice. On the other hand, practitioners in the field of sport psychology can inform our theory, drive our research questions and refine application through documenting practice-based evidence.

The topics that have engaged sport psychologists for the last century (the first study was in 1896–see Kremer and Moran, 2008) are many and varied, and the trajectory of sport psychology has not been linear. To explain, 'the journey has been an interesting one and not without a few detours along the way – some of which have caused us to check our map again for directions' (Walker *et al.*, 2006, p.30). Initial diversions took researchers into cul-de-sacs, such as the quest for personality and intelligence as the key variables in understanding sport performance. To explain, *personality* comprises 'those characteristics of the person that account for consistent patterns of feeling, thinking, and behaving' (Pervin and John, 2001, p.4). It is a pervasive characteristic and largely unchanging. A consensual scientific definition of intelligence is explained as follows: 'intelligence is a very general mental capacity that … involves the ability to reason, plan, solve problems, think abstractly, comprehend abstract ideas, learn quickly and learn from experience (Gottfredson, 1997, p.13). Unsurprisingly, research failed to support a single-factor explanation for understanding success in sport. Instead, two landmark papers mapped out the field for decades to come. In 1977, a study reported that elite athletes (e.g. gymnasts) could be differentiated from less proficient performers on the basis of a number of factors, termed *psychological skills*, including positive self-talk, imagery and stress control (Mahoney and Avener, 1977). In the same year Bill Morgan and Michael Pollock discovered that elite athletes had a distinct psychological profile – but rather than personality being the key, mood (i.e. a temporary emotional state) was the main factor (Morgan and Pollock, 1977). Sport psychology prospered as a result of a *psychological skills training* approach (see Moran, 2012) for two reasons. It was possible to measure the individual psychological skills using questionnaires and, second, evidence emerged that these skills were *trainable*. The typical mood profile of elite athletes, reported by Bill Morgan across several decades of research, was known as the *iceberg profile*. On negative mood factors (e.g. aggression, depression, etc.) athletes scored below the population norm and they scored significantly higher on vigour or energy. Subsequent research demonstrated that exercise had proven benefits not just for athletes but for the general population and even in the treatment of depression (see Fiske, Wetherell and Gatz, 2009). The original studies from 1977 guided the future route of *applied sport psychology* and *exercise psychology,* respectively (see Lavallee *et al.*, 2008). Focusing on the former field, an evidence-based applied sport psychology now exists, one that is informed by theory and has made a major contribution to sport performance, particularly in Olympic sports (see Moran, 2012).

Expertise paradigm, deliberate practice and talent identification

> Imagination is not enough. Knowledge is necessary.
>
> Paul Scott

In the Harvard Business Review, Anders Ericsson and colleagues (2007) summarise the evidence that outstanding performance or expertise is the product of years of deliberate practice and coaching, not of any innate talent or skill (Ericsson, Prietula and Cokely, 2007). Their account, while contrary to the traditional view of talent development, is supported by both recent theory and evidence. In a landmark paper in 1993, Ericsson *et al.* proposed that skilled practice over a sustained period of time (e.g. 10,000 hours) was a more valid predictor of expertise than the physiological variables that previous research alluded to (Ericsson *et al.*, 1993). For instance, if we use the computer metaphor of the mind, there was little evidence to support the contention that there were hardware differences between experts and non-experts (e.g. reaction time), but instead, software differences occurred (e.g. ability to pick up attentional cues). Cognitive skills such as attention, anticipation, decision-making and memory characterise expertise. Cumulative research across sport, the arts and chess has reported the following as among the characteristics of expertise: 1) more elaborate taskspecific knowledge; 2) more efficient use of their knowledge; 3) superior ability to predict outcomes; 4) enhanced planning ability; 5) visually detecting greater accuracy and speed and locating patterns in the visual field faster and more accurately and; 6) more insight into, and control over, their own mental processes. The evidence clearly suggests that expertise is domain specific; for instance, within sport one does not become an expert by virtue of perfor-mance in a different domain (e.g. a professional golfer becomes a soccer player). However, some skill transfer does occur, for example, between different codes of motorsport because of the similar task demands (a topic we will address later in this chapter).

Now we shall address what type of practice is involved in the accumulation of expertise. In an interview in 2005, Anders Ericsson outlined what is meant by deliberate practice: 'Deliberate practice is defined as training activities that have been specifically designed to improve some aspect of an individual's target performance' (Schraw and Ericsson, 2005, p.397). In other words, deliberate practice is rehearsing a skill you can't do well or even at all. According to Ericsson, 'The research on expert performance has, I believe, demonstrated convincingly that neither a magical bullet nor an innate talent can allow someone to attain an expert level of performance rapidly and effortlessly.' Instead, he contends that 'even for the most *talented* individuals, the road to excellence takes many years of daily deliberate practice to acquire the complex mechanisms and adaptations that mediate expert performance and its continued maintenance and improvement' (Schraw and Ericsson, 2005, p.391). The implications of the aforementioned research on expertise are that there is a need to provide an environmental context that enhances the psychological and cognitive characteristics of those pursuing excellence.

Case Study: UAE Motorsport Star assessment in Dubai

As part of its mission to have UAE-licensed racing drivers competing at the top level of global motorsports, the Automobile and Touring Club of the United Arab Emirates (ATCUAE), with support from the University of Ulster, established UAE Motorsport Stars. This annual programme will allow talented young drivers based in the UAE the opportunity to receive professional training from qualified and highly experienced sport scientists from the University of Ulster in Northern Ireland, providing them with the skills and knowledge needed to further their careers in motorsport. The skills taught by the university will focus on off-track areas and will cover topics including psychological training, media training, career management, nutrition, and athletic conditioning. Before we examine the detail of the case study, it is instructive to explore the task demands of motor sport from a sport science perspective and the subsequent evidence-based performance matrix that results.

Horsepower versus brainpower

'Sports people of all kind need to be psychologically and mentally prepared for the tasks they face in their careers and this is one of the keys to success', Mohammed Ben Sulayem (2011b). This quote is arguably a truism, and yet motor sport has been primarily focused on horsepower instead of brainpower. That lack of attention given to the mental side of motor racing is surprising given that the *task demands* of motor racing include route planning, track/course memorisation and attentional switching. Furthermore, drivers may have to perform under conditions of cognitive load (i.e. while talking to the engineer) and in both closed-skill (e.g. qualifying) and semi-closed-skill (e.g. race conditions) environments. Essentially, it is a *natural laboratory on wheels*, in which an array of psychological factors can be investigated. These include communication (e.g. with co-driver), stress control (e.g. controlling emotions), concentration (e.g. ignoring distractions like a minor incident in your field of vision) and mental imagery (e.g. ability to visualise the track). One applied psychologist, with experience in motor sport consulting, highlighted the impact of goal setting, visualisation and imagery, anxiety control, and effective communication as effective interventions (Klarica, 2001). Interestingly, qualitative research with motor sports performers has indicated that imagery is a key variable in sports performance. In one study, that of MacIntyre and Moran (2007), a motor racer described in detail how he used imagery not just to rehearse the track and the braking points, but also how they used imagery in a creative way to imagine various scenarios and their most adaptive response to them. If we return to the previously described mental travel effect, it is also noteworthy that the driver was able to imagine his lap close to real time. Furthermore, it is possible to measure imagery abilities with objective tests (e.g. mental rotation tests) to overcome any biases in typical self-report methods. Mental rotation tests have been shown to have predictive validity in sporting activities that require route planning and extensive imagery rehearsal (MacIntyre *et al.*, 2002).

The psychological demands of motor racing occur in a physically demanding environment. For example, according to Klarica (2001) 'heart rates close to maximum are endured for extended periods of time (20–60 minutes), and it is not uncommon for a driver to lose 5–10% of body weight during a race because of dehydration' (p.291). The FIA Institute, in a recent publication, noted that 'a fitness routine focused on generalised strength, endurance and flexibility is now required as part of any driver's training routine (2011, p.62). Standardised measures of physiological variables such as anthropometry, flexibility, strength, lung function, aerobic capacity and endurance all exist.

One question that evolved in the development of the performance matrix – a weighted decision tree that included the variables under scrutiny – was the respective roles in talent identification of the psychological and physiological factors. To explain, talent identification is a process of recognising current participants with the potential to become elite performers. It usually includes three aspects of measurement and assessment: physical, psychological and sociological. If measured correctly, 'these elements may provide ... relevant information on the young prospects' abilities' (Lidor *et al.*, 2009, p.131).

However, the challenge is in the interpretation of the data, for example, should a factor like endurance (e.g. bleep test score) have a minimum criterion level in the matrix or should a higher level of achievement be factored into the model? Consideration of the assessment of different factors by a minimum criterion or high achievement approach is necessary. Furthermore, given the paucity of published research on the psychological skills of world-class performers in motor sport, caveats must be added to the equation. For example, in a talent-identification scenario, social desirability may influence performance in subjective tests, whereas performance in objective tests may be untainted. Employing multiple measures, within reason, both objective and subjective tests may facilitate the development of a more valid and accurate model.

UAE Motorsport Star assessment programme objectives

- To provide young talent from the UAE with the opportunity to learn the skills necessary to be a successful racing driver.
- To increase the knowledge and understanding of sport science in the UAE.
- To act as a qualifying stage for the ATCUAE's nomination to the FIA Institute Young Driver Excellence Academy.

Links with the FIA Institute Academy

In 2011, the FIA Institute, which is the education division of the governing body of world motorsport, developed a Young Driver Excellence Academy. Like UAE Motorsport Stars, the FIA Institute aims to prepare young drivers to compete at the pinnacle of the sport and does so through the delivery of six separate training workshops at locations around Europe for a period of three to five days each. The FIA Institute Young Driver Excellence Academy is being led by former Formula One star and two-time Le Mans winner Alex Wurz and former World Rally Championship winning co-driver Robert Reid. In its first year, the Academy selected 12 drivers to take part, with at least one driver chosen from each of the following five regions: North, Central and South America; Western and Northern Europe; Central and Eastern Europe; Middle East and Africa; and Asia and Oceania.

Each FIA-accredited National Sporting Authority (ASN) is allowed to nominate two drivers each for consideration by the FIA Institute. The ATCUAE will use UAE Motorsport Stars to identify which of its own drivers to nominate.

7.3
Finalists at the
expert panel
interview in the
UAE Motorsport
Star programme,
July 2011

Source: Getty
Images

Eligibility criteria

Eligible candidates for the UAE Motorsport Stars programme were required to meet the following criteria:

- having an age of 16 to 25 years old
- competing successfully in four-wheel (rallying, karting or circuit racing) competition to at least a national level
- holding a valid national racing license issued by the ATCUAE
- having adequate ability in spoken and written English.

Selection process

The selection of the first candidates for UAE Motorsport Stars followed a stepwise process:

1 A shortlist of five candidates was compiled by ATCUAE staff, with support from senior club officials across the Emirates.
2 A two-day assessment centre was held in the UAE comprising of the following stages:

- A psychological assessment was conducted by Dr Tadhg MacIntyre from the University of Ulster.
- A physiological assessment was performed by Dr Gareth Davison from the University of Ulster.
- A 'media skills' test was conducted by Mr Sean O'Connor and recorded at the Dubai television centre.
- The expert panel, which interviewed the candidates individually, was chaired by Mohammad Ben Sulayem,

president of the Automobile and Touring Club of the UAE (ATCUAE) and vice president of the Fédération Internationale de l'Automobile (FIA), and also featured Mahir Badri, ATCUAE chief executive, Khalid Al Hussain of the General Authority of Youth Welfare and Sports and Dr David Hassan, Senior Lecturer in Sport at the University of Ulster.

3 Following the assessment process, the selection panel reviewed each candidate and, finally, two drivers were selected, Mohammad Al Mutawaa and Mohammad Al Dhaheri.

The two drivers were awarded a one-week intensive training and driver education course at the Ulster Sports Academy which is located on the University of Ulster's Jordanstown campus, Northern Ireland. As Mohammed Ben Sulayem (2011a) explained

> Education is a very valuable thing to carry with you and these young drivers will certainly benefit strongly from this excellent programme … This experience that the drivers are getting will be incredibly beneficial to their racing career and their aspirations of racing on a world stage.

During this week-long training course, the driver(s) will receive expert coaching and support in the following areas:

1 lifestyle management
2 introducing deliberate practice, practice histories and performance profiling
3 structuring physical practice, scheduling and understanding of skill acquisition
4 goal-setting techniques
5 positive self-talk strategies
6 developing mental skills, metacognitive abilities and self-awareness
7 strength and conditioning training to build the muscles required for racing endurance
8 injury avoidance
9 nutritional advice and hydration procedures.

A driver will also be nominated for the FIA Institute's Young Driver Excellence Academy.

Summary

In this chapter, we reviewed the Arab roots of sport science, explored the current approaches of this interdisciplinary domain and highlighted how sport science has the capacity to influence research and practice in allied fields. The discipline of sport and exercise psychology was elucidated and particular attention was given to the scientist–practitioner model. Furthermore, limitations of particular research topics were noted and the role of both PST and metacognition was alluded to. Debates between two routes to explain the development of expertise were resolved on the basis of recent theories and evidence. And, furthermore, the ability of the theory of deliberate practice to provide a road map for talent identification is clarified. Finally, the case study exemplifies an integrated applied sport science-based approach to talent identification in motorsport. The consequences of this approach are two-fold. First, as stated by Mohammed Ben Sulayem (2011b), 'this experience that the drivers are getting will be incredibly beneficial to their racing career and their aspirations of racing on a world stage.' And, second, the case study demonstrates the potential of sport science to describe, explain and predict performance to key stakeholders in the Middle East. To paraphrase the poet Robert Frost, sport science can make all the difference.

References

Arora, S., Aggarwal, R., Sirimanna, P., Moran, A., Grantcharov, T., Kneebone, R., Sevdalis, N. and Darzi, A. (2011). Mental practice enhances surgical technical skills: a randomized controlled study. *Annals of Surgery*, 253 (2), 265–270.

Ben Sulayem, M. (2011a). UAE launches Motorsport Star scheme. http://www.khaleejtimes.com/displayarticle.asp?xfile=data/theuae/2011/July/theuae_July151.xml&section=theuae&col=.

Ben Sulayem, M. (2011b). UAE motorsport stars programme tests drivers' mental edge. http://www.ameinfo.com/270181.html.

Berryman, J. W. and Park, R. (1992). *Sport and exercise science: Essays in the history of sports medicine*. Chicago: University of Illinois Press.

Brewer, B. (2009). *Sport psychology: Olympic handbook of sports medicine*. West Sussex: Blackwell.

Brown, J. L., and Cogan, K. (2006). Ethical clinical practice and sport psychology: When two worlds collide. *Ethics and Behavior*, 16, 15–20.

Carretta, T. R. (1987). *Spatial ability as a predictor of flight training performance*. Brooks Air Force Base, Texas: USAF Manpower and Personnel Division.

Colgan, R. (2003). *Advice to the young physician: On the art of medicine*. Springer: New York.

Daprati, E., Nico, D., Duval, S., and Lacquaniti, F. (2010). Different motor imagery modes following brain damage. *Cortex*, 46, 1016–1030.

Decety, J. and Grezes, J. (2006). The power of simulation: Imagining one's own and other's behavior. *Brain Research*, 1079, 4–14.

Decety, J., Grezes, J., Costes, N., Perani, D. and Jeannerod, M. (1997). Brain activity during observation of actions. Influence of action content and subject's strategy. *Brain, 120*, 1763-1777.

Decety, J., Jeannerod, M., and Prablanc, C. (1989). The timing of mentally represented actions. *Behavioural Brain Research*, 34, 35–42.

Driskell, J., Copper, C. and Moran, A. (1994). Does mental practice enhance performance? A meta-analysis. *Journal of Applied Psychology*, 79, 481–492.

Ericsson, K. A., Krampe, R. Th. and Tesch-Römer, C. (1993). The role of deliberate practice in the acquisition of expert performance. *Psychological Review*, 100 (3), 363–406.

Ericsson, K. A., Prietula, M. J. and Cokely, E. T. (2007). The making of an expert. *Harvard Business Review*, 85 (7–8), 114–21.

FIA Institute for Motor Sport Safety and Sustainability (2011). Medicine in Motor Sport. Online publication accessed 11 July 2011. http://medicineinmotorsport.fiainstitute.com/.

Fiske, A., Wetherell, J. L. and Gatz, M. (2009). Depression in older adults. *Annual Review of Clinical Psychology*, 5, 363–389.

Fletcher, D. and Wagstaff, C. R. D. (2009). Organizational psychology in elite sport; Its emergence, application, and future. *Psychology of Sport and Exercise*, 4, 427–434.

Foster-Wallace, D. (2006). Federer as religious experience. Online article accessed 1 May 2011: http://www.nytimes.com/2006/08/20/sports/playmagazine/20federer.html.

Frost, R. (1916). *Mountain interval*. New York: Henry Holt and Company.

Garrett, W. E. and Kirkendall, D. T. (2000). *Exercise and sport science*. Philidelphia: Lippincott, Williams & Wilkins.

Gottfredson, L. S. (1997a). Mainstream science on intelligence: An editorial with 52 signatories, history, and bibliography. *Intelligence*, 24, 13–23.

Guillot, A. and Collet, C. (2005). Duration of mentally simulated movement: A review. *Journal of Motor Behavior*, 37(1), 10–20.

Harwood, J. (2011). Is the F1 season already over as Vettel wins again? Online news article downloaded on 24 May 2011: http://www.thefirstpost.co.uk/79291,sport,other-sport,is-the-formula-1-season-already-over-as-sebastian-vettel-and-red-bull-win-again-spanish-grand-prix.

Heaney, S. (1993). *Seeing things*. New York: Farrar, Straus and Giroux.

James, W. (1890). *The principles of psychology*. New York: Henry Holt & Company.

Jeannerod, M. (1994). The representing brain: Neural correlates of motor intention and imagery. *Behavioural and Brain Sciences*, 17, 187–245.

Jeannerod, M. (1997). *The cognitive neuroscience of action*. Oxford: Blackwell.

Jeannerod, M. (2001). Neural simulation of action: A unifying mechanism for motor cognition. *NeuroImage*, 14, 103–109.

Jeannerod, M. (2006). *Motor cognition: What actions tell to the self*. New York: Oxford University Press.

Klarica, A. (2001). Performance in motor sports. *British Journal of Sports Medicine*, 35 (5), 290–291.

Kremer, J. and Moran, A. (2008). Swifter, higher, stronger: The history of sport and exercise psychology. *The Psychologist*, 21 (8), 740–742.

Lavallee, D., Jennings, D., Anderson, A., Martin, S. (2005). Investigating Irish athletes' attitudes towards sport psychology. *The Irish Journal of Psychology*, 26, 115–121.

Lavallee, D., Williams, M. and Jones, M. (2008). *Key studies in sport and exercise psychology*. Columbus, OH: McGraw-Hill.

Lidor, R., Côté, J. and Hackfort, D. (2009). ISSP position stand: To test or not to test? The use of physical tests in talent detection and in early phases of sport development. *International Journal of Sport and Exercise Psychology*, 9, 131–146.

Lippi, G., Guidi, G. C., Nevill, A. and Colin Boreham, B. (2008): The growing trend of scientific interest in sports science research, *Journal of Sports Sciences*, 26 (1), 1–2.

MacIntyre, T. (2012). What have the Romans ever done for us? The contribution of sport and exercise psychology to mainstream psychology. *The Psychologist,* 25 (7), 2–3.

MacIntyre, T. and Moran, A. (2007). Exploring imagery use and meta-imagery processes: Qualitative investigations with an elite multi-sport sample. *Journal of Imagery Research in Sport and Physical Activity* Vol 2, Article 4.

MacIntyre, T. and Moran, A. (2010). Meta-imagery processes among elite sports performers. In A. Guillot & C. Collet (eds). *The neurophysiological foundations of mental and motor imagery* (pp. 227-244). Oxford: Oxford University Press.

MacIntyre, T., Moran, A. and Jennings, D.J. (2002). Are mental imagery abilities related to canoe-slalom performance? *Perceptual and Motor Skills*, 94, 1245–1250.

Mahoney, M. J., and Avener, M. (1977). Psychology of the elite athlete: An exploratory study. *Cognitive Therapy and Research*, 1, 135– 141.

Maughan, R. (2009). *Olympic textbook of science in sport*. West Sussex, UK: Wiley-Blackwell.

Moran. A. (2009a). Cognitive psychology in sport: Progress and prospects. *Psychology of Sport and Exercise,* 10 (4), 420-426.

Moran, A. (2009b). Thinking in action: Some insights from cognitive sports psychology. Keynote at International Conference on Thinking, Belfast, 22 June 2011. Published proceedings. Belfast, N.I: QUB.

Moran, A. (2011a). Thinking in Action: Some insights form cognitive sports psychology. Keynote at International Conference on Thinking, Belfast, June 22nd, 2011. Published proceedings. Belfast, N.I.: QUB.

Moran, A. (2011b). *Sport* and *exercise psychology: A critical introduction* (2nd ed.). London: Routledge.

Moran, A. (2012). *Sport and exercise psychology: A critical introduction* (2nd edn.). London: Routledge.

Moran, A. and MacIntyre, T. (1998). 'There's more to an image than meets the eye': A qualitative study of kinaesthetic imagery among canoe-slalomists. *The Irish Journal of Psychology*, 19, 406–423.

Moran, A. and MacIntyre, T. (2008). 'Motor cognition and mental imagery: New directions'. Paper presented on 16 May at conference on 'Functional, Algorithmic and Implementational Aspects of Motor Control and Liverpool Hope University, 15–16 May 2008. Abstract published in M. Ziessler and E. Hossner (eds). *Functional, Algorithmic and Implementational Aspects of Motor Control and Learning*, p.16.

Morgan, W. P. and Pollock, M. (1977). Psychological characterization of the elite distance runner. *Annals of New York Academy of Science*, 301, 382–403.

Pervin, L. A. and John, O. P. (2001) *Handbook of personality: Theory and research*. New York: Guilford Press.

Robinson, T. (2008). David Beckham: Soccer's superstar. Berkeley Heights, NJ: Enslow Publishers.

Rogozkin, V. A. and Maughan, R. (1996). *Current approaches in sports sciences: An international perspective*. New York: Plenum Press.

Salmela, J. H. (1996). Expert coaches strategies for the development of expert athletes. In V. A. Rogozkin and R. Maughan (eds.), *Current approaches in sports sciences: An international perspective*. New York: Plenum Press.

Schraw, G., and Ericsson, K. A. (2005). An interview with K. Anders Ericsson. *Educational Psychology Review* 17, 389–410.

Seligman, M. E. P. and Fowler, R. D. (2011). Comprehensive soldier fitness and the future of psychology. *American Psychologist*, 66 (1), 82–86.

Syed, M. (2011). *The psychology of choking*. Online news article accessed 11 June 2011. http://news.bbc.co.uk/sport2/hi/front_page/13185266.stm.

Thatcher, J., Thatcher, R., Day, M.C., Portas, M. and Hood, S. (2009). Sport Science. In J. Thatcher, R. Thatcher, M. C. Day, M. Portas and S. Hood (eds) *An introduction to sport and exercise science*. Exeter: Learning Matters.

Tschanz, D. W. (2003). Hunayn bin Ishaq: The great translator. *JISHIM Journal of the International Society for the History of Islamic Medicine*, 1, 39–40.

Vandell, R. A., Davis, R. A. and Clugston, H. A. (1943). The function of mental practice in the acquisition of motor skills. *Journal of General Psychology*, 29, 243–250.

Walker, G., Kremer, J. and Moran, A. (2006). Coming of age in sport psychology. *Sport and Exercise Psychology Review*, 2, (1) 43–49.

Wilson, P.H., Thomas, P.R. and Maruff, P. (2002). Motor imagery training ameliorates motor clumsiness in children. *Journal of Child Neurology*, 17, 491–498.

Yarrow, K., Brown, P. and Krakauer, J. W. (2009). Inside the brain of an elite athlete: The neural processes that support high achievement in sports. *Nature Reviews: Neuroscience*, 10, 585–596.

8

The management and development of association football in the Middle East

A focus on AFC's 'Vision Asia' document

Philip O'Kane and Luke McCloskey

Overview

This chapter provides a brief introduction to association football in the Middle East. It outlines the initial development of the game, from the colonial era to the formation of respective national football associations in the period following colonisation, and the affiliation of these football associations with the Asian Football Confederation (AFC). A summary of the success of Middle Eastern nations and clubs in AFC-sanctioned tournaments is promoted, together with an analysis of the AFC's football development plan for the region. The potential legacy of the Qatar 2022 World Cup is also discussed, along with the wider significance of association football in the Middle East.

Case Study: The FIFA World Cup

Every four years the FIFA World Cup represents the preeminent showcase for association football in the world; it has been competed for by national teams since 1930. There is no bigger global sporting event than the FIFA World Cup and no other sporting tournament can inspire the same level of passion and commitment. For example, the average audience viewing figures per match for the 2002 World Cup was 314 million people worldwide (Hunt, 2006). Middle Eastern countries have qualified on numerous occasions for the FIFA World Cup, but to date none has made a significant impact on the final stages of the tournament, with the recent exception of Saudi Arabia and Iran at the 1994 and 1998 finals, respectively.

At the 1994 World Cup Finals, held in the United States of America, Saudi Arabia met 1986 World Cup semi-finalists Belgium in a game they had to win to progress to the second round of the competition. Saudi Arabia had lost its opening group game to Holland 2–1, despite taking an unexpected early lead, and had then beaten Morocco by the same score line in their second game. In the match against Belgium, which was played on 29 June 1994 in front of 52,959 spectators at the Robert F. Kennedy Memorial Stadium in Washington, DC, Saudi Arabia won 1–0 to secure a famous victory. This was due to a remarkable individual goal by Saeed Al Owairan who ran from his own half past five Belgian defenders and the goalkeeper before scoring (Hunt, 2006). This performance earned Al Owairan the nickname of the 'Desert Pele' and with it the 1994 Asian Footballer of the Year award. Saudi Arabia went on to lose 3–1 to eventual semi-finalists Sweden in the second round, but their legacy was guaranteed as the first Middle Eastern country to make it through to the knock-out stages of the World Cup finals.

At the next World Cup finals, held in France in 1998, the national team of Iran also caused quite a stir with some fine performances. In their second group game Iran faced the USA in a match laden with political rhetoric and was labelled by the media as something of a grudge match (Hunt, 2006). The USA were strong favourites for the game played in Lyon on 21 June 1998 in front of a crowd of 49,000, as Iran had never won a match in the World Cup finals, despite famously drawing with Scotland in 1978. Both teams needed to win the game to keep their chances of qualifying for the knock-out stages alive. In a pulsating, end-to-end game, Iran won 2–1, thanks to goals from Hamid Estili and Mehdi Mahdavikia. It was an historic first ever win at the World Cup finals for Iran and a victory that was celebrated throughout the

Middle East (Chehabi, 2006) with the Iranian players returning home as heroes, despite losing their final group game 2–0 to Germany.

These two examples show the importance attached to performing well on the world stage at the FIFA World Cup, as it integrates otherwise comparatively marginalised countries in the context of football more fully on the global stage. Following the 1998 World Cup a number of Iranian players secured offers to play overseas for European clubs, particularly in Germany (Chehabi, 2006). Middle Eastern countries will be hoping for more such impressive performances when Qatar becomes the first ever Middle Eastern country to host the finals of the FIFA World Cup in 2022. The significance of this and the potential legacy of the tournament for the Middle East are dealt with later in this chapter.

Introduction: The origins of association football in the Middle East

Association football is the most popular spectator sport in the world, reflecting, as it does, national identity, ethnicity and community (Bandyapadhyay, 2006). As in many other regions of the world, football is woven tightly into the lives of the people of the Middle East and is undoubtedly the region's most popular sport. It is seen as the 'game of the people' in that it reflects society, whilst the management of the game can arguably be used as a model of development off the field of play as well as on it. This is because football, it can be argued, offers a sense of identity for a nation's people and can also promote social cohesion, as has been apparent in many other countries throughout the world (Middle East Institute, 2010).

The game of association football dates from the mid-nineteenth century, with the laws of the game first being officially codified by the English Football Association in 1863. From the late nineteenth century the game spread all over the world, during a period when Victorian imperialism was at its height, as the colonisation of other parts of the world, mainly by Britain but also by other European nations such as France, Russia, Germany and Portugal, led to the spread of the sport throughout Africa, Asia and the Middle East. The British in particular were instrumental in introducing the game into the Middle East due to a number of distinctive factors that they were able to utilise. In nineteenth-century British missionary schools throughout the Middle East the game of association football was part of the curriculum, and it is here that the game was first introduced to the offspring of the region's elite (Chehabi, 2006). Elsewhere, the game was introduced to the working class through other, less direct, methods. Oil was first discovered in the Middle East in 1908 (Cleveland, 1994) and the influx of British employees of the Anglo-Persian oil companies into the Middle East led to many working-class people in the region becoming acquainted with the game. The legacy of the colonial powers' military presence was also instrumental in introducing football to the Middle East. For example, the British officers of the South Persian Rifles in the early twentieth century, introduced the game to the indigenous troops over whom they commanded and who in turn spread the sport throughout the remainder of the region (Chehabi, 2006). The presence of colonial powers in the Middle East was therefore the main catalyst for the introduction and spread of the game of association football across the Arabian Peninsula in particular.

At the same time as Western colonial powers were introducing the game throughout the globe, its structures and management were becoming more established, particularly in Europe. This was best illustrated by the foundation of FIFA (Fédération Internationale de Football Association), the world governing body of association football, in Paris in 1904. FIFA oversee the administration of football worldwide and manages a number of competitions, most notably the FIFA World Cup, held every four years since the early twentieth century and regarded as the pinnacle of world football (see case study). FIFA's mission statement is 'Develop the game, touch the world, build a better future' (ww.fifa.com). Despite the formation of FIFA in 1904, the management and structure of the game throughout the Middle East and the rest of Asia did not become established or recognised until the end of the colonial era, that is post-World War II, when the majority of the nations in the what may be referred to as the 'modern' Middle East gained independence from European colonial powers.

As these newly independent nations became more stable, they in turn founded official football associations to oversee the game domestically. The earliest football federation established in the Middle East was the Iranian Football Federation founded in 1920 (itself a legacy of colonialism), quickly followed by the foundation of the Lebanon Football Association in 1933 and the Syrian Football Federation in 1936. Post-World War II the Iraqi Football Federation was founded in 1948 the Football Associations of Jordan in 1949, Kuwait in 1952, Bahrain in 1957 and the Saudi Arabia Football Association in 1959. The most recent national football associations founded in the Middle East include the Qatar Football Association in 1960, Yemen Football Association in 1962, the United Arab Emirates Football Association in 1971) and the Oman Football Association in (1978. These 12 countries of the Middle East now form part of the Asian Football Confederation, which was itself founded in 1954 and currently has 46 member countries.

The Asian Football Confederation and the Union of Arab Football Associations

The Asian Football Confederation (AFC) is responsible for the overall governance and management of association football in Asia, including the Middle East, in

conjunction with FIFA, the world governing body. The AFC is responsible for implementing and delivering a football development strategy throughout the continent and staging competitions featuring both national teams and club sides. The most prestigious of the competitions currently being sanctioned and managed by the Asian Football Confederation is the Asian Nations Cup. First promoted in 1956 it is the second oldest continental football competition in the world after the Copa America of South America. Middle Eastern countries have been quite successful in the Asian Nations Cup, as nations representing this region have won eight out of the 15 tournaments staged to date: Iran (1968, 1972, 1976), Saudi Arabia (1984, 1988, 1996), Kuwait (1980) and Iraq (2007) (www.the-afc.com). This is also reflected in the fact that ten Middle Eastern footballers have won the coveted 'Asian Footballer of the Year' trophy, first awarded in 1988 when it was presented to Ahmed Radhi of Iraq. He has since been followed by Saeed Al Owairan, Saudi Arabia (1994), Khodadad Azizi, Iran (1996), Ali Daei, Iran (1999), Nawf Al Tenyat, Saudi Arabia (2000), Mehdi Mahdavikia, Iran (2003), Ali Karimi, Iran (2004), Hamad Al-Montashari, Saudi Arabia (2005), Khalfan Ibrahim, Qatar (2006) and Yasser Al-Qahtani, Saudi Arabia (2007) (www.the-afc.com).

The AFC also sponsors the prestigious Asian Champions League for club teams throughout the continent. This competition is contested annually by the top 32 clubs representing the top ten Asian leagues. The tournament has been staged in its present guise since 2002, but prior to this existed in various different guises, including the Asian Champion Club Tournament (1967–1972) and the Asian Club Championship (1985–2002). Traditionally the most successful club sides have emerged from the strong domestic leagues of South Korea and Japan; however, in recent years teams from Iran and Saudi Arabia have triumphed. Saudi Arabian teams, Al-Hilal (1992, 2000) and Al-Ittihad

(2004, 2005), have won the tournament twice, as has Esteghlal Tehran from Iran (1970 and 1991). The other Middle Eastern teams to have won the coveted championship are PAS Tehran from Iran in 1993 and Al-Sadd from Qatar in 1989 (www.the-afc.com). The recent victories of the sides from Saudi Arabia in particular the ongoing work and financial investment in developing domestic football in the country by the Saudi Arabian Football Association, which in turn is leading to its club sides challenging the traditional dominance of the teams from the Far East.

In addition to the AFC, the countries of the Middle East have also formed a number of regional football associations designed to manage the sport of association football specifically within the Middle Eastern domain. In 2001 the 12 Middle Eastern members of the AFC, plus Palestine, formed the West Asian Football Federation and have subsequently organised a fledgling West Asian Football Federation championship, which has been dominated by Iran with four victories (2000, 2004, 2007 and 2008), with Iraq winning in 2002 and Kuwait winning the most recent tournament, defeating Iran 2–1 in the 2010 final. A precedent for this move, the formation of a new football federation within a federation, had existed as the countries of the Middle East had already formed the Union of Arab Football Associations (UAFA) as far back as 1974. Interestingly UAFA included not only the AFC nations (later to form the West Asian Football Federation), but also a number of nations from the Confederation of African Football (CAF), namely Algeria, Morocco, Egypt, Tunisia, Libya, Mauritania, Somalia, Sudan, Djibouti and Comoros. The reasons for this are complex and are as a result of the close political and cultural ties that many countries in North Africa have with the Middle East. The 'Arab' nations of North Africa are known collectively as 'The Maghreb', which means 'the west' or literally 'when and where the sun sets' in Arabic, referring as it does to these western Arab states. These countries have been traditionally seen as part of the Arab world of the Middle East since the Islamic conquest of the region during the middle ages. These countries were also colonised by European powers in the nineteenth century (Cleveland, 1994). The fact that the countries of the Middle East are seen as being linked more strongly culturally and ethnically with these North African countries than with Asia illustrates the extremely difficult task that the AFC has in managing and developing association football within the region. As Asia is such a large continent, with an extremely cultural and politically diverse population in which cultural and ethnic boundaries overlap with continental, political and administrative ones, the task of implementing a football development plan for the continent is something which, whilst by no means straightforward, the AFC has been able to achieve quite effectively.

The Union of Arab Football Associations has sponsored a number of international competitions, including The Arab Nations Cup, which has taken place sporadically since 1963. The first tournament was won by Tunisia, the only victory to date by an African team. Iraq has won the tournament four times, a notable achievement, especially given the fact that it was banned from international competition from 1991–2003 as a result of international sanctions issued against it. In recent years Saudi Arabia has been the competition's dominant side. It is however debatable how effective UAFA has been in promoting joint collaboration between North African and Middle Eastern football federations, as African teams have not fully embraced the tournament since Tunisia won the aforementioned, inaugural competition in 1963. The Middle Eastern countries have also organised a 'Gulf Nations Cup' over recent decades. The inaugural competition was won by Kuwait in 1970, with the early years of the competition being dominated by Kuwait and Iraq, albeit with other nations such as Saudi Arabia (2003) and Qatar (2004) winning it in recent years. The United Arab Emirates won the competition for the first time in 2007 thanks to a 1–0 victory over Oman in Abu Dhabi, with the newest member of the Asian Football Confederation, the defeated Oman, in turn claiming its first ever title in 2009.

8.2

Fans of Egypt's Al-Ahly cheer for their team during their Egyptian League football match against rival club Zamalek in Cairo on 29 June 2011

Source: © MOHAMED HOSSAM/AFP/ Getty Images

The 'Vision Asia' football development plan

As previously stated, the AFC has quite a difficult task in managing and promoting the game of association football over such a vast and diverse cultural and geographical domain. It has addressed this difficulty by devising a football development strategy entitled 'Vision Asia'. In order to effectively implement the plan, the AFC has divided the continent into four zones, East Asia, South East Asia, Central/South Asia and West Asia, the latter of which takes in the countries of the Middle East. 'Vision Asia' is a continent-wide programme aimed at raising the standards of Asian football at all levels. The Vision promotes a pyramid structure within clubs, with a broad participation base, supported by effective coaching structures and adequate facilities (www. the-afc.com).

Vision Asia comprises of 11 disciplines identified as key development themes through which football in the Middle East can develop, prosper and nurture soccer talent. These disciplines form the foundation for development across all 46 member associations, representing more than half of the world's population (www.the-afc.com).

The Vision's central disciplines are wide-ranging and reflective of the current development status of football in the Middle East. They represent the blueprint around which national associations will strategize, plan and deliver success, ultimately on a par with their counterparts in Europe and around the world. The plan's key areas are: National Associations, Marketing, Grassroots and Youth, Coach Education, Referees, Sports Medicine, Competitions and Clubs, Women's Competitions, Futsal, Media and Fans (www.the-afc.com).

Central to the strength of the AFC's enduring plan in the Middle East will be its implementation across each individual nation-state. The dynamics of each national association will provide a unique challenge in the full execution of this strategy. While national associations will provide the driving force for the development of football in the Middle East, Vision Asia seeks to assist each association in having the best structures suited to the inimitable football environment present within that country. Consequently, the potency of this strategy will depend greatly on the willingness of each association to embrace development, change and, in some instances, marked revolution.

The Vision Asia strategy engenders clear and cohesive development principles for national associations, extending across amateur and professional structures. Associations should be structured into key departments, to include Coach Education, Youth Development and Sports Science, thus allowing for growth and change to occur organically. Furthermore, the statutes of each national association should ensure conformity with FIFA directives, providing further dissemination of effective practice. More pertinent perhaps, will be the self-sufficiency of each member association as a result of developing this key strategy. It is anticipated that, through more effective operational structures at national level, football in the Middle East can generate greater levels of revenue and commercial potential, which in turn will allow them to reinvest in the development of the sport for the betterment of future generations.

Effective marketing of the football product in the Middle East will be decisive in providing a sound financial footing for national associations. Furthermore, this will cultivate further growth and interest in their games, in turn leading to expanded sources of revenue. Marketing is viewed as a tool with which national associations can use to broaden their participation base, promote their games around the world, whilst producing an important financial stream for reinvestment. It remains clear that football in the Middle East is quite some way off commercial saturation point, as currently being experienced by their counterparts in Europe. Moreover, this discipline will require specific marketing expertise and effective branding of their games. Indeed, it's reasonable to assert that a significant investment in the promotion of football in the Middle East will undoubtedly yield generous commercial returns.

Youth and Grassroots development represent another fundamental component in the broader development policy for football in the Middle East. It will underpin the future success of national teams, whilst maximising their most valuable asset available, the players. Widening the participation base, supplemented by effective coaching, will heighten the quantity and quality of players being developed. Equally important, however, will be the scope of grassroots development. National associations will need to target clubs, schools and community-based groups so as to have maximal impact. Additionally, a clear and cohesive player development pathway will be critical to ensure systematized progression (www.scottishfa.co.uk). Many national associations in Europe develop a modified youth games structure from that of the adult game, which in turn promotes greater technical ability at a younger age (www.thefa.com).

A simultaneous process of coach education and grassroots development is also critical. Quality players will come from quality coaching structures and practices. Moreover, national associations in the Middle East will need to build refined coaching structures, sustained by a progressive coaching accreditation framework. Building a new coaching ideology will undoubtedly take time. However, it is a prerequisite to success at national level, yet, once formulated, will provide longevity and durability to the development strategy. A minimum coaching requirement policy in all competitions will also raise coaching standards throughout the region. The current practice of importing coaching knowledge from outside the region will provide valuable support for emerging talent. Nonetheless, the more enduring philosophy of developing home-grown coaching talent should take precedence. Expanding the skills base of players and the knowledge disseminated to them by quality coaches, will have significant implications for the future of football in the region.

Not dissimilar to the formation of coaching structures, will be that of referee development. The plan sets out the need for progress at both policy and structural levels (www.the-afc.com). Similarly, a coordinated referee accreditation framework that creates an obvious progression route will be critical. Training referees, refereeing mentors and creating the necessary support mechanisms for officials will be equally significant. Furthermore, producing the appropriate structures to develop refereeing will ensure greater uniformity within the profession and indeed, across the region. In summary, Vision Asia constitutes a framework which will engender opportunities for refereeing from grassroots to elite level.

In an effort to reduce disparity between mature, developing and emerging national associations, advances in sports medicine are viewed as fundamental (www.the-afc.com). Indeed, an emerging coaching strategy will need to run concurrently with innovative sports science methodologies and practices. As MacIntyre has correctly identified elsewhere in this collection, sports science will fortify the coaching process and the precision of data given to players at all levels. The plan sets out criteria which underpin a need for greater numbers of trained sports science personnel, with the aim of delivering comprehensive healthcare and clinical treatment for players at all levels (www. the-afc.com). Conversely, sports science alone will not deliver the realisation of this vision; yet will form an integral element in the journey to sustained success.

What binds many of the elements of this plan together are an array of individual clubs and competitions. The aims of the plan in this regard are bilateral, i.e. to provide coordinated competition at two levels, elite/professional and amateur/youth level. When deconstructed, though, it becomes evident that the overarching objective is to produce elite players via a multifaceted strategy. For a vision to be realised, it must resonate through all levels of participation. Consequently, it sets out principles for the involvement of key stakeholders, most notably community-based clubs, schools and local associations. By giving local clubs and associations the tools to formulate their own destiny, success nationally will be much more probable and sustainable. Although this suggests a 'bottom-up' approach, local clubs will still need considerable direction and leadership from their national associations. This could also come in the form of national football centres, which will help nurture new talent (www.thefa.com). Indeed, it's reasonable to assert that an interdependent process between national associations and local associations will yield positive results at all levels.

Women's football represents another element in the framework of the game's development in the Middle East. Clearly, there is disparity between levels of engagement across the Middle East. Indeed, the AFC acknowledge the social and cultural issues which have impeded the growth of the women's game (www.the-afc.com). Irrespective of this, the need to popularize and broaden participation in football is imperative. Grassroots and youth involvement will be critical, nonetheless; using effective marketing opportunities and providing role models for younger participants will indeed increase the attraction on the part of many to participate. Female integration into all aspects of football will also be invaluable, especially in coaching, admin-istration and officiating. In summary, maximising the opportunities for female participants and coaches at local level will sustain growth at the national level. Futsal is an emerging game within the region. The AFC view it as a means of improving the technical ability and proficiency of players (www.the-afc.com). Considerable work is required to integrate it into the current development structure.

Delivering the football brand across the Middle East is complicated by the diversity of languages and cultures within the region. For that reason, regionalised media exposure of local and national games carries greater significance. The vision sets out a clear need for established, professional relations with all media forms. Establishing closer links with the media will in itself market and promote football, thus increasing participation across its key target groups. The regionalisation of media structures is evident in the AFC's plan; however, each country can itself contribute to the football brand in the Middle East through their own activities.

In metaphoric terms, fans represent the 'strikers' within the Vision Asia development team (www.the-afc.com). They are deemed paramount to the success of football in the region. In many ways, football fans encapsulate the appetite and passion required to realise the potential of football in the Middle East. They underpin many of the key elements previously discussed in this chapter. They will inspire commercial success, provide future generations of players and give such athletes the motivation to reach the pinnacle of their game. It is clear that this vision recognises that fans will provide a voice for their team and help inform national associations in their work and encourage them in the right direction.

In summary, it is evident that the 11 distinct elements outlined in the Vision Asia document are actually interdependent and can provide a vehicle for growth and sustainable development in the Middle East. Evidently, the plan may not establish itself neatly within each individual national association, especially considering the divergence in their stages of development. Indeed, national associations will need to provide the 'fuel' for this plan, in the form of investment, leadership and effective governance. With this in place, football in the Middle East can achieve accelerated growth and provide success affiliation of the passion and devotion expressed by their fans with those of the game itself.

8.3
Football can be used to promote healthy lifestyles

Source: PhotoAlto/ Ale Ventura

The Qatar 2022 World Cup, its potential legacy and wider significance

On 2 December 2010 FIFA made the historic announcement that the World Cup will be held for the first time in the Middle East when Qatar hosts the tournament in 2022 (www.fifa.com). The bidding process to host the 2022 World Cup finals began in February 2009, when each potential host country submitted their bid. Qatar finally defeated Australia, Japan, South Korea and the United States of America in the race to win the right to host the tournament amid scenes of unprecedented jubilation. Thirty-two teams will compete over four weeks at venues in Qatar and in front of a global audience of tens of millions for the right to be regarded as World champions. The hosting of the World Cup finals brings many benefits to the host nation and will leave a legacy that will resonate far beyond 2022 (www.fifa2022qa.com).

Indeed, the staging of the World Cup in Qatar 2022 has the potential to yield benefits beyond the borders of Qatar itself. World Cups can underpin nation-building potential, with its legacy and enduring impact reverberating through the Middle East. The World Cup in 2022 represents an unprecedented opportunity for football's development in the Middle East. While it will leave a significant economic footprint within the region, the development of the game of football itself will be a key priority. This will extend to football administration, grassroots development and the promotion of non-elite football, to include youth, women and people with special needs (www.fifa. com). These key target areas could witness unparalleled growth, with the World Cup providing a window of opportunity to broaden the participation base currently evident within the 'people's game'. Specifically, the Qatar World Cup bid outlines a lasting educational, commercial and cultural impact for the country and, by extension, the region (www.fifa.com). More significantly, its football legacy has the potential to stimulate participation at local and national levels.

Ultimately however the enduring legacy of Qatar 2022 is inextricably linked with the key aims of the AFC's 'Vision Asia' document (www. the-afc.com). The tournament will have profound implications for grassroots participation, coaching education and the proficiency through which national associations can deliver football to the people. Aspiring players will be afforded enhanced opportunities to perform their skills, through improved playing facilities, better coaching and games administration. For the region itself, it remains crucial that the prosperity and opportunities that come to Qatar, certainly in sporting terms, are dispersed throughout the Middle East.

In contrast to the corporate impact of the tournament, its ability to impact football at community level will provide its sternest, yet most rewarding, challenge. National associations will need to capitalize on this unique opportunity by having long-term player development models in place. This will ensure the legacy is a sustainable one, rather than a temporary and ephemeral experience.

More immeasurable, perhaps, will be the sense of pride and

confidence gained by people in Qatar and the Middle East region. The FIFA World Cup will leave a lasting sporting and social legacy, cultivating social cohesion and widening participation in football. This is exemplified in the proposal to deliver sport and leadership programmes to schools in both Nepal and Pakistan (www.fifa.com).

Qatar will experience the customary effects that a World Cup can bring to a nation. It will create jobs and improve transportation infrastructure (www.fifa.com). Nonetheless, its impact on football within and beyond its borders will be particularly fascinating. Managed appropriately, the World Cup could have a seismic impact on the development of football talent in the region, creating a new generation of players.

Summary

In an overall sense therefore, it is clear that association football has a wider global significance beyond merely the promotion of the sport. Football can also be used to promote educational, cultural and humanitarian values, whilst the governing body of the game worldwide, FIFA, interpret football as constituting a symbol of hope and integration throughout the world:

> Football is no longer considered merely a global sport, but also as unifying force whose virtues can make an important contribution to society. We use the power of football as a tool for social and human development, by strengthening the work of dozens of initiatives around the globe to support local communities in the areas of peacebuilding, health, social integration, education and more.
>
> (www.fifa.com)

For fringe nations which remain at the periphery of world football, it holds a place of central importance in the everyday lives of the population and can be seen as a focus for identity and a source of national pride (Bandyopadhyay, 2006). For developing nations in particular, football plays a key role in programmes of national development on account of many of the reasons detailed in this chapter. An example of football being used to help promote national pride and identity in the Middle East is apparent in Yemen, which is one of the poorest countries in the Middle East. However, as football is a great leveller and despite the fact that the Yemen Football Federation was only founded in 1962, the country can compete on a level playing field with the richer Gulf states, in turn providing the Yemeni people with a much needed morale boost (Stevenson, 2010). For example, a first ever victory for the Yemen national team over wealthier neighbours Bahrain in 2010 was a source of unbridled joy for the people of this small nation.

Football can also be used to promote health and education in many developing nations. This is a key focus of the AFC's 'Vision Asia' football development plan, covered in depth earlier in this chapter. Various charity organisations and NGOs worldwide therefore use football in a developmental capacity as it promotes healthy lifestyles. Football is also not confined to any particular locality or any ethnic, religious or political domain (Rookwood, 2011). As a result of this, football is also being used in some areas of the Middle East to help promote peace. In many conflicts, young people become socialised into warfare, and therefore there is a need to produce peaceful alternatives, often through the use of sport to overcome historical differences and disputes. Work undertaken with young people who live in areas where unrest and conflict persist – through the medium of football – can help to underwrite other peace initiatives as it brings people together in a neutral environment. One region of the Middle East which has witnessed conflict for the past number of decades is Israel. Sport in Israel is highly politicised but, since the globalisation and liberalisation of Israeli society from the late 1980s onwards, association football has become more accessible to all sections of the community there. In this way, football has been used as an instrument of peace and a tool for bringing people together; this fact is illustrated by the number of Arab football teams and players participating in the Israeli league. During the late 1990s and 2000s three Arab teams advanced to the major Israeli soccer league, namely Hpoel Taibe, Maccabi Akhi Nazareth and Bnei Sakhnin. In the context of Israeli society this is quite a significant development and suggests that football may hold the key to bringing societies together within areas in the Middle East that have experienced conflict in recent times.

There are many challenges, therefore, for the management of association football in the Middle East over the next number of years, but arguably the region is well equipped to deal effectively with these as they arise. In order to successfully develop football in the region, it is crucial that the football federations of the Middle East embrace the AFC's 'Vision Asia' football development plan if the game in the region is to become more sustainable. By concentrating on improving the structure of football domestically, specifically at grassroots level, as embedded within the 'Vision Asia' plan, the football associations of the Middle East can succeed in nurturing young talent, instead of employing foreign players and managers from South America and Europe, as has traditionally been the case in the past. Evidently, this will result in a more sustainable management structure for developing football in the region. The sporadic success of Middle Eastern teams on the world stage in both the FIFA World Cup and AFC Champions League shows that the natural talent is present, it just needs to be nurtured properly if this success is to prove more regular and sustained. The Vision Asia development plan lays the basis for this, and the potential impact of the Qatar 2022 World Cup should leave a lasting sporting and social legacy, cultivating social cohesion and widening participation in football throughout the Middle East. The football associations of the Middle East will be hopeful that, following the successful implementation of the Vision Asia plan, the national teams of the Middle East will make a significant impact on the World Cup in Qatar in 2022 and emulate the Saudi

Arabian team of 1994 that remain the only Middle Eastern country, to date, to advance to the knock-out stages of the World Cup finals.

The effective delivery of the 'Vision Asia' plan 'on the ground' has also been made easier by changes in Middle East society over the past number of years as a result of globalization which has widened the societal perspective of many states in the region (Stetter, 2008). Globalization in the Middle East has particularly affected communications within society, with information being much easier to access than has previously been the case. This has strengthened the sense of pan-Arab identity across the region, especially amongst new generations in the Middle East (Yamani, 2002). This should make delivery of region-wide development plans such as Vision Asia easier, as the various football associations involved can work in partnership to implement the plan utilising this new galvanised sense of identity. The same is true for the legacy of the Qatar 2022 World Cup, which should create benefits right across the Middle East region.

There can be little doubt, therefore, that with the delivery of the Vision Asia football development plan, the ongoing grassroots work in many of the Middle Eastern countries and the upcoming World Cup in 2022 it is a very exciting time for football in the Middle East. If the development and management of association football in the Middle East over the next decade continues at the pace at which it has done so over the past decade, then it can only be a matter of time before Middle Eastern nations, clubs and players make a significant impact on the world stage of the so-called 'beautiful game'.

References

The Asian Football Confederation – http://www.the-afc.com

Bandyopadhyay, Kausik (2006) 'The Real People's Game', *Soccer and Society*, Vol. 7, pp. 157–164.

Chehabi, Houchang E. (2006) 'The Politics of Football in Iran', *Soccer and Society*, Vol. 7, pp. 233–261.

Sports in Society, Issues & Controversies

Cleveland, William L. (1994) *A History of the Modern Middle East*, Oxford: Westview Press Inc.

Dodge, Toby and Higgott, Richard (2002) *Globalization and the Middle East: Islam, Economy, Society and Politics*, London: Royal Institute of International Affairs.

The FA's VISION 2008–12 – www.thefa.com

FIFA, 2022 FIFA World Cup Bid Evaluation Report: Qatar – www.fifa2022qa.com.

Hunt, Chris (2006) *The History of the FIFA World Cup: World Cup Stories*, Cambridge: Interact Publishing Limited.

International Football (Soccer) Competitions in the Middle East: Arab Nations Cup, Gulf Cup of Nations, UAFA Competitions, Milton Keynes: Books LLC.

Montague, James (2008) *When Friday Comes: Football in the War Zone*, Edinburgh: Mainstream Publishing.

The Middle East Institute (2010) *Viewpoints: Sports and the Middle East*, Washington, DC: The Middle East Institute. May – www.mei.edu.

Rookwood, Joel and Palmer, Clive (2011) 'Invasion Games in War-torn Nations: Can Football Help To Build Peace?', *Soccer and Society*, Vol. 12, pp. 184–200.

The Scottish FA, Developing Talent Plan – www.scottishfa.co.uk

Shor, Eran (2010) 'In Search of a Voice: Arab Soccer Players in the Israeli Media', in *Sports and The Middle East*, Washington, DC: The Middle East Institute.

Sport for Development & Peace (2008) *Harnessing the Power of Sport for Development and Peace, Recommendations to Governments*

Stetter, Stephan (2008) *World Society and the Middle East: Reconstructions in Regional Politics*, New York: Palgrave Macmillan.

Stevenson, Thomas B. and Alaug, Abdul Karim (2010) 'Yemeni Football and Identity Politics', *Sports and The Middle East*, Washington DC: The Middle East Institute.

Sugden, John and Wallis, James (2007) *Football for Peace? The Challenge* of *Using Sport* for *Co-existence in Israel*, Oxford: Meyer & Meyer Sport.

UEFA Eleven Values – www.uefa.com

9

Sport and women in the Middle East

Awista Ayub

Overview

While this chapter aims at providing a broad perspective about the role of sports in the lives of women in the Middle East, it should be noted that, whereas there are general statements which can be made about this population, the region is not homogeneous as each country has a host of unique issues specific to their nation and the pace of change as it relates to women's rights both on and off the sports field. With that said, the author will thus highlight key benchmark moments within the evolution of sport for women in the Middle East, showcasing the success to date. Further, the author will discuss areas where future issues may arise specifically as they relate to the rules and regulations being made by various international sports federations (IFs) that directly affect this population, particularly now that more women from the region are participating in competitive sports on the global stage.

Background and context to women's participation in sport throughout the region

In recent years, the participation in sport by women in the Middle East has increased tremendously, which has not only brought about many positive values to the young women who are members of this emerging community, but their participation has, at times, provoked furious discussion regarding what role sports has, if any, in the lives of young female athletes both living in and around the Middle East.

At times, in these Muslim-majority countries, scriptures from the Qur'an have been used either to support the argument that women have a

9.1
Morocco's Nawal El Moutawakel celebrates her gold win in the Women's 400m hurdles final with her country's flag in the 1984 Olympic Games, Los Angeles

Source: ©Bob Thomas/Getty Images

rightful place in the sports domain or have equally been used to exclude them from the arena. But, in spite of this debate, many female athletes in the Middle East have proven these skeptics and critics wrong by showing the broader world that they do have a rightful place in the athletic arena, not beside men but, rather, beside other female athletes from around the world. They have further proven that, if given the space and time to practice and compete in their respective sports, they will succeed and will do so while gaining vital life lessons along the way that can then be taken off the field as well.

The chapter starts with a case study that is an excerpt from the author's book *Kabul Girls Soccer Club* (2010). This particular excerpt derives from interviews with various adult sports officials in Kabul, Afghanistan during a 2007 research trip. This case study will provide the reader with a perspective of the dynamic and, oftentimes, competing issues that sports officials in the Middle East face as they look to either introduce or expand sports opportunities for women within their country.

Case Study: a closer examination of the debate surrounding Afghan women's participation in sports

(This section from *Kabul Girls Soccer Club* is reproduced here with the expressed permission of the publisher, Hyperion.)

> In Afghanistan no one I spoke with embraced the Taliban or had enjoyed life under their regime. But I did meet brothers who thought their sisters should stay at home and not go to school, and high-ranking sports officials who questioned whether girls' soccer could be reconciled with religion.
>
> In the center were girls who considered themselves Muslim. They prayed daily, respected scriptures, dressed modestly. However, they also wanted to be educated, pursue careers, marry men they loved at a time they chose, and to play soccer – or any sport – without asking permission. They would eagerly seize every opportunity given to them.
>
> For society at large the question has become: What opportunities should be offered? And at what pace?
>
> That depended on whom you asked.

In 2005 while I was working at the Embassy of Afghanistan in Washington, D.C., all the news was about a young female basketball player determined to win a seat in that year's parliamentary elections – it seemed unreal, even more so when she won.

Sabrina Saqib, at twenty-seven, was one of the youngest members of the Afghanistan Parliament.

I met with her on my trip to Afghanistan in 2007. On the day of our interview, a burly security man greeted me. Like every Parliamentarian, Sabrina had an armed guard assigned to her. He led the way up five flights of stairs, past the broken elevators, with their call buttons smashed.

As Sabrina welcomed me into her apartment, the guard took up his post outside her door.

Sabrina was born in Kabul in the late 1970s. Her parents immigrated to Iran when she was a child. She went on to graduate from Tehran University, where she played basketball in female-only gymnasiums.

Iran had created one model for female sports participation in an Islamic country. Their stable athletic infrastructure included women's coaches, trainers, and referees – as well as dedicated gymnasiums where girls and women could compete in a female-only environment. These gender-segregated arenas provided a way for women to play sports, while also respecting the culture.

In 2001, Sabrina returned to Kabul and looked for basketball programs for women. There weren't any.

"So I did the only sensible thing," she told me. "I joined a men's basketball team."

For practice games, Sabrina and the male players tried to avoid any physical contact – hard in a sport where contact is the norm. It meant the men couldn't really guard her. Even though there were no public games, and Sabrina dressed in loose shirts and long pants, people talked. After a while, one of her teammates told her: "Please, you can't come anymore. Your presence is causing too many problems for us."

"I wasn't surprised," Sabrina said.

As luck would have it, soon after, Sabrina was invited to help start a women's basketball program through the ANABF (Afghanistan National Amateur Basketball Federation). Although the program expanded to included hundreds of girls across Kabul, many players dropped out, stopped by marriage, husbands, or family pressure.

So Sabrina spoke directly to the families themselves.

"We have to have strong women," she'd tell them. "If women want to be good mothers, fit mothers, sports can help. For healthy children it's not just enough to go to the doctor – if the mother has exercised, it can help her to have strong children." She was appealing to what many families felt was the main responsibility of women.

Sometimes there was nothing to be done.

"We have to let the girls come and go, come and go. One day they will stay forever."

Did the struggle for a women's sports program prepare her for her run for political office? Definitely.

In 2004, Afghanistan's first parliamentary elections in thirty-five years were being organized. Sabrina's mother encouraged her to run.

She was twenty-six years old.

Colored posters with a photo of Sabrina were plastered throughout Kabul. In them, she wore a yellow *hijab* and smiled directly into the camera. Young people in particular were so enamored with the posters that many were stolen and pasted up in their homes.

Some, though, found her poster too forward. It was very different than the typical black-and-white photo of a grim-faced candidate, surrounded with dense text.

On September 18, 2005, millions of Afghans made it to the polls to cast their vote. According to the 2040 Constitution, 25 percent of the parliament – sixty-eight seats – was reserved for women. When the results were in, seventy-four women had won their districts, accounting for 28 percent of the seats in parliament. Sabrina was one of them.

Sabrina Saqib is determined to create opportunities for women through sports in Afghanistan. "Sports are a sign of peace in Afghanistan," she said. "Step by step, we will have both."

Shukria Kahmat, thirty-nine, is the deputy for Afghan women's partici-pation in the Olympics. I interviewed her, aptly enough, at Ghazi Stadium. She was just completing her first year in the women's office, managing eighteen women's sports programs.

Shukria remembered the thriving sports program she'd grown up with – competitive teams, western sports clothing, intensive coaching, and stands packed for the games, with men and women cheering. She herself played basketball during this time, in the early seventies.

With war, she and her husband left for Pakistan, and returned to Kabul in 2002. The state of women's sports then came as a shock.

"The day I came, there was nothing. At the first practices in Ghazi Stadium, the girls were barefoot. They didn't have the sneakers or the right kind of clothing. We had to start everything from the ground up."

At the time, she said, people were "very *bay-tarbya*, dark-minded."

Even so, Shukria was encouraged. Slowly, "people are more open and accepting toward women playing sports."

Bit by bit, she and her office were piecing together sports opportunities for women within the Olympic Committee. It was still a struggle, however. Like Sabrina Saqib, Shukria Hakmat frequently visited families, personally encouraging them to let their daughters play. It was slow going, with a notable success here and there.

"Deena's a volleyball player. A really good one. At first, her husband wouldn't let her play," Shhukria told me.

Shukria visited Deena's husband and family, appealing to their nationalism. "If you let Deena play, you will be making a contribution to our country," she told them.

They agreed.

Then Deena's volleyball team made it to the championship game of the Volleyball Federation's tournament. This game would be televised. This was another obstacle, but Shukria overcame it.

Shukria understood that change would be wrought slowly.

"I respect all views," she said softly. "But we can find a middle way."

The middle way, according to Shukria, was female-only gymnasiums. Until then, Shukria would continue visiting homes one by one, convincing parents, husbands, and in-laws to let women play.

"I have a dream, more important than where athletes play or the uniforms they wear," she said. "One day we will get Olympic medals. Until then I will never leave my country. I will never stop."

If Sabrina Saqib and Shukria Hakmat saw women's sports as a sign of peace and progress in Afghanistan, Safiullah Subat represented both its hope and obstacle. When I interviewed him, he had been the chief of physical education for the Afghanistan Ministry of Education for six years.

An accomplished soccer player, Safiullah's government job came not long after the fall of the Taliban. Now in his sixties, he'd played soccer for more than forty years.

Regarding sports in Afghanistan, his opinion was that slow progress was best. "We should have limited number of sports federations, and they should be ones that we can put more focus and attention on," he said.

Which sports? Four: soccer, boxing, wrestling, and track and field.

In response to a query about volleyball, a popular sport for girls, he replied, "I believe volleyball is a very ordinary game, and even if you go to the most remote area in the country, you will find people playing volleyball there." The implication was that since it was played everywhere, a federation for it wasn't necessary.

"For some sports, women are physically not ready or it's not appropriate for them," he said. "For example, boxing, weight lifting, soccer. Physically, they are not good for women. I believe a women's body, by nature, is weaker as compared to a man's. Allah created women to be very delicate."

Safiullah leaned forward. "If I give you this ball, would you be able to break the glass?" he asked. "Even though I'm twice your age, if

I throw this ball on the wall, that wall would shake," he continued. "But you wouldn't be able to break the window glass. It doesn't mean that women are less capable than men."

This question of strength has been debated throughout the world. In many countries, there isn't a sport women haven't tried, or, for that matter, excelled in.

However, Safiullah's thinking was common, especially among older Afghan men, whether in America or Afghanistan.

"I am not against women in sports," he added firmly. "But, for example, men in our society do not want their women to go bareheaded to play soccer. They want them covered. You know that for soccer players it's very important to wear shorts. If you wear long pants, you won't be able to shoot as well."

Safiullah knew about the work of the Afghan Youth Sports Exchange and my role in it, so he clarified his position. "I don't mean that women should not play soccer. Since I am a soccer player myself, I would never stop the advancement of soccer in any way for any type of purpose."

His only concern was to find the right conditions for them to play.

"I want them to be in their own separate gymnasiums … among themselves. I want them to play soccer, but in their own area, with women trainers."

Safiullah stressed that there had to be a process. "No one will be happy if we go from zero to sixty overnight," he said. It was just a few years ago, under the Taliban, that he had had a long beard, women weren't allowed in school, and executions took place on the same field where women played soccer today.

"How would it be possible, after what we went through, for women to already be out in the stadium, wearing shorts and competing while men watch along the sideline? If I take it too fast, and I do every-thing too quickly, then reactions will come and [girls' sports] will stop completely. The community will stand against it and they will ban the whole thing for good."

As if he'd heard a protest, he pressed on: "I know my people and the situation in my country – that is why I am telling you that it's important to go slowly, respect the culture and the situation in the country right now." During the thirty years the United States was imple-menting Title IX, Afghanistan was overtaken by a different history. The year the U.S. women won the World Cup, the Taliban took Kabul. After years of war and destruction, Safiullah seemed to be saying that time would be needed to rebuild, to heal.

It seemed that the "slow pace" referred to by Safiullah Subat, and the resistance to progress in this area outlined by Sabrina Saqib and Shukria Hakmat, found voice and reality in the experience of Abdul Saboor Walizada. Walizada, the Women's National team head coach, and I had worked together on the girls' soccer clinic and tournament in Kabul.

Twenty-five girls represented Afghanistan on the National Team. Although all the players hailed from Kabul, Walizada – what he prefers to be called – had plans to expand beyond the capital and establish a truly national team.

His work has been marked by extraordinary success, and controversy. In some ways he has been the pivotal person in women's soccer.

"People laugh at me for training women and mock me for what I am doing," Walizada said. "I can't say that I am completely comfortable with my position for that reason. I do get public harassment."

Even younger generations of Afghan men were not ready, or willing, to accept a man coaching a women's sports team, he believed.

Six months after he started coaching the women's team, Walizada had been pulled from his car and beaten up by two armed men. He was not surprised by the attack, and referred to it in an offhand manner. Violence in the country was ubiquitous, and Walizada was only glad he hadn't been seriously hurt.

"I never found out who they were or their reason, he said. "Maybe I was training their sister or somebody from their family without permission, I don't know. After that, I wanted to drop this work, but we'd had some progress with the program, and my colleagues wanted me to continue."

At one point, a group of boys and men scaled the wall to *Bagh-e-Zanana*, the Women's Garden, as the team was practicing, and hurled stones at the girls. Military personnel manning one of their practice fields taunted Walizada, and once, at a tournament, outraged university students tried to storm the field.

"Bright, open-minded, educated people," Walizada said with a weary smile. "I am very tired of the continuous struggle … sometimes it is beyond my tolerance. But still, I love soccer."

Traditional spheres for women in the public space and their evolution into sports

As was apparent from the above case study, the discussion which is taking place among key decision makers and stakeholders within the female sports arena not only addresses issues as they relate to access to space for women and sports, but it also presents an 'on-the-ground perspective' as to how some countries, while providing access to sports for their female athletes, have been able to structure that space in accordance with the local culture and religion.

Generally speaking, today, the role that women in the Middle East play within their daily lives has changed dramatically, especially so in recent years, both inside and outside of the home. Historically, women in this region lived within a dichotomous space – the private world at home and the public world outside. Although the line between the two may have become less distinct today, throughout many parts of the Middle East, in the not so distant past, the lines between these two spaces were much more clearly demarcated and as a result, women were oftentimes forced to adopt a different persona depending on what space they were occupying at any given point in time.

Within many communities in the Middle East, the public space oftentimes consists of the outside world of the city streets, and the market place – areas mostly dominated by men – while the private space for women consists solely of the home (Sadiqi, 2006). Traditionally, men have controlled the public space, and even the private space too, as there is still some degree of negotiating between men and women on decisions made within the home. According to Sadiqi who writes about the women's rights movement in Morocco, "the private space is associated with powerless people (women and children) and is subordinated to the public space, which is culturally associated with men – who dictate the law, lead business, manage the states, and control the economy, both national and domestic" (Sadiqi, 2006).

Although many rural areas within the various countries of the Middle East still adhere to the public space dichotomy, more cosmopolitan cities such as Casablanca in Morocco, Istanbul in Turkey and Cairo in Egypt have transformed dramatically in recent years toward becoming more "liberal" in regard to the role that women play within society, as they are able to flow more freely from one domain into the next. The result has allowed for a major shift to occur towards achieving a more integrated society where men and women can control the public space – albeit not necessarily always with equal levels of control.

While some cities within the region can boast about this shift, it did not, and still does not, come without some resistance. Often, in order for this new cultural shift to take hold, men in their respective communities are forced to adjust to new gender roles within their public sphere – a sphere they have historically dominated. It is important to note that, although strides were made toward expanding the public sphere for women within many communities in the Middle East, men can at times still expect the women to tend to the same responsibilities in the house, as that gender role expectation had not necessarily always shifted in response to the advancement of the role of women within the broader society (Sadiqi, 2006). In many ways, this societal expectation has, and still, affected the pace of growth for sports among women in the Middle East.

In recent years, although previously dominated by men, the athletic arena has become a new space for women in the Middle East to stake their claim. According to Martha Brady from the Population Council, the sports arena for women in developing countries has finally emerged as a safe space for women to congregate, and also challenge themselves which can, and does, have broader implications for the women's rights movement throughout the Middle East (Brady, 2006). But this growth has not come without restrictions and some degree of struggle.

Evolution of women into sports comes with stipulations

Sports within the broader culture of the Middle East have always constituted a dominant presence within the social fabric of the culture of the region, but that domain, as was seen in the case study, has typically been reserved for men. That was until now.

As a result of the strides made locally by women to increase access to the sports domain, today, the number of girls participating continues to grow having fought for these rights both on and off the field. Further, because many of these young women grew up watching their fathers and brothers play sports, many have questioned their own participation in sports, oftentimes negotiating their rights at home and, as a result, have been able to take their success further. As they pushed for their right to participate in sports, with time, female athletes in the Middle East have proven some critics wrong, including family members, along the way.

In an interview with Ceyla Kutukoglu, the Corporate Communication Supervisor with the Turkish Football Federation, she stated that:

> Some parents actually changed their minds because at first they thought that girls can't play football, but some fathers are so addicted to football they saw that their kids, even though they don't have a son, their girls also can play football and they started to like it … for example a younger girl could join a football team and [a father] actually became proud of it because he's passionate about football and now he's encouraging [his] daughters to play football.
> Kutukoglu, Ceyla, 2011. Interview with the author on 11 May 2011, Istanbul, Turkey. Audio recording with the author.

Certainly, while these major societal shifts are taking place, which has helped to change the traditional mindset of women within this sphere, the participation of young women in this mostly male domain can still sometimes come with stipulations, regardless of the strides being made.

In a 2006 report about a youth program in Egypt, which was published through the Population Council, entitled "Providing new opportunities to adolescent girls in socially conservative settings," the authors noted that those girls who participated in soccer were oftentimes required to obtain special permission to play, and sometimes not only from parents:

> Parents, male siblings, and community representatives were consulted at all stages to ensure that girls' right to play was protected and had their families' support. It was crucial that girls' uniforms were modest and that basic sports skills were taught in an enclosed space, at the youth center away from prying eyes.
>
> Brady (2006)

Given that these issues still exist at the local level of the game, it is important to realize that, while great strides have been made by women in the Middle East within the sports domain, there is still room to grow, as many of these athletes are still pushing up against barriers amid a battle for their right to play. But, as you will soon see, success, as well as emerging opportunities on the international stage, can play a significant role toward overcoming these local barriers at a rapid change of pace.

Olympic glory for a Muslim female athlete and its impact in the region

Much of the forward shift as it relates to sport and women in the Middle East, particularly in Morocco, can be attributed to one woman, Nawal El Moutawakel – the country's former Minister of Youth and Sport. El Moutawakel's journey as a women's sports advocate began after winning the gold medal in the women's 400m hurdles at the 1984 Los Angeles Summer Olympic Games (www. olympic.org/uk/athletes/profiles). After that win, she not only became the first Moroccan woman to win an Olympic gold medal, but she also became the first African and Muslim woman to have achieved this feat as well.

In her return back to Morocco, with her gold medal in hand, El Moutawakel then possessed a platform to promote sports for girls at the national level as well as on the global stage. Understanding that she now had this capacity, and the legitimacy, to create broader social change for women in sports within Morocco, El Moutawakel started her work at the grassroots level and founded the Casablanca 10K Women's "Run for Fun" that in 2011 was held for the thirteenth time. Today, the "Run for Fun" which started with only a few hundred female participants, now has over 25,000 women, aged 15–75 years, who participate in the race (www.changemakers.com/users/nawal-el-moutawakel).

In addition to the 10K "Run for Fun", El Moutawakel founded the Moroccan Association of Sport and Development, a sports and development organization, serving as its President before stepping down in 2007 to take on the role as Morocco's Minister of Youth and Sport until 2009. Furthermore, outside of Morocco and within the broader global sports movement, El

Moutawakel is currently an International Olympic Committee (IOC) Executive Board member, and, since 1996 has been an active member of the IOC's Working Group on Women and Sport. In addition, she has the distinction of becoming the first woman in IOC history to have been appointed Chair of the IOC Evaluation Committee.

It can easily be said that El Moutawakel has been a key advocate toward changing the perception of female athletes in Morocco, and the broader Middle East, to what it is today, and oftentimes this is only possible after having achieved success at the highest level of sports – something that takes years of development and training. However, eventually, with that success the ability to rapidly shift change becomes easier.

The Olympics, FIFA and the Women's Islamic Games

Today, as more women from the Middle East, as well as across the broader Muslim community, participate in sports, opportunities for them to compete either in already established international tournaments or in new tournaments have increased.

For example, at the 2008 Beijing Summer Olympic Games, several Muslim countries increased their female delegations from previous years, which included Iran, Pakistan, and Bahrain, and two, Oman and the United Arab Emirates, sent their female athletes to the Games for the first time (Bannayan, 2008).

If one examines women's soccer, during the 2011 FIFA Women's World Cup qualifying matches, several women's teams from the Middle East – Iran, Palestine, Jordan, and Turkey – as well as several from North Africa and Asia, made serious attempts to qualify for the championships. While none eventually did qualify, they did gain the experience of competing in games against other high-ranking teams and, along the way, many of the teams representing the Middle East also improved upon their FIFA rankings (www.fifa.com/worldfootball/ranking/lastranking/gender=f/fullranking.html).

As one looks ahead to the 2015 FIFA Women's World Cup, to be held in Canada, the hope would be that one of these teams does indeed qualify, given FIFA's recent decision to increase the team pool to 24 from 16 (www.fifa.com). To that end, FIFA, too, sees the Middle East and surrounding region as an area for greater growth of the game and, toward the end of 2009, FIFA held a conference in Tunisia where delegates from 14 Middle East and North African nations, predominantly Muslim countries, met to discuss and share ideas about how best to promote the advancement of the game among young girls within their respective communities. While this was certainly a positive push forward from FIFA to develop the women's game in the region, it would only be several months later that they would make a decision to ban female players or teams of players from wearing the *hijab* during all FIFA-sanctioned games, a decision whose impact may have negative consequences for the growth of the sport, as will be discussed and outlined later in this chapter.

As the number of women in the Middle East, and the broader Muslim world, participate in sports in record numbers, there proved to be a demand to create a space and opportunity to directly meet the unique needs of this community on the international competitive stage as well. As demonstrated by the case study at the beginning of the chapter, the participation of female athletes from the Middle East can sometimes be accompanied with stipulations such as the requirement to remain covered and/or to play in female-only spaces with no male spectators around; these are two stipulations which, were a female athlete from the region to strictly adhere to, would be virtually impossible to adhere to in international competitions.

Thus, the response to these needs of the female athletes from the region resulted in the creation of the Women's Islamic Games. The tournament, which was established in 1993, has been held in Iran every four to five years since its inception, with the most recent Games taking place in 2010. In looking at the enrollment numbers for these Games, in 1993, 407 athletes representing ten countries participated and, by the fourth Games in 2005, 1,316 athletes representing 44 countries had competed – participant numbers for the 2010 Games had not yet been released at the time of this publication (www.ancientolympicgames.net/womens-islamic-games.html).

What makes the Women's Islamic Games unique, beyond the group of women who participate in them, is the environment in which they compete – which is an all-female one. By providing this type of environment, the Games has opened a new window of opportunity to girls who might not have been otherwise able to compete in international competition and, as Safiullah Subat during the case study mentioned earlier in this chapter remarked, sometimes providing this "safe space" is a necessity in order to both increase participation numbers and to also garner adequate support at the local level, whether that be from the athletes, the parents or various sports officials.

If one looks to the examples of growth with the Women's Islamic Games as well as to the increased enrollment levels of female athletes from the Middle East in other established sports competitions, they have proven that, if given the opportunity and space to compete, they will participate. As we look toward the future of sports for women in the Middle East, it will be important to continue to measure these outputs as an indicator of what is taking place within the region to either provide or, equally, fail to provide, sports opportunities for women. But, certainly, the hope is that these numbers will continue to grow for years to come.

Further, beyond seeing a positive growth within the participation level of women from the region as a positive sign of growth, it is important to also see how countries in the region are now portraying this growth to their advantage. In recent years, several countries in the Middle East have been looking to win bids to host future large-scale international tournaments, like the Olympic Games as well as FIFA's World Cup, and, just recently, those efforts have proved successful.

In December 2010, FIFA awarded the 2022 World Cup bid to Qatar, making it the first country in the Middle East to host such a large-scale global tournament. While it is a great achievement for the region, receiving the bid did in no way stop critics from voicing their concerns about women's rights within the country and region. Given that Qatar is considered one of the more progressive countries in the Middle East, many critics argue that there are still many strides yet to be made on this front and have made it a point to use the tournament as a platform to expand the dialogue as it relates to women's rights in the region (sportsillustrated.cnn.com/2010/writers/ann_killion/12/14/qatar/index.html). Now that Qatar has had time to consider the feedback as it relates to women's rights, as they look to host the World Cup in 2022 and resubmit its bid to host the 2020 Summer Olympic Games, one would imagine that they would be proactive in the coming years to not only address the issue locally, but regionally as well.

9.2
Bahrain's Ruqaya Al Ghasara celebrates after winning the women's 200m final on the fourth day of the athletics competition for the 15th Asian Games in Doha, 11 December 2006

Source: ©FRANCOIS-XAVIER MARIT/ AFP/Getty Images

The *hijab* debate
(This section from A Closer Look at FIFA's *Hijab* Ban is reproduced here with the expressed permission of The SAIS Review.)

As mentioned earlier, the debate about the *hijab* and what place it has in the athletic arena for female athletes is a fairly new one, and one that has become an issue as it, oddly enough, highlights progress made in the athletic arena in recent years and speaks volumes to the continued progress of women's rights within each region. This trend also represents the progress being made by local sports bodies (often male run) to provide an avenue that has allowed women to participate in athletics with increased numbers, both within and outside of the country.

Though sports opportunities for women in the Middle East have increased in recent years, there is still a period of growing pains taking place today as international sport governing bodies are forced to evaluate their own rules in regards to dress and determine what it means for the increased participation of Muslim women in sports today. And no case has resulted in more controversy than a ruling made by FIFA in 2010 to ban an Iranian girl's soccer team from competing in the Youth Olympic Games (YOG).

The inaugural Games, sanctioned by the International Olympic Committee, took place in August 2010 in Singapore and, according to the Games' site, saw over 3,500 athletes from more than seventeen countries compete in various sporting events (www.singapore2010.sg/public/sg2010/en/en_about_us/en_youth_olympics_games.html). But what was to be a tournament exhibiting the Olympic values of "excellence, friendship and respect" became tainted with controversy months before the opening ceremony.

In April 2010, FIFA banned the Iranian girls' youth national soccer team from competing in the YOG, citing two rules that prohibit the *hijab* from being worn during all FIFA sanctioned games.

The two rules cited from FIFA's current 2010–2011 rule book in support of the ban were:

> Advertising on Equipment: "Basic compulsory equipment must not have any political, religious, or personal statement" and Safety: "A player must not use equipment or wear anything that is dangerous to himself or another player.
>
> www.fifa.com/worldfootball/lawsofthegame.html

While both rules were added to FIFA's 2007–2008 rulebook and have remained there since, only recently – three years later – were they implemented more strictly to ban, for the first time, an entire team of Muslim players who wear the *hijab*. Previously, a case in 2007 resulted in a ban of an eleven-year-old Canadian player from competing in a local youth soccer match after a referee decided that, according to the Quebec Soccer Federation's "Safety" rule which was derived from FIFA's rule book, the *hijab* was not to be worn during a match. It was after this case that FIFA decided that players do not have permission to wear a *hijab* in any FIFA sanctioned games (www.cbc.ca/canada/story/2007/02/28/soccerhijab.html).

Based on the "Safety" rule as stated in its rule book, FIFA's main policy aim is that of protecting the well-being of all players on the field as they work toward meeting its mission to "develop the game, touch the world, build a better future." But one must also question the timing of the broader policy implementation, as an anti-*hijab* sentiment has swept across Europe in recent years.

After initial outrage, and after intense discussions took place between FIFA and Iran's Football Federation, discussions which also saw the IOC support FIFA's ban, the Iranian team was eventually reinstated into the tournament in May of that year. However, adjustments were made as to how the players covered, wearing uniforms that consisted of a cap, long-sleeved tops, below-knee length trousers, and long stockings. These adjustments, all parties agreed, allowed the players to adequately cover while also respecting the international rules of the game and, more importantly, allowed the team to compete in the YOG.

While the debate has died down with a temporary solution to this one case, it is still not clear how FIFA will handle future *hijab* cases for both individual players and teams of players who cover, particularly now as more Muslim women are participating in the game. Furthermore, the broader questions still remain as to what place the *hijab* has in the game, and more importantly, given that these young players are adhering to their religious stipulations, how FIFA, and other sports federations for that matter, should respond to future debate on this issue.

FIFA's ruling to ban Iran's national team not only potentially alienated those Muslim female athletes who eventually played in the YOG, but, in a broader sense, its decision to ban the *hijab* entirely from the game discriminates against one segment of its player population – Muslim girls. As an increasing number of young Muslim women participate in athletics around the world, the larger impact and implementation of FIFA's ruling have yet to be seen, and the fear among many Muslim female athletes today is that other international sports federations may follow FIFA's lead to ban the *hijab*, particularly among those Federations that do not have a *hijab* policy already in place.

Still, as uncertainty looms regarding future *hijab* cases, there are lessons to learn from how this most recent issue was handled. Lessons which should help guide how other Federations can enforce their own *hijab* policy as they strive to both separate religion and politics from their games, while also respecting the individual rights of their players – two priorities that are not mutually exclusive.

While the increased level of participation of Muslim women in sport is a positive sign representing the cultural shift taking place in many countries today, this success could be on the verge of contracting if governing bodies, like FIFA, fail to appropriately address the issue of the *hijab* and determine how to both respect an athlete's right to play as well as her right to adhere to her religion.

Future of sports for women in the Middle East

As we look to the future of sport for women in the Middle East, certainly there is much to be hopeful about – girls are participating in greater numbers across the region and they have proven that they can both respect cultural expectations while still being able to compete on the international stage. While there is room still to grow as we look ahead to the development of this sector, we must acknowledge too that there will be 'growing pains' along the way, but ones that can be overcome if various IFs are able to think creatively about how to work with and within this unique and growing sector of female athletes.

Summary

After reading this chapter, the reader should now have a better understanding about the local issues that affect the growth, or lack of growth in some cases, as it relates to the participation level in sport for women in the Middle East, as well as in the surrounding region. While it is important to note that some generalizations can be made about this topic, it is important too to note that each country has a host of unique issues that is must work through. Yet, as was proven by the case study and other supporting text, it is evident that, as this player population continues to grow, sports officials must take into account the unique needs that this population sometimes require and be able to find a middle ground that both respects the rules of the game as well as the individual rights of this still growing demographic of athletes.

References

Ayub, Awista (2010) *Kabul Girls Soccer Club*. New York: Hyperion.

Bannayan, Aline (2011) *Muslim Sportswomen Gain Standing in Beijing*. Available: http://www.womensenews.org/story/athleticssports/080807/muslim-sportswomen-gain-standing-in-beijing (Last accessed 15 May 2011).

Brady, Martha *et al.* (2006) Providing new opportunities to adolescent girls in socially conservative settings: The Ishraq program in rural Upper Egypt. *Population Council*, http://www.popcouncil.org/pdfs/IshraqReport.pdf.

Killion, Anne (2010) *Human Rights? Women? Heat? FIFA Didn't Look at Issues with Qatar*. Available: http://sportsillustrated.cnn.com/2010/writers/ann_killion/12/14/qatar/index.html (Last accessed 15 May 2011).

Kutukoglu, Ceyla (2011) Interview with the author on 11 May 2011 Istanbul, Turkey. (Audio recording in possession of author.)

Sadiqi, F. and Ennaji, M. (2006). The feminization of public space: Women's activism, the family law, and social change in Morocco. *Journal of Middle East Women's Studies*, Vol. 2, No. 2, pp. 86–114.

All Africa.com (2009) *Tunisia: Women's Soccer, a Model Worth Following*. Available: http://allafrica.com/stories/200911200931.html (Last accessed 15 May 2011).

Ancient Olympic Games (2009) *Women's Islamic Games*. Available: http://www.ancientolympicgames.net/womens-islamic-games.html (Last accessed15 May 2011).

CBC News (2007) *International Soccer Body to Discuss Quebec Hijab Ban*. Available: http://www.cbc.ca/canada/story/2007/02/28/soccerhijab.html (Last accessed 15 May 2011).

Changemakers (2011) *Nawal El Moutawakel.* Available: https://www.
changemakers.com/users/nawal-el-moutawakel (Last accessed 15 May
2011).

FIFA (2010) *Laws of the Game 2010/2011.* Available: http://www.fifa.com/
worldfootball/lawsofthegame.html (Last accessed 15 May 2011).

FIFA (2011) *The FIFA Women's World Rankings.* Available: http://www.fifa.
com/worldfootball/ranking/lastranking/gender=f/fullranking.html (Last
accessed 15 May 2011).

International Olympic Committee (2011) *Ms. Nawal El Moutawakel.* Available:
http://www.olympic.org/ms-nawal-el-moutawakel (Last accessed 15 May
2011).

Youth Olympic Games (2010). *Facts and Figures.* Available: http://www.
singapore2010.sg/public/sg2010/en/en_about_us/en_youth_olympics_
games.html (Last accessed 15 May 2011).

10

Developing elite sporting talent in Qatar

The Aspire Academy for Sports Excellence

Conor Kilgallen

Overview: Sport in Qatar

Qatar's National Vision 2030 seeks to transform the country into a leading global power by the year 2030, capable of sustaining its own development and providing high living standards for its entire population. The vision is built around four major pillars, one of which includes a commitment to human development. Within this specific commitment sport can play a decisive role.

In fact, much work has already been undertaken in Qatar to provide access to, and encourage participation in, a wide variety of sporting activities. Moreover, there are few better ways to promote a sport and, by extension, the country in which it is played, than by hosting major sporting events. For several years now, Qatar has been a regular destination on the international tennis, cycling, golf and motorcycling circuits. Additionally, in recent years, Qatar has won the right to stage an impressive list of other international sports events. These include: 2006 Asian Games; 2006, 2007, 2009 and 2010 International Fencing Grand Prix; 2009 Indoor Athletics Grand Prix Championships; 2009 FINA World Cup Diving competition; 2010 and 2011 World Indoor Athletics Championships; 2011 Asian Football Championships; 2011 Asian Indoor Games; 2011 Pan-Arab Games; and 2011 World Table Tennis Championships. The ambition does not end there, however. Qatar continues to look to host sporting events on an even greater scale. Indeed, perhaps its most defining achievement to date in this regard has been the successful bid to host the FIFA World Cup in 2022. With this success, Qatar has firmly arrived on the world's sporting stage. Undoubtedly, the preparations for this major tournament will have a galvanizing effect on Qatar's National Vision 2030. While the country, its economy and people, as a whole, can benefit from this project, sport in Qatar is also a very likely beneficiary. It is unprecedented for a country to learn almost 12 years in advance of this particular tournament that it is to host a FIFA World Cup. Qatar will endeavour not to forgo this opportunity to promote and manage sport generally, as well as specifically developing, and preparing football players for the tournament itself. As the host country, Qatar will automatically qualify, as of the right, for the World Cup in 2022.

The opening section of this chapter will briefly outline how Aspire Zone Foundation, a government-funded organization, is structured and is well placed to contribute to Qatar's sports economy, while simultaneously managing world-class infrastructure and events, developing elite sports performers, and promoting healthy lifestyles. Its role is therefore industry wide. Subsequently, the spotlight will then turn to one of Aspire Zone Foundation's business units, ASPIRE Academy for Sports Excellence, with a detailed case study of how it seeks, through its everyday work, to develop adolescent student-athletes in Qatar.

Aspire Zone Foundation

Given the scale of sporting ambitions in Qatar, it is essential that the management of sport is handled effectively. Aspire Zone Foundation (AZF) plays a major role in sports management, development, and facility management. AZF was established by Emiri decree in 2008. As indicted thus far, its mission is in fact fourfold: to develop sports champions; to manage world-class sports infrastructures and events; to promote healthy lifestyles; and to contribute to the development of the sports sector in Qatar. The precinct managed by AZF, known as Aspire Zone, houses, among others, ASPIRE Academy for Sports Excellence, a state-of-the-art academy for developing student-athletes; ASPETAR, a sports medicine and orthopaedic hospital, which is FIFA-accredited; and award-winning, world-class sporting arenas and venue management services for sports, such as association football, athletics, martial arts, squash, table tennis, swimming, diving, basketball, volleyball, gymnastics, handball and fencing. With such facilities, Aspire Zone has already proved to be a perfect venue for hosting, not only major sporting events, but also large international conferences, such as Aspire4Sport, a sports management conference, which was staged in November 2010.

Aspire Zone Foundation in turn consists of three main Strategic Business Units (SBUs) which each play a role in realizing the AZF mission. These SBUs include:

1. Aspire LOGISTICS, which is the supporting organization for all Aspire Zone's building, operations and management needs.
2. As mentioned above, ASPETAR is a hospital specializing in orthopaedics and sports medicine. ASPETAR is FIFA-accredited and features centres of excellence for sports medicine, orthopaedics and rehabilitation, as well as sports science.
3. Finally, founded in 2004, ASPIRE Academy for Sports Excellence (see Figure 10.1), aims to develop its student-athletes into exceptional sports champions who are highly educated leaders, and to assist individuals to lead healthy, active and sporting lifestyles.

Aspire Academy for Sports Excellence

ASPIRE Academy for Sports Excellence, henceforth referred to simply as ASPIRE, is unique in that it provides sports training, education, and sports science/sports medicine services on-site to developing, adolescent male student-athletes. While this case study will examine how sports training, education/student care, and sports science/sports medicine are managed individually through different departments, it is worth noting that the key to ASPIRE's success is the integrated approach that is adopted between its three different, yet interlocking, departments. Moreover, these departments are given efficient support from a further centralised department, corporate

10.1
Local children participate in a football training session at the ASPIRE Academy for Sports Excellence in Doha, Qatar, 2011

Source: Getty Images

services. This department will also be discussed briefly later in this analysis, as it is no less important in underpinning the success of ASPIRE. Furthermore, this case study, which forms the basis of the entire chapter, will explore how a 'Quality Management' approach is employed by ASPIRE in order to reach and maintain the highest international standards of service in its chosen field.

Sports department

ASPIRE is home to approximately 200 full-time student-athletes each academic year, plus a smaller number of part-timers who attend for afternoon sports training only. Of the sports practiced at ASPIRE, association football accounts for the majority of these student-athletes. Athletics is the second largest sport, in terms of participant numbers. Finally squash and table tennis account for the remaining sports, which are trained 'in-house' by ASPIRE coaches. In addition to the aforementioned sporting codes, however, ASPIRE also has student-athletes from what are referred to as 'federation sports'. This is a situation in which some student-athletes come to ASPIRE for the purposes of education attainment, but sports training is shared with the respective national sports federations in Qatar. Examples of 'federation sports' include golf, tennis, gymnastics and trampoline, judo and taekwondo, fencing, swimming, shooting and rowing.

Although ASPIRE has been operational for a relatively short period of time, it has already achieved some notable sporting successes. These include a World Junior High Jump Champion and some graduates already making an impact with the Qatari national football team. However, ASPIRE seeks not to become complacent as an academy for sports excellence. As with any organization, there is always room for improvement. As will be outlined, the sports management leadership model in ASPIRE tends to favour a transformational approach – as opposed to a transactional one – in an effort to progress continually (Howell and Avolio, 1993).

Unlike transactional leadership, which involves a highly structured environment and places a large emphasis on managerial authority, transformational leadership uses different methods to inspire and motivate employees (Boje, 2000). A shared vision is used to 'inspire followers to transcend their own self-interest for the good of the organization' (Allen, 1998). An organization can be transformed and improved through this form of leadership, as the manager creates a powerful bond with his or her followers, which fosters confidence, dedication and creative problem-solving (Allen, 1998). As mentioned thus far, a transformational leadership model is utilised in ASPIRE's sports department amid its continual quest for sports excellence. The following section will outline how, through a pyramid analogy, this sporting excellence is sought and, to date, largely achieved in the case of ASPIRE.

In order to strive for sports excellence, one must have clear end goals in mind. A goal is simply 'a target, or specific standard, that one strives to attain' (Locke and Latham, 1990, 6). Once clear end goals, as to what constitutes elite performance, are established, and indeed how these are to be measured (key performance indicators) are agreed and understood, the process of working towards these aspirations can begin. In ASPIRE, a clear process has been established within its sports department in order to allow the best possible likelihood of achieving its sporting excellence goals. As mentioned, a 'pyramid' analogy is typically used. If the end goal (sporting excellence) can be considered the apex of a pyramid, then the base of this structure is where the journey of transformation begins. This journey begins by gathering information on existing processes. Then the pathway becomes more focused (midpoint of pyramid) as the process of analysis and how to improve each athlete unfolds, with some adjustment and implementation also typical at this point. Finally, as implementation of change takes hold, the journey towards the pyramid apex nears its conclusion, with some evidence of sporting excellence as the product (see Figure 10.2). A more detailed examination of the work carried out at the base and middle of the 'pyramid' will be outlined in the following paragraphs.

10.2
Pyramid of sporting
excellence

Base of pyramid

For each sport, a comprehensive programme overview is required from time to time to document existing processes and consider whether these are achieving the desired outcomes. By bringing everything together in one place, nothing is left to chance and there is little room for misunderstandings or a lack of coherency around individual sports planning. This provides a solid foundation for a focused, continual improvement process to take hold, which clearly benefits the athletes in their desire to achieve success. In gathering information about an individual programme, the first and most important issue is to understand and appreciate the mission of that particular sport, its goals and objectives. It is also important to know the philosophy of the head coach for the sport in question, as this will influence the practice of all employees and athletes concerned with it. Moving forward, clear information about the organizational structure within the sport should be documented, as this influences channels of leadership, management and communication. With this information in place, it is then appropriate to examine in more detail the 'what, why and where' of the particular sport under review. By way of explanation, a summary of such necessary information is provided below:

Coaches: A summary and overview of all coaches' backgrounds, philosophies and roles within each sports programme is required.

Programmes: An overview of programmes for different age groups or disciplines within an individual sport is also necessary as part of this process.

Student-athletes: A concise, updated list of active student-athletes within a sport is fundamental, with status information (full-time or part-time), date-of-birth and a unique student-athlete code completing this database.

Training: An overview of the training programme for a sport is required, as is the timetabling and structure of the programme to be followed, which can vary depending upon the sport in question.

Facilities: A comprehensive list of facilities available to student-athletes within each ASPIRE sport is required. Quality, availability and ease of access are also necessary details to understand the complete level of service available to the athlete in question.

Apparel: Quality, quantity and type of apparel for both staff and student-athletes, and the reasons why, must be outlined and justified.

Equipment: Again a list of the quality and quantity of equipment available to student-athletes and coaches is required, as are the reasons why these are required.

Competition: An overview of competition type and frequency for each sport is essential information to gather as the specific training programme for each athlete will be dependent upon it.

Camps: Information required in relation to camps includes strategy, frequency and venues, as such athlete-centred residential services perform a vital role in the development of the individual or team.

Having completed a review of a particular sport within these parameters, it is then appropriate to seek an overview of the services provided from outside the sports department to support its work and, as part of this, the status of relationships with key stakeholders. For example, many services are provided by ASPIRE's sports science/sports medicine department for each sport. A clear understanding of these services (role, structure, and relationship) is necessary. Services are also provided by the education and student care department which can have a direct, or indirect, impact on a given sport. Therefore, it is necessary to understand the roles of the staff in this department, including team guides, residential educators and career management consultants. Finally, relationships with key stakeholders, such as parents, require clarification, with a view to developing strategies moving forward.

Middle of pyramid

Once the essential information has been gathered to provide a detailed overview of a sports programme, the next step is to analyse the programme, with a view to improving it still further. Improvement is sought by making appropriate minor adjustments, or implementing larger-scale changes, if the latter is deemed necessary. These are done with the end goal of elite performance in mind. The process of analysing needs for change or adjustment, and the actual implementation of change, is a four-step process. First, discussions should take place among relevant staff to agree Critical Success Factors common to all elite sports programmes. A Critical Success Factor (CSF) is an element that is necessary for an agreed strategy to be successful (Daniel, 1961). A SWOT (strengths, weaknesses, opportunities, threats) analysis (Hill and Westbrook, 1997) is used as the discussion medium. The second step is to identify gaps between the current situation and the desired situation around each CSF. Priorities should be identified, depending upon the urgency of action required. Third, ideas or solutions need to be agreed on how to address the gaps that are identified. This involves, among others, a resource-needs analysis. Resources may include human resources, facilities, technology or finance. Finally, the fourth and last step is to identify 'next step' meetings with relevant staff or experts (based on step three outcomes), with a view to addressing the CSF gaps.

When identifying Critical Success Factors (step one of the above process), it is important to be as concise and as detailed as possible. To give greater depth to the analysis, CSFs should be broken down into sub-factors where possible. These sub-factors may also be broken down further, if necessary. Given that this chapter deals with the work of ASPIRE, an ASPIRE sports department-specific example of Critical Success Factors and sub-factors will now be outlined.

CSF 1: *High performance management*

    Sub-factor (a): Human resources/standards
- Examines such things as code of conduct for departmental staff, position job descriptions, appropriateness of appraisal tools, and self-evaluation strategies.

    Sub-factor (b): Database
- Examines what is documented on company database and its usefulness.

    Sub-factor (c): Planning
- Examines how planning (e.g. annual schedule) is conducted and how efficient it is at the time of review.

    Sub-factor (d): Organization structure
- Is the structure functional, and does it maximise potential within the department?

    Sub-factor (e): Individual athlete long-term development plan
- What are the issues concerned and where is/are the athlete(s) on this continuum?

CSF 2: *Athlete number and quality*

    Sub-factor (a): Athlete number
- How is optimum number decided and what is the justification for this?

    Sub-factor (b): Identification and talent scouting
- What is the process by which talented young sportsmen are identified?

    Sub-factor (c): Selection process
- What is the process for admission and does it require amendment?

    Sub-factor (d): Reasons for student-athletes not coming to ASPIRE
- Why are some of the selected student-athletes not sent to ASPIRE by their parents?
- What are some of their concerns and can these be addressed?

Sub-factor (e): Student-athlete mortality
- What are the reasons behind some student-athletes' decision to drop out of academy training?

CSF 3: *Education, life skills, career*

Sub-factor (a): Post-ASPIRE career pathways
- What support does ASPIRE provide after the student-athlete has graduated?
- Do graduates leave ASPIRE with appropriate life skills?

Sub-factor (b): Career support
- What support does ASPIRE provide for graduates to find employment?

Sub-factor (c): Status and recognition
- Is being at ASPIRE a status symbol within Qatar?

CSF 4: *Training*

Sub-factor (a): Standards
- Are current training times, volumes and recovery times suitable?

Sub-factor (b): Environment
- Is the environment suitable for training for each sport?

Sub-factor (c): Training camps
- Do these meet ASPIRE's needs?
- Are there appropriate risk management guidelines in place?
- What is the code of conduct when travelling with minors (athletes under the age of 18 years)?

CSF 5: *Facilities, equipment and apparel*

Sub-factor (a): Facilities
- What is the current demand on facilities?
- Are facilities meeting ASPIRE's needs?

Sub-factor (b): Equipment
- How adequate is the equipment used in respective sports?
- How efficient is the maintenance of this equipment?

Sub-factor (c): Apparel
- Is apparel satisfactory and of good quality?
- Is the distribution of apparel fair?

CSF 6: *Coaching*

Sub-factor (a): Identification and selection of coaching staff
- Are identification criteria clear?
- Is recruitment smooth and quick?
- How is orientation and assimilation handled?

Sub-factor (b): Development
- What are the requirements of a good coach?
- What development opportunities are available to coaches and others?

CSF 7: *Competition*

Sub-factor (a): Selection process
- How is competition selected?

Sub-factor (b): International competition
- On what basis are international competitions chosen?

Sub-factor (c): Annual calendar
- How soon in advance can annual planning be done?

CSF 8: *Performance monitoring*

Sub-factor (a): Database
- How is the current database performing and what are some of the emerging trends?

Sub-factor (b): System of measure
- What is available from the sports science/sports medicine department?

CSF 9: *Sports science/sports medicine and research*

Sub-factor (a): Servicing
- What is most useful?
- What are the priorities?
- Is the sports staff informed of the latest research?

Sub-factor (b): Problem-solving
* How is information from sports science/sports medicine being used?

CSF 10: *Stakeholder Relationships*

Sub-factor (a): Parents
* How involved and informed are parents?

Sub-factor (b): Strategic allies
* How enhanced are relations with clubs, schools and federations?

As mentioned already, identifying CSFs is just the first step towards improvement. Any gaps between the current and desired situation then need to be identified, before prioritizing what needs to be addressed first, coming up with proposed solutions, and finally arranging 'next step' meetings to commit to action without undue delay. By committing to such a transformational process systematically, it allows for better opportunity to achieve sporting goals (apex of pyramid), while continually improving the service provided by the sports department.

Sports science/sports medicine department

As is evident from the above section dealing with the work of the sports department, achieving sporting excellence is predicated upon the management of a range of diverse factors. Given the athlete population of ASPIRE (developing student-athletes), it is essential that sports staff are informed with up-to-date, evidence-based, relevant information on every facet of their athletes, with a view to maximizing their ongoing development. For this, collaboration with ASPIRE's sports science/sports medicine department (SS/SM) is of crucial importance.

The primary goal of the SS/SM is to provide world-class applied sports science and sports medicine services (biochemistry, physiology, sports psychology, strength and conditioning, biomechanics, nutrition and health services) to improve the sports performance of ASPIRE student-athletes for the purpose of increasing the number of quality athletes in future national squads. This section will illustrate how SS/SM services are utilised to maximise the potential of each individual student-athlete in ASPIRE. Particular attention will be devoted to the concept of 'service teams', which, through an integrated and evidence-based approach, determine elite athlete development pathways for each sport and/or student-athlete. Closely linked to service teams is, on the one hand, research and, on the other, the concept of long-term athlete development. These two concepts will be explained in detail over the course of the ensuing section. Before this, however, the role of the talent identification section within SS/SM will be examined, to explain how the best young sporting talent in Qatar is identified and selected to participate in many of ASPIRE's sports.

Talent identification (TID)

The objective of ASPIRE's talent identification (TID) programme is to find students who have exceptional athletic talent and provide to them an invitation to join ASPIRE. Ultimately, less than 1 per cent of those tested are given the opportunity to enrol. The TID programme tests local school students with a screening process consisting of valid and reliable test measures. It profiles children, not currently involved in sport, to help match their natural talent to a particular skill-set that may in turn indicate a predisposition to a given sport. This enables the children to receive a maximum return for their efforts and avoid the frustration of pursuing an interest in a sport for which they are not suited. Talent selection is based on the combination of hard science and years of experience and observation by appropriately qualified personnel.

10.3

Lebanese al-Riyadi player Hussein Tawbe vies for the ball against US player Brandon Christopher Crump of Saudi Arabia's al-Hilal club during the 21st FIBA Asia Champions Cup in Doha in 2010

Source: © KARIM JAAFAR/AFP/Getty Images

The process of identification and selection consists of three distinct phases, referred to as Bronze, Silver and Gold. The Bronze phase comes first. This focuses on testing as many students as possible in order to find suitable talent amongst a defined cross section of young people. Anywhere from 6,000 to 8,000 students each year are tested during this phase. Measures and tests during the Bronze phase include body shape measurements, speed, upper body power, lower body power, over-arm throwing ability and endurance. Approximately 5 per cent of students tested at the Bronze phase are invited to attend the next stage of testing, the Silver phase, a few weeks later.

At the Silver phase, observations are made on the students' overall ability to cope with an increased competitive environment, while testing is slightly more complex. The test battery includes speed, endurance, upper body power, lower body power, over-arm throwing ability, reflex ability, agility and body shape measurements. Students are divided into groups, depending on their performance in the previous Bronze phase of testing. Groups may, for example, be divided into fast, strong, and aerobically-gifted students. Those who score highest in each group, and meet body shape standards, are invited to the Gold phase of testing. Approximately 25 per cent of Silver phase participants make it through to the final stage, the Gold phase.

The objective of the Gold phase is to observe how the athletes actually perform and train in a typical sporting environment. This phase of testing and observation takes the form of a two day mini-camp. While further scientific tests take place to determine, for example, physiological, bio-mechanical and psychological qualities, the experience of coaches is also invaluable in assessing suitability and desire for particular sports. At the end of the Gold phase, approximately 10 per cent are given scholarship invitations to attend ASPIRE full-time from the beginning of the following academic year.

In addition to targeting children who are unattached to particular sports, TID staff are also actively involved with sports coaching personnel throughout Qatar to recruit suitable talent from clubs or federations where children have already settled on a chosen sport. Moreover, TID staff also work closely with ASPIRE main sports in sport-specific talent search programmes. These include, for example, table tennis, squash and soccer goalkeepers.

Service teams

ASPIRE has adopted a multidisciplinary 'service team' model that reflects best practice among many successful sports programmes worldwide. Essentially a 'service team' is a group of key professional support staff who work with, and support, coaches of a particular sports team or athletic discipline. Functions of a service team include the following:

1. effective service planning
2. rigorous evaluation of plans to meet coaches' goals and targets for individual athletes and team development

3   effective management of resources available to coaches (servicing and support)
4   presentation of analytical debate and options to the coach
5   provision of assistance, support, ideas and advice to coaches during the training programme planning process
6   identification of existing research or research opportunities which can provide additional value to an applied programme
7   professional challenging of coaching staff on support details and philosophy to ensure a mentality of continual improvement.

To ensure that the above functions are carried out in an efficient manner, a proper structure within each service team is required. Each service team in ASPIRE has a named physiotherapist, medical doctor, physiologist, sports psychologist, sports dietician, bio-mechanist, strength and conditioning expert (all from SS/SM) and a team leader (from the education and student care department) to support coaches from the sports department. Meanwhile, a service team coordinator is appointed to each team. The coordinator may come from any of the above SS/SM disciplines. The coordinator effectively acts in the role of a 'high performance advisor' to the coach of his sport or team. The coordinator is the key contact person for both service team members and ASPIRE management. Meetings are organized and chaired regularly by these coordinators. Facilitation of testing and servicing is also a duty of the coordinator, while they play a key role in negotiations about staffing for foreign training camps and tournaments. Appointments of coordinators are reviewed annually and are considered very important selections.

While service team coordinators provide a form of indirect leadership beside the senior coach, there is also a smaller group of SS/SM professionals who form a 'core' team at the heart of every sport, team or athletic discipline. Services of physiotherapists and strength and conditioning experts are compulsory for each service team. These staff members are involved on a day-to-day basis with the sport in question. Each service team also has a designated 'team leader' (from the education and student care department) within the core group. Team leaders perform a crucial administrative role and act as a key contact person with families of student-athletes and other stakeholders. Outside of the core group are other SS/SM professionals, who are involved to varying degrees, depending on the aims and philosophies of particular coaches. These staff may, or may not, be involved on a day-to-day basis.

For service teams to operate successfully, the word 'team' should be given due recognition and priority. Rather than operating as a collection of individuals who come together occasionally for meetings, the service team members are obliged to work and collaborate together in an integrated manner, where possible. In doing so, it reduces the impact of potentially poor internal communication, while simultaneously eliminating the possibility of unnecessary, overlapping roles. At the heart of this integrated approach is the student-athlete, whose development and welfare are the focus of attention. In devising plans or programmes for student-athletes, service teams adopt approaches which are evidence-based. Considerable attention is also given to the developmental stage of the student-athlete. For this, a long-term athlete development (LTAD) curriculum is employed in ASPIRE. The following paragraphs will look at the role of, first, research in ASPIRE and, second, the importance of an LTAD strategy.

Research

Sports science and sports medicine professionals in ASPIRE use proven test protocols to establish various physical and mental qualities of all student-athletes two or three times a year. Extensive data on these developing boys has been gathered over the years. From this, applied plans are devised through the service teams. Having applied research programmes in place, characterized by rigorous quality assurance standards, is a key driver of continuous improvement. The unique opportunity to test the same student-athletes over a long time period allows for some exciting research questions to develop. However, it must be noted that research is not carried out at ASPIRE for the sake of research itself or academic publications. Instead, the emphasis is placed on ensuring that output can demonstrate improved support to the performance of student-athletes. Hence, research and applied work co-exist in a mutually harmonious fashion. This proves to be professionally fulfilling for staff, as well as contributing to a niche international reputation for ASPIRE's quality applied approach.

Long-term athlete development

Long-term athlete development (LTAD) is essentially an athlete-centred approach or philosophy, which is sensitive to the developmental stages of an athlete, and which typically focuses on developing physical literacy in young people. According to Whitehead (2001), a physically literate person 'moves with poise, economy and confidence in a wide variety of challenging situations' (p. 45). LTAD is a vehicle for change within sports cultures and provides a framework for accountability. LTAD models are always evidence-based, and also reflect knowledge and experience of coaches from around the world. Such models should be flexible enough to accommodate the particular needs of a given sport, be it early or late specialization. In ASPIRE, work is in progress to follow an LTAD model with a view to holistically developing student-athletes. While the development of physical literacy is at the heart of the plan, consideration is also given to the cognitive, social and emotional development of student-athletes.

It is an aim of the strength and conditioning unit within ASPIRE's SS/SM to develop, through a six-year period of LTAD, 18–19 year-old athletes who can repetitively produce and tolerate the required mechanical and physiological loads of their chosen sports throughout their season. In order to achieve this, specific training is prescribed and implemented in accordance with the concerned sport's annual training plan. This training from the strength and conditioning coaches has an intentionally proportioned blend of injury-prevention and performance-enhancement elements, based on outcomes from SS/SM tests, and taking the development level of the athlete into account. If plans are successfully implemented, it should help minimize dropout from sport, overuse injuries and performance decrement/movement dysfunction, all of which can contribute positively to a successful sports programme.

Education and student care department

Regardless of the success or otherwise of ASPIRE's student-athletes in their respective sport, the Academy has a duty to ensure its graduates emerge as well-rounded people, with qualifications to serve them well in the future, whatever their chosen path beyond, alongside, or instead of, sport. With this in mind, the education of the student-athletes is of prime importance, while student care is given due attention to ensure none of the approximate 200 full-time student-athletes each year go without the highest level of academic, social or career support.

School

The largest section of the education and student care department is the school itself. The school, staffed by an experienced multinational workforce of educators, and equipped with state-of-the-art learning technologies and resources, aims to have every student-athlete, first, graduate, and second, gain the necessary qualifications for tertiary education, should he choose to follow this route. The school curriculum, which is for grades seven through twelve, is aligned with Supreme Education Council of Qatar standards, offering a foundational and advanced programme to meet each student's needs and potential for success. English mastery is afforded high priority in ASPIRE school, as this is a significant factor in being accepted on tertiary courses. All courses, with the exception of Arabic and Islamic Studies, are taught in the English language. Furthermore, student-athletes practice taking the TOEFL exam from the tenth grade onwards, while days of English immersion are regularly scheduled to assist them in mastering the language.

Keys to academic success include academic support services and a 'commitment to learning' approach. Academic support services range from testing for learning disabilities to pro-active education about learning strategies. Meanwhile, the 'commitment to learning' approach is unique to ASPIRE. A primary goal is to become a 'learning community' in all its forms. The process for this particular goal stresses five important themes:

1 holistic learning
2 interconnection of important ideas
3 responsibility for own learning
4 basis of personal effectiveness
5 embrace rich variety of human differences.

These themes are briefly described below.

Holistic learning: ASPIRE aims to educate the 'whole person'. That is, meaningful learning experiences and activities are provided to challenge and inspire the student-athletes by exploring the academic, physical, emotional, spiritual and social elements found in all aspects of both the school curriculum and sports programme.

Interconnection of ideas: Exposed to multiple teaching modalities, cultural and sports training experiences, student-athletes learn and understand how the ability to make connections between ideas, information, experiences, academic disciplines, sport and the world around them is essential.

Responsibility for own learning: Success in academia, sport and life requires a high level of discipline and commitment. Student-athletes are encouraged to take responsibility for their own learning and task assignments, while simultaneously understanding that success requires a high degree of involvement, independence and responsibility for one's own work.

Basis of personal effectiveness: Student-athletes learn that effective critical thinking, problem-solving and communication, in both academia and sport, are central to success, and, therefore, are essential for the development of personal effectiveness.

Embrace rich variety of human differences: As ASPIRE is such a multicultural environment, with employees coming from all over the world, student-athletes learn the importance and richness of diversity. ASPIRE seeks to develop a broad understanding and acceptance of a wide range of persons, including people of different cultures, races, socio-economic backgrounds, and natural abilities.

Career and university networking

ASPIRE has a duty of care to ensure its graduates have the best possible life after they have left the Academy, whatever path they choose. The education and student care department has its own designated 'career and university networking' section to manage this important part of student life. This section focuses on providing a career counselling programme for ASPIRE's student-athletes and on promoting exceptional further education and career opportunities. Student-athletes are assisted in identifying potential career opportunities, while being supported in qualifying for tertiary education, all the while promoting a continuing sports development. Furthermore, ASPIRE has a duty to support its graduates (alumni) upon graduation, to ensure that the transition to the next stage of their career is as smooth as possible.

Interdepartmental cooperation

The three key aspects of ASPIRE described in this chapter (sports, sports science/sports medicine, education and student care) are the primary departments with direct access to student-athletes within the Academy. The success of the Academy depends on these departments working together in cooperation, rather than isolation. If experience is anything to go by, this integrated approach of sharing information and having common goals (as illustrated through, for example, the 'service team' approach above) is highly recommended for such institutions, especially when there is a large workforce.

Naturally enough, the aforementioned departments could not survive alone without sufficient professional support from other sectors. To ensure the smooth running of operations, ASPIRE has a corporate services department. Corporate services, which has a shared-services approach with *Aspire Zone Foundation*'s other SBUs, provides the administrative 'backbone' for the Academy. In ASPIRE, numerous employees work in corporate services in the following sections: information technology, marketing and communications, finance, procurement, human resources, and administration. The more efficient these sections are, the more efficient ASPIRE can be, and therefore, by extension, the more successful the student-athletes are in their chosen pathway.

Quality management

Given the vast range of services across all departments discussed here, it is necessary for a system to exist in order to monitor how the organization is holistically managed as it strives towards achieving its mission. For this, ASPIRE has its own dedicated 'quality management' team, which is charged with ensuring the organization is well positioned against best practice worldwide.

'Quality management' focuses on service quality and the means to achieve it. A central tenet is making sure the people delivering services are aware of general principles. ASPIRE has chosen the European Foundation for Quality Management (EFQM) model as it fits well with educational/sports settings. The EFQM approach consists of an 'excellence model', the so-called 'RADAR' measurement system, and the method of self-assessment.

1 The 'excellence model' is a non-prescriptive assessment framework for a holistic overview of an organization. It is made up of 'enablers' (e.g. leadership, policy and strategy, people, partnerships, resources, and processes) and 'results' (outcomes of the organization).

2 Next to the 'Excellence Model' lies the measurement system, referred to as 'RADAR' (results, approach, deployment, assessment, review). To gather evidence against the 'excellence model', the 'RADAR' system provides the reference for what needs to be assessed during the self-assessment.

3   Finally, the self-assessment process is a comprehensive, systematic and regular review of an organization's activities and results, referenced against the EFQM 'excellence model' and 'RADAR'. Such a positioning allows the organization to gauge its strengths and weaknesses and culminates in planned improvement actions that are then monitored for progress periodically (EFQM, 2003).

Applying this approach is seen as a catalyst for driving organizational improvement. Ultimately, if desired, an organization can be (and in ASPIRE's case has been) externally assessed by trained EFQM assessors to verify scores and commitment to the process. This is done through the EFQM's 'recognition scheme.' The main aim of this scheme is to help organizations to improve their performance and competitiveness through excellence (EFQM, 2003). Ultimately, by having such a quality management system in place, ASPIRE is well positioned to maximize the quality and efficiency of its services across all departments.

Summary

In aiming to encapsulate how sporting talent is developed in the state of Qatar, a general overview of sport in the country has been provided in this chapter, highlighting the important role sport aims to play in Qatar's National Vision 2030. The Aspire Zone Foundation (AZF) plays, and will continue to play, a big part, in realizing Qatar's sporting ambitions through its various strategic business units (SBUs).

The main focus of the chapter, by means of a case study, addressed one of AZF's SBUs, ASPIRE Academy for Sports Excellence, as this is the organization where the development of sporting talent primarily takes place. This academy is unique in the Middle East, in that it aims to develop adolescent student-athletes holistically in terms of sport and education.

Three departments within ASPIRE – sports; sports science/sports medicine; and education and student care – exist in harmony, and this success serves to demonstrate how an integrated approach between departments is vital for success, together with strong backing from administrative personnel in this case the corporate services department.

All in all, the chapter seeks to demonstrate the importance of a structured and integrated approach to develop young sporting talent in the Middle East. Clearly, none of this would be possible without strong financial support. Most important of all, however, is that all of this effort is only made possible due to the grand visions existing for both sport and the Qatari nation. In this regard, the case of ASPIRE should stand as a role model for other countries across the region.

References

Allen, G. (1998) *Leading*. Available online: http://ollie.dcccd.edu/mgmt1374/
book_contents/4directing/leading/lead.htm (15 February 2011).

Boje, D. (2000) *Transformational Leadership*. Available online: http://cbae.
nmsu.edu/~dboje/teaching/338/transformational_leadership.htm (28 April
2011).

Daniel, D.R. (1961) 'Management information crisis', *Harvard Business
Review*, 39(5): 111–121.

European Foundation for Quality Management (EFQM) (2003) *Assessing for
Excellence: A practical guide for successfully developing, executing and
reviewing a self-assessment strategy for your organization.* Brussels:
EFQM.

Hill, T. and Westbrook, R. (1997) 'SWOT analysis: It's time for a product recall',
Long Range Planning, 30(1), 46–52.

Howell, J.M. and Avolio, B.J. (1993) 'Transformational leadership, transactional
leadership, locus of control, and support for innovation: Key predictors of
consolidated-business-unit performance', *Journal of Applied Psychology*,
78(6), 891—902.

Locke, E.A. and Latham, G.P. (1990) *A Theory of Goal-Setting and Task
Performance*, Englewood Cliffs, NJ: Prentice Hall.

Whitehead, M. (2001) 'The concept of physical literacy', *European Journal of
Physical Education*, 6, 127–138.

Index